British Political Parties

The emergence of a modern party system

SECOND EDITION

Alan R. Ball

Principal Lecturer in Politics, Portsmouth Polytechnic

MACMILLAN
EDUCATION

First edition 1981
Second edition 1987

Published by
MACMILLAN EDUCATION LTD
Houndmills, Basingstoke, Hampshire RG21 2XS
and London
Companies and representatives
throughout the world

Printed in Hong Kong

ISBN 0–333–44501–5 (hardcover)
ISBN 0–333–44502–3 (paperback)

To Frances

BRITISH POLITICAL PARTIES

Also by Alan R. Ball

Modern Politics and Government (Third Edition)
Pressure Politics in Industrial Societies (with Frances Millard)

Contents

Preface to the First Edition

This book is intended to introduce students to the study of British political parties within the framework of their development. Its theme is the British party system and the organisation, ideology and power structure of the major parties within that evolving system. There has been no attempt to present a detailed chronological survey, but in dealing with each party within the context of the existing party system of each period, the student will, I hope, become familiar with the more detailed historical background by continual cross-references. I have avoided the use of political-science jargon as much as possible, and to avoid confusion to students new to this historical period I have aimed at consistency in the use of party labels rather than exact historical accuracy. Thus the label 'Conservative' is used throughout and I have resisted the temptation to use 'Unionist' or 'Tory'. The same is true for the other political parties discussed.

The book is an attempt to summarise, condense, explain and present in simpler form the vast numbers of monographs and specialised texts that have appeared in recent years. I hope I have not done too much damage to the original material.

I am grateful for the initial helpful comments of Jean Blondel and the many constructive suggestions of Andrew Gamble. My thanks to Flora Gennings, who assisted in the proof reading, and to Marilyn Bosworth of Portsmouth Polytechnic library who helped in tracing the material. My four children were invaluable in leaving me alone as much as possible during the gestation period. My warmest thanks must go to Frances Millard for her patient and inestimable advice and support on matters of presentation and structure. She cannot be associated with the interpretation of the material, factual errors, or the conclusions reached; they remain entirely my own responsibility.

Portsmouth Polytechnic   Alan R. Ball

Preface to the Second Edition

The changes in the British party system since 1981 have provoked this second edition. Events since 1981 have seen the birth of the Social Democratic Party and the creation of the Alliance with the Liberal Party, threatening to undermine the post-1945 two-party system. The 1983 general election sealed the contemporary triumph of Thatcherism and the defeat of the patrician element within the Conservative Party. The Labour Party, beset with internal difficulties, staggered to a massive 1983 electoral disaster and then set about attempting to recover.

These significant developments have produced stresses within the party system which have not yet developed into a clear pattern. The Liberal–SDP Alliance has not yet broken the 'mould' of British politics; the Conservative Party is not securely 'Thatcherite' and the permanent revival of the Labour Party is not assured. Therefore, I have attempted in Part Four of this second edition to look at the factors in this transition and to capture the flavour of British party politics in the 1980s within the total context of the historical emergence of British political parties. The revised Part Four is not an analysis of the modern party system but a discussion of its continuing evolution.

Although I have made extensive changes to the chapters concerned with the post-1964 period, I have made few in the earlier sections besides updating the references and adding clarity where necessary.

I would like to thank Terry Hanson of Portsmouth Polytechnic Library for his help and my colleague Rob Atkinson made valuable and constructive suggestions. Again my main thanks must go to Frances Millard who gave valuable assistance and kept me sane during the reproductive process.

Portsmouth, September 1986   Alan R. Ball

List of Abbreviations

AMS	Additional Member System
BBC	British Broadcasting Corporation
BUF	British Union of Fascists
BUI	British United Industrialists
CLP	Constituency Labour Parties
CPC	Conservative Political Centre
EEC	European Economic Community
ILP	Independent Labour Party
LCA	Liberal Central Association
LRC	Labour Representation Committee
NATO	North Atlantic Treaty Organisation
NEC	National Executive Committee (of the Labour Party)
NHS	National Health Service
NLF	National Liberal Federation
NUGMW	National Union of General and Municipal Workers
NUM	National Union of Mineworkers
NUR	National Union of Railwaymen
NUWSS	National Union of Women's Suffrage Societies
PEST	Pressure for Economic and Social Toryism
PLP	Parliamentary Labour Party
PR	Proportional Representation
SDF	Social Democratic Federation
SDLP	Social Democratic and Labour Party

SNP	Scottish National Party
STV	Single Transferable Vote
TGWU	Transport and General Workers' Union
TRG	Tory Reform Group
TUC	Trades Union Congress
UDI	Unilateral Declaration of Independence
USDAW	Union of Shop, Distributive and Allied Workers
UUC	Ulster United Council
WSPU	Women's Social and Political Union

Introduction: Political Parties and the British Party System

British political parties exist because there is conflict within the political system. The party system has a long-established tradition in Britain; it has reflected political conflicts in British politics over the last three centuries. But if parties arise out of conflict, they do not necessarily cause it. Indeed, the theme of this book is that parties are beneficial and also inevitable. They are beneficial because they provide a mechanism for the peaceful resolution of political tensions. They are inevitable because they have developed historically as a fundamental element of the system of representative government.

Political parties already existed as recognisable groupings in the legislature in the seventeenth century, and these groupings gradually acquired a greater degree of permanence. However, throughout the eighteenth and early nineteenth centuries these parliamentary groupings lacked durability and were confined exclusively to the legislature. It was not until the first moves to electoral reform that organisations with links with extra-parliamentary groups began to emerge. The 1832 Reform Act was important in this development. It led to the appearance of local registration societies to organise the newly enfranchised voters and encouraged the creation of central organisations to co-ordinate electoral activity. The Tory Carlton Club was formed in 1832, followed by its Whig equivalent, the Reform Club, in 1834.[1]

However, it was not until after the 1867 Reform Act that political parties in the modern sense began to emerge in the British political system; by the time of the 1883 and 1885 reforms these new organisations were clearly identifiable. Although it is impossible to fix clear dates for the emergence of this modern party system, certainly by the last quarter of the nineteenth century we can identify the following three important elements:

(1) Cohesive and durable groups exist in the House of Commons.

(2) There are coherent and persistent organisations outside the Commons with clear links and similar political labels to the groups in the Commons.

(3) Both the parliamentary and extra-parliamentary organisations systematically and continually interact with the electorate.

It is these three characteristics of the modern British party system that provide us with a means of defining our subject. One could escape with Epstein's definition of a political party: 'Almost everything that is called a party in any Western democratic nation can be so regarded for the present purpose.'[2] Or, in Hodgkin's words, parties may be said to be 'all political organisations which regard themselves as parties and which are generally so regarded'.[3] Yet such open-ended definitions will not suit our purposes here. There are several problems in the development of British political parties that necessitate a clear use of the label 'political party'. For example, if a party splits, as did the Liberal Party in 1886, should one regard it as two political parties? If there is a clear drift to the fusion of two political parties, as with the National Liberals and the Conservatives after 1931, at what stage do we regard the separateness of the two organisations to have ceased? There are examples in succeeding chapters of political parties that are clearly part of another political party for most of their relevant existence despite their distinctive labels and separate organisations. Such was the case with the Independent Labour Party (ILP) between 1900 and 1932. The ILP in this period was so firmly part of the federal Labour Party that it cannot really be regarded as an independent political party, though its electoral strength was greater than that of the contemporary Communist Party, which must be regarded as a political party for the purposes of this study.

Thus problems of definition abound. None the less, to examine such questions as whether Britain had a two-party system at a particular time, or whether it has always displayed characteristics of a multi-party system, we need some guidance. For our purposes, then, a political party is a political institution which has the following characteristics:

(1) An organisation that has a recognised degree of permanence.
(2) This organisation contests elections and seeks to place its members in positions of influence in the legislature.
(3) It either attempts to occupy executive positions in the political system, such as those in the Cabinet, or to exercise influence on those occupying such offices by virtue of its position in the legislature.
(4) It has a distinctive label which distinguishes it from other political groupings.

Perhaps it is the third feature which gives rise to the greatest difficulty. Here the problems are caused by the nationalist parties, which are clearly parties in that they possess distinctive organisations and seek to increase their power by winning seats in the legislature. However, they do not seek executive office, for their ultimate goal is often their own removal from the British Parliament after the establishment of separate parliaments in their respective countries. Thus we are trying uneasily to bridge the definitional gap between a political party and a pressure group. On the above terms, the modern Ecology Party is clearly a political party, albeit as yet an unsuccessful one. Similarly, the followers of Ramsay MacDonald after August 1931, National Labour, did not constitute a political party even though the leader of this parliamentary group was the prime minister.

Functions of Political Parties

Having specified what we mean by a political party, we may find it useful at this stage to offer some generalisations about the functions or roles of these parties in the political system. A function in this sense is 'productive of consequences'.[4] In other words, as a result of the activities of political parties, certain repercussions are felt in the political system. On the whole these are beneficial in that if these roles were not performed by the parties, then other organisations would probably perform them. We do not mean to imply, however, that these functions are unchanging. Nor are they necessarily always performed effectively. Indeed, controversy has always surrounded the discussion of functions.

Generally, we can identify four groups of functions performed by political parties:

(1) *Representative functions.* Political parties are important prerequisites of liberal democratic government. Perhaps, they 'are not a sufficient condition for democracy. There is more reason to believe that they are a necessary condition since no modern democracy exists without parties.'[5] Parties widen the extent of popular participation. They provide mechanisms for organising the choice of representatives to act on behalf of their electors. They also provide some guidance to the electorate concerning the policies which those representatives commit themselves to pursue.

(2) *Electoral functions.* This is not necessarily a function of parties only in liberal democracies, though it is obviously closely linked with the representative function. Parties structure the vote. They organise the electorate. They present labels to the electorate and seek electoral support. This in turn leads to a two-way system of communication between the governed and the government or potential government. Parties may go further, as they have always done in modern British politics, attempting to convert the electorate to their programme.

(3) *The governing function.* Political parties almost monopolise the organisation of government in Great Britain. Independents scarcely exist in the House of Commons. Cabinet posts are always occupied by the nominees of the political parties and the main source of political recruitment in the British political system is the party system. In other political systems a variety of agencies, such as the army or the church, may perform the task, but not in Britain. Still, one must

exercise some care here. There are other avenues to political power such as the civil service or the judiciary that are relatively independent of political parties.

(4) *The formulation of policy.* This is the most difficult function to deal with. There is no doubt that political parties formulate demands, but it is less certain that they always translate demands into government policy. Richard Rose has concluded that there are a great many obstacles to 'party government' and cites the civil service as a most important barrier.[6] However, in spite of these important qualifications, the party is certainly one of the agencies engaged in the formulation of government policy; how weak that engagement is is a continuing question.[7]

The Party System

The wider relationships of political parties constitute what is known as the party system. Any system is composed of inter-related, interdependent elements. The constituents of a party system are the parties themselves. They are not isolated, autonomous organisations. The actions of one will affect the actions of others in a variety of complex ways. It is frequently argued that the *number* of parties is the most important clue to explaining the nature of this interaction. Thus we can speak of a two-party system, a multi-party system, or even a two-and-a-half-party system.

If we are to regard numbers as central, then obviously questions of precise definition become extremely important. Counting requires us to be quite clear what we are including in the count. However, precise counting is not enough. It does not give us a guide to important distinctions between systems which are similar in the numbers of their parties. For example, using our definition of political parties, we would need to view Britain as a multi-party system. None the less, the British party system is universally considered to be very different in important respects from, say, the Italian multi-party system, where the large Communist Party has been permanently excluded from cffice since 1947. Therefore, we need to introduce factors other than numbers into our discussion.

Once we introduce other factors, the emphasis on numbers is attenuated. Political scientists have indeed stressed a variety of other features in their examination of different types of party systems. For example, the type and structure of the parties will affect their interaction: parties may be regional or national, more or less centralised, enduring or ephemeral. The relative strengths of the parties are also important: the Irish Nationalists at the end of the nineteenth century could at times determine the fate of governments, but the British Communist Party has never enjoyed that luxury. Finally, the ideological relationships of the parties also has an impact on party behaviour. A two-party system of Communists and Fascists would surely prove short-lived, while a highly fragmented multi-party system with little ideological distance between the numerous parties would not necessarily be so unstable.

In considering these additional variables the very act of counting may also be different. This is why Britain is commonly regarded as a two-party system, despite the fact that there are clearly more than two parties in existence: two of the parties are regarded as more important than others. Giovanni Sartori has provided a convincing set of criteria for judging whether a two-party system exists at any given time:

(1) Two parties are in a position to compete for the absolute majority of seats.
(2) One of the two parties actually succeeds in winning a sufficient parliamentary majority.
(3) This party is willing to govern alone.
(4) Alternation or rotation in power remains a credible expectation.[8]

These are the criteria which we shall use. In this sense it is apparent that Britain has been a two-party system for extended periods of its recent history. This is not to imply that it has always been so. Nor is it to preclude the possibility of change in the future: party systems are not static features of the political scene, for the parties which constitute them are themselves dynamic organisations. It is one of the tasks of this book to examine the changing nature of the British party system.

Change and the Party System

An important factor affecting the stability of a party system is the electoral system. Thus the widening of the franchise, the elimination of corruption, the method of registration and the distribution of seats are all factors which have influenced the nature of the British party system. Throughout much of the twentieth century these elements have remained largely unchanged and uncontroversial. However, the method of translating votes into seats, i.e. the first-past-the-post method, has not remained uncontroversial and is currently the subject of debate. If the latter were changed to some form of preference voting, or a type of proportional representation, there is little doubt that the nature of the British party system would also change. However, the electoral system is not the only factor influencing party-system transformation. Thus the growth of clerical occupations and the revolution in suburban transport affected the nature of Conservative Party support after 1880. At the end of the nineteenth century social-class divisions replaced local issues and religious cleavages as the major dimensions of British politics. This shift was an important factor in the displacement of the Liberals by the Labour Party in the first quarter of the twentieth century. Economic crisis (1931) and wars (1916 and 1940) have had repercussions for the party system. The rise of nationalism in the British Isles, the Irish parliamentary nationalism at the turn of the century and the appearance of Welsh and Scottish variants on the parliamentary scene in the 1960s again affected the working of the system. Neither do the parties operate in a political vacuum. The party system interacts with other political structures such as the Cabinet and Parliament, as well as with political conventions about the nature of representative and responsible government.

Thus the determinants and agents of change in the party system are many and varied. The complexity makes one wish for a more straightforward explanation of the two-party system, like that advanced by Macauley in the nineteenth century. Speaking of the 1641 political crisis he said:

> The recess of the English Parliament lasted six weeks. The day on which the Houses met again is one of the most remarkable epochs in our history. From that day dates the corporate existence of the two great parties which have ever since alternatively governed the country. In one sense, indeed the distinction which then became obvious had always existed, and always must exist. For it has its origin in the diversities of temper, of understanding, and of interest, which are found in all societies, and which will be found till humans cease to be drawn in opposite directions by the charm of habit and by the charm of novelty . . . Everywhere there is a class of men who cling with fondness to whatever is ancient . . . we find also everywhere another class of men sanguine in hope, bold in speculation, always pressing forward . . . But of both the best specimens will be found not far from the common frontier. The extreme section of one class consists of bigoted dotards: the extreme section of the other consists of shallow and reckless empirics.[9]

Unfortunately, reality fits into no such neat compartment. It is inherently dishevelled and untidy in its appearance. Still, each observer tries to make sense of history by imposing an order of some kind. Many will disagree with the emphasis placed and the conclusions drawn in this book. It deems the continuities of the British party system to be far more significant and revealing than the changes. The method may also be open to doubt. It seeks to dissect the individual components of the party system and to assess their interrelation firmly in the context of their historical development.

Notes to the Introduction

1. For histories of the British parties before the middle of the nineteenth century see I. Bulmer-Thomas, *The Growth of the British Party System*, vol. 1, 2nd edn (London: John Baker, 1967) pp. 3–101.

See also Sir I. Jennings, *Party Politics: The Growth of Parties*, vol. 2 (Cambridge University Press, 1961) pp. 1–124.
2. L. D. Epstein, *Political Parties in Western Democracies* (London: Pall Mall, 1967) p. 5.
3. T. Hodgkin, *African Political Parties* (Harmondsworth: Penguin, 1961) p. 16.
4. This is King's term; see A. King, 'Political Parties in Western Democracies: Some Sceptical Reflections', *Polity*, vol. 2, no. 2, Winter 1969, p. 119.
5. Epstein, p. 8.
6. R. Rose, *The Problem of Party Government* (Harmondsworth: Penguin, 1976) pp. 371–416. Rose develops this argument in *Do Parties Make a Difference?* (London: Macmillan, 1980).
7. Many other categories of functions have been suggested; there is little agreement among functionalists as to what functions should be included. It is important to stress that functions are being used here merely to provide an analytical framework for dealing with the role of political parties and this particular list of functions is intended to simplify. An alternative list would be: (a) structuring the vote, (b) integration, (c) mobilisation, (d) leadership recruitment, (e) organisation of government, (f) policy formation. See King, pp. 111–41. Sometimes the list is reduced to: communication, representation, participation, legitimation.
8. G. Sartori, *Parties and Party Systems*, vol. 1 (Cambridge University Press, 1976) p. 188. See A. Beattie, 'The Two-Party System: Room for Scepticism', in *Adversary Politics and Electoral Reform* (London: Anthony Wigram, 1975) p. 294 for a variant.
9. Lord Macauley, *The History of England*, vol. 1 (Everyman edn, 1906) p. 74.

PART ONE

The Making of the British Party System, 1867–1922

1

The Electoral System and the Party System, 1867–1922

Recent British political history shows a high degree of continuity and an absence of sharp breaks with the past. This is particularly true with regard to the development of party structures and the party system in the late nineteenth and early twentieth centuries. The period after 1867 saw important political changes in the British party system accompanied by extensive reforms in the electoral system, but it is difficult to fix these changes by an exact date. It is perhaps tempting to cling to the dates of significant legislative reforms: the four major Reform Acts of 1832, 1867, 1884 and 1918 and, equally important, the Secret Ballot Act of 1872, the Corrupt Practices Act of 1883 and the Redistribution of Seats Act of 1885. Certainly, the parliamentary legislation of the 1880s makes those years crucial in the evolution of the party system. Yet each of these reforms has its seeds in a previous formative period and the results of the reforms were neither immediate nor clearly detached from other important changes in the nature of the political system.

However, to compare the British party system of 1867 with that of 1922 illustrates how far reaching was this transformation. In 1867 the two parties, the Conservative and Liberal Parties, were mainly parliamentary groupings with weak internal cohesion, loosely associated under a party label. There were almost no national extra-parliamentary organisations, the local associations were often *ad hoc* self-appointed bodies of local elites, while the candidates fought the elections with scant regard to national issues. There was much electoral corruption and religion was much more important than social class in determining voting behaviour. Elections were expensive, MPs unpaid and uncontested seats were common.[1] Nearly half of Conservative MPs were landowners, as were one-quarter of the Liberal Party in the House of Commons. The contrast with the early 1920s is sharp. The once powerful Liberal Party was split and had been overtaken in terms of votes and seats by the Labour Party. An Irish Home Rule Party had appeared, exerted tremendous political leverage, and had completely disappeared. The main parties were more organised at parliamentary level and had developed systematic, coherent political organisations at national and local levels. Elections, more democratically conducted, were based on national themes revolving round issues of social reform and economic management by the state. Social class, as measured by the electoral success of the Labour Party and the flight of the middle classes to the Conservatives, was now the most important single determinant of voting behaviour and party allegiance. Religious Nonconformity had lost its political force. Even before the First World War half of the Conservative MPs had commercial-industrial backgrounds, and the landowning element had declined to a quarter. This group had almost disappeared from the pre-war Liberal Party. Thus the changes in the party system and elections in this period were quite far reaching, but they were a product of gradual change and evolution.

The Party System, 1867–1922

The Second Reform Act of 1867 was followed by the clear emergence of two political parties dominating the House of Commons. In the election of 1868, of the 670 seats, the Liberals won 384 and the Conservatives 274. (It is difficult throughout this period to be precise on the election results because of the relative looseness with which party labels were worn.) However, the rise of the Irish Home Rule Party, with its geographical base in the southern part of Ireland, was soon to blur the two-party system in the House of Commons, though not in the constituencies. The Home Rulers won 57 seats in the 1874 election to the Conservative total of 350 and the Liberal total of 245, and in 1880 the Irish increased their total to 61, the Conservatives and Liberals winning 238 and 353 respectively.

The two elections of 1885 and 1886 further disturbed the existing party system. First, the Irish Home Rule Party increased its representation, and for a short time it held the balance of power in the House of Commons with crucial political consequences for government stability. Second, the Liberal Party's espousal of Home Rule led to the 1886 split in the party with opponents from both the Whig and Radical wings leaving to constitute the Liberal Unionists, who soon became indistinguishable from the Conservatives. (The Conservative Party was then known as the Unionist Party, not reverting to the title 'Conservative' until the 1920s.) The split in the Liberal Party contributed to the long period of Conservative domination to 1905, punctuated only by the interlude of weak Liberal government between 1892 and 1895. Exploiting the patriotic fervour raised by the Boer War, the Conservatives maintained their gains in the 'khaki' election of 1900. (See Table 1.1.)

TABLE 1.1

Election	Total seats	Conservatives	Lib. Unionist	Liberals	Home Rule	Labour
1885	670	250	—	334	86	—
1886	670	316	79	190	85	—
1892	670	268	47	274	81	2
1895	670	341	70	177	82	—
1900	670	334	68	184	82	2

Source: M. Kinnear, *The British Voter* (London: Batsford, 1968) pp. 13–26.

The emergence of the new Labour Party in 1900, together with the fortuitous combination of issues and the divisions in the Conservative Party, gave the Liberal Party the most remarkable and decisive election victory of the period in

1906, a victory that was to give the Liberals their last over-all majority in the Commons. Of course, as we will note later, the number of seats won by the Liberals was far greater than the proportion of votes gained. Yet in spite of this massive victory the over-all Liberal majority was only to last until 1910, when the two elections were to reduce the Liberal government to dependence on their Irish and Labour allies for an over-all majority over the Conservative Party.

The First World War added to the confusion of the British party system. The tensions of the struggle put great stress on the existing political parties. The Irish Home Rule Party was effectively to disappear from British politics after the 1918 election, and both the Liberal and Labour Parties split. The establishment of an electoral truce in 1914 and the emergence of the coalitions of Asquith in 1915 and of Lloyd George in 1916 seemed to herald important developments in the British party system. The 1918 election was fought on the new rules introduced by the Reform Act of that year and saw the clear emergence of the Labour Party as the main challenger to the powerful Conservative Party. The election produced a most bewildering array of political groupings in the House of Commons. The following election in 1922 did not appear to untangle the confusion. (See Table 1.2.)

TABLE 1.2

Election	Seats	Con.	Lib.	Lab.	Home Rule	Coalition Libs	Coalition Labour	Others
1906	670	157	400	30	83	—	—	—
1910 (Jan)	670	273	275	40	82	—	—	—
1910 (Dec)	670	272	272	42	84	—	—	—
1918	707	335	28	63	7	133	10	131
1922	615	345	54	142	—	62	—	12

Note: The Coalition Liberals constituted the Lloyd George wing of the Liberal Party after the 1916 split (see Chapter 3, pp. 75–9). The 131 members of the other parties elected in 1918 included 73 Sinn Fein MPs from Ireland who never took their seats but set up their own Parliament in Dublin.

Source: D. Butler and A. Sloman, *British Political Facts 1900–1979*, 5th edn (London: Macmillan, 1980) pp. 206–7.

The Electoral System, 1867–1918

The electoral system is an important determinant of party structure, of party ideology and of the party system. Between 1867 and 1918 the electoral system in Britain underwent profound change. However, although the relationship of the electoral system to the party is central, it is also a complex one. There are three basic misunderstandings concerning the electoral system in the period after 1867. The first is that Britain was a formal and practising liberal democracy by the end of the nineteenth century. In fact, it was not until the Fourth Reform Act of 1918 that all adult males were given the vote, and universal suffrage had to wait until 1928. The reforms of 1832, 1867 and 1884 certainly widened the franchise, but none achieved the goal of complete manhood suffrage. The existence of administrative barriers, plural voting and an undemocratic distribution of seats added to the over-all picture of an incomplete liberal democracy. Second, there was no relentless pattern of progress to universal adult suffrage and few were conscious of working to such a goal. History always looks a smoother pattern of development in retrospect. The attainment of the post-1928 position was achieved by a series of haphazard jerks and 'leaps in the dark'. The third point that is not always appreciated is that the electoral laws were in a great state of legal and practical confusion throughout most of this period. The 1918 Reform Act was really the first measure of consolidation. It was the first to even attempt to impose clarity, and above all uniformity, on the heterogeneity of the electoral laws.

There were three important aspects of the electoral system which had vital consequences for the political parties after 1867: the franchise; the administration of elections; and the distribution of seats and the simple plurality system. Before turning to the 1918 Act, these will be considered in turn.

The Franchise

Before the Fourth Reform Act of 1918 probably 40 per cent to 50 per cent of adult males were excluded from the voting register. Briefly, the first three reform bills enfranchised the following groups:

1832   The forty shilling freeholder, the £50 tenant in the counties, and the £10 householder in the boroughs.
1867   All householders in the boroughs and the £12 tenant in the counties.
1884   All householders in the counties.

However, there was an absence of over-all uniformity in the distribution of the vote. By 1911 it has been estimated that there were still at least seven categories of franchise in the United Kingdom. The most important of these were the household and occupation franchises, amounting to over 84 per cent of the electorate.[2] The total votes on the register represented less than 30 per cent of the total adult population. Women constituted the main body of the disenfranchised in general elections, but sons living with parents, servants living in the same house as their employers, soldiers in barracks, and those in receipt of poor law relief, added to the total. Complicated administrative procedures swelled the numbers of the voteless, and (as we shall see later) discriminated particularly against working-class lodgers.

The class bias of the electoral system was exacerbated by the existence of plural voting. In the elections of 1910 there were at least half a million voters, constituting 7 per cent of the electorate, with more than one vote. Plural voting was mainly a consequence of the property franchise, and the university graduates with an extra vote were colourful reminders of the inequalities of the system: graduates elected nine Members of Parliament (this particular franchise survived until 1948). Plural voting gave Joseph Chamberlain six votes in the 1885 election and one individual was said to have had twenty-three votes.[3]

However, in spite of the haphazard nature of the changes brought about by the three Reform Acts, and in spite of the absence of adult male suffrage before 1918, the political consequences of nineteenth-century legislation were indeed vast. The 1832 Act produced an increase of almost 50 per cent in the electorate; the 1867 Act increased the vote in the boroughs by 13 per cent and in the counties by 38 per cent;[4] the 1884 Act led to an increase of 66 per cent. The increase in the number of voters as a result of this legislation had, as we shall see, profound consequences for the party system and the structure of political parties.

Yet party development was also affected by the exclusion from the voting registers of almost half the adult male population. The electoral system ensured that the middle-class areas of the industrial cities had a proportionately higher number of registered voters than the working-class areas. The legal and *de facto* exclusion of so many working-class voters could be seen to be as deliberate as the exclusion of women, and this middle-class bias may have ensured the dominance of the Liberal Party as the party of the left until after 1918.[5]

There were various attempts to extend the franchise after the 1884 Reform Act, but one problem was that the political beneficiaries possessed neither the vote nor other means of political leverage. The major parties had to be convinced that they would benefit from any further reform. The Liberal Party was chiefly interested in the abolition of plural voting, but its several legislative attempts, particularly after 1906, were defeated in the House of Lords. The Conservatives wanted a redistribution of seats before any change in the franchise. In particular they wished to reduce the over-representation of Ireland which worked to their parliamentary disadvantage.

Ironically it was the increasing demands of women for the vote that did most to wreck any important reforms of the franchise between 1884 and 1918. The activities of the National Union of Women's Suffrage Societies (NUWSS) and particularly after 1906 the activities of the more militant Women's Social and Political Union (WSPU) led by the Pankhursts caused internal splits within all the political parties on the question of female suffrage; this probably delayed female enfranchisement because it was not an issue between the parties.[6] The Irish saw the issue as a device to delay Home Rule. The Conservative Party wanted a reduction in the number of Irish MPs first. The Labour Party wanted adult suffrage first, since the enfranchisement of women on the basis of the existing male franchise would have swollen the number of middle-class voters. (Women already possessed the vote for local government elections.) The Liberal Party was more sympathetic, but the hostility of certain party leaders frustrated the aims of the parliamentary rank and file. It needed a war and a coalition government, and perhaps the cessation of female agitation,[7] before the franchise could be extended.

The Administration of Elections before 1918
Irrespective of the extent of the franchise, the administration of elections had significant repercussions for the political parties, for election results and for democratic practice before the 1918 Act introduced uniform and fairer procedures into election organisation. The Ballot Act of 1872 allowing secret voting helped to limit some corrupt practices such as bribery and treating and it almost succeeded in eliminating widespread violence at election time. It has been said that the 1880 general election was probably the last that witnessed widespread corruption in Great Britain.[8] The spread of the new party organisations by the 1880s and the passage of the 1883 Corrupt Practices Act furthered the cause of electoral purity. It is as well to note, however, that certain corrupt practices were never entirely eliminated during this period and could still be observed in the last two elections before the enactment of the 1918 Reform Bill.[9]

Elections before 1918 extended over many weeks because of scarce police resources to deal with possible disorders, and candidates could stand in different seats hoping to ensure at least one success. In the election of 1900 Keir Hardie was successful in the two-member constituency of Merthyr Tydfil already knowing of his defeat in Preston.

However, by far the most important factor in the administration of elections before 1918, and the one that significantly affected the fortunes of the political parties, was the method of registering voters: 'it was registration that made votes'.[10] The electoral register was compiled on 1 January of each year on the basis of information collected prior to the previous July. The complexities of the various franchises by which adult males were entitled to vote provided a fertile field for the election agents of the political parties. It is fair to say that most of the energies of the party agents and the bulk of party election funds were devoted to filling the electoral register with one set of supporters and stripping the same register of the opposing voters through the Registration Courts, machinery that pre-dated the Second Reform Bill. It is vital to stress the importance of registration in terms of party activity and party success. The lodger vote illustrated some of the complexities and undemocratic features of the registration procedure. If the landlord lived on the same premises or the lodger moved, the lodger lost his vote. He lost his vote even if he moved to new lodgings in the same constituency. Unlike other voters, he had to claim his vote annually, and appearing before the revising barrister could, and generally did, mean time off work and loss of pay.[11] Thus the intricacies of the electoral system hit the lower classes in the larger towns most severely and certainly reduced the size of the electorate.

There were other cumbersome difficulties associated with registration. The whole procedure had two important consequences. First, it contributed further to the undemocratic features of the electoral system. Second, it gave the political parties tremendous power over the administrative aspects of elections and so in great measure it was the parties which decided who could vote.

The Distribution of Seats and the Simple Plurality System

The pattern of seat distribution throughout the United Kingdom had significant consequences for the electoral successes and failures of the political parties in this period. The politicians constantly recognised the importance of the issue: witness the bargaining before the 1885 Act and the opposition of the Conservative Party to female suffrage and to the abolition of plural voting before 1914, at least until the question of Irish overrepresentation had been tackled.

The redistribution of seats in 1832 was important in removing the most glaring examples of rotten and nomination boroughs. The smaller towns in the South continued, however, to be overrepresented in terms of their population throughout the nineteenth century, and the larger towns of the North and the Midlands continued to have fewer seats than their population size merited. In 1866 one-half of the membership of the House of Commons was elected by one-fifth of the electorate. The redistribution of seats in 1867 was small, and the anomalies generally favouring the landed interest in the counties and the small boroughs continued. It was the 1885 Act which dramatically lessened the electoral advantages of the South and the South-West by giving more seats to the larger cities, while the number of English constituencies electing more than one MP was substantially reduced.

Yet it is important not to exaggerate the democratic effects of the 1885 Act. Small boroughs were still overrepresented and the drawing of electoral boundaries separating classes again favoured the 'landed' and Conservative Party interests.[12] The distribution of seats allowed a Conservative domination of suburbia by the late 1880s; after the Third Reform Act and the Redistribution Act the Conservatives established parity with the Liberals in English boroughs.

The existence of multi-member seats, although reduced after 1885, did encourage third parties and the maintenance of coalitions, especially in the Liberal Party. Before the Liberal split of 1886 Radicals and Whigs could be run in harness. Keir Hardie continued to hold his Merthyr Tydfil seat until his death in 1915 by winning enough Liberal votes to finish second to a successful Liberal and pushing the second Liberal into third place. The distribution of seats and the existence of multi-member seats encouraged an agreement between the Liberal and Labour Parties in 1903 designed to avoid the splitting of the anti-Conservative vote.

The simple plurality method of choosing MPs remained unchanged before and after the Fourth Reform Act. The method obviously had important repercussions on the relationship of seats won to votes cast, as did the distribution of seats. In the election of 1874 the Liberals won over 52 per cent of the total vote yet gained fewer seats than the Conservative Party, which won just under 48 per cent of the vote. A similar discrepancy can be observed in the 1880 election: the Conservatives won 44 per cent of the vote yet only 37 per cent of the seats. In 1906 the advantage clearly swung to the Liberal Party, for with less than half the votes it won 60 per cent of the seats. It has been estimated that if a system of proportional representation had been used in that election, the Liberals would have lost 30 per cent of their seats.[13]

However, much care has to be exercised before 1918 and especially before 1885 in drawing too simple conclusions from the relationship between votes and seats. The number of uncontested seats in British elections consistently declined towards the end of the nineteenth century, but in 1880, for example, there were still 109 seats uncontested, and even by 1906, outside Ireland, 32 were uncontested. When one election followed closely on the heels of another, as in 1910, the number of uncontested seats rose.[14]

It is true that the Conservatives did better when the number of uncontested seats was higher, but the claim that the Conservatives did better on a low poll has been contested.[15] However, it does appear that throughout the period the votes for the Conservative Party, especially after 1885, tended to increase gradually and show fewer fluctuations than the votes for the Liberal Party.[16]

Thus the simple plurality method, the distribution of seats and the drawing of constituency boundaries all contributed to the distortion of the relationship between seats and votes. Changes were made in the two latter variables by various reforms before and including the 1918 Act, but the simple plurality system remained unaltered. There were certain proposals to change this method of counting the votes and deciding the electoral winner. In 1867 there was an attempt to introduce a system of proportional representation (PR) into the Reform Bill, but the attempt failed partly because it appeared to be aiming at the separation of members from their constituency base by introducing national lists of candidates.[17] In 1905 the PR Society was revived, and in 1910 a Royal Commission on Electoral Reform advocated the use of the *alternative vote* system. In fact, a form of PR was proposed for the Irish Senate in the Liberal government's Home Rule Bill of 1914. Proposals for the single transferable vote method of PR were discussed by the Speaker's Conference on Electoral Reform in 1917 and subsequently by Parliament. They were finally defeated on the grounds of perceived party advantage, possible threats to local party organisations, and their apparent complexity. The proposal for the introduction of the 'alternative vote' was also defeated. The 1918 Act did allow for the single transferable vote system (a form of PR) for the twelve university seats which remained in existence until 1948. PR was also included in the Irish legislation of 1921 and 1922.

The Fourth Reform Act, 1918
The 1918 Act virtually ended the debate on electoral reform
for the next fifty years. Subsequent changes were relatively
minor and were the result of party agreements. The Act
established adult male suffrage based on residence and gave
the vote to women over the age of 30 (so that they would
not outnumber the males, an anomaly that was remedied in
1928). It furthered the equalisation of constituencies and
produced more equitable procedures for periodic redistribution. Most importantly, the Act simplified and democra-
tised the electoral administrative procedures. The electorate
was doubled, elections took place on one day, and party
agents could no longer decide who was to be on the register.
Traces of plural voting remained with the university and
business vote until 1948 and 18-year-olds were not enfranchised until 1969, but in practice the Act achieved the goal
of an electoral system that complied with the basic principles
of liberal democracy. A few two-member constituencies
remained, but with a wider franchise, the removal of most
inequalities in the distribution of the seats and the elimination of undemocratic administrative practices Britain could
be described as a 'liberal democracy'. After 1918 it was the
simple plurality system and the absence of any form of PR
outside the universities and Northern Ireland that was, at
times, to affect the electoral fortunes of the political parties.

Notes to Chapter 1

1. See T. Lloyd, 'Uncontested Seats in British General Elections,
   1852–1910', *Historical Journal*, vol. 111, no. 2, 1965, pp. 260–5.
2. See N. Blewett, 'The Franchise in the United Kingdom 1885–1918',
   Past and Present, vol. 32, 1965, p. 32.
3. A. K. Russell, *The Liberal Landslide: The General Election of 1906*
   (Newton Abbot: David & Charles, 1973) p. 19.
4. See F. B. Smith, *The Making of the Second Reform Bill* (Cambridge
   University Press, 1966).
5. H. C. G. Matthew *et al.*, 'The Franchise Factor in the Rise of the
   Labour Party', *English Historical Review*, vol. 91, no. 361, October
   1976, pp. 723–52.
6. See D. Morgan, *Suffragists and Liberals* (Oxford: Blackwell, 1975)
   p. 149.
7. See M. Pugh, *Electoral Reform in War and Peace 1906–18* (London:
   Routledge & Kegan Paul, 1978) pp. 131–43.

8. T. Lloyd, *The General Election of 1880* (Oxford University Press, 1968) p. 133.
9. N. Blewett, *The Peers, the Parties and the People: The General Elections of 1910* (London: Macmillan, 1972) pp. 372 and 375.
10. P. F. Clarke, 'Electoral Sociology of Modern Britain', *History*, vol. 57, 1972, p. 32.
11. There was a change in 1907 which allowed more lodgers to vote, known as the 'latch-key' decision; see M. Pugh, *The Making of Modern British Politics 1867-1939* (London: Blackwell, 1982) p. 15.
12. See H. Pelling, *The Social Geography of British Elections, 1885—1910* (London: Macmillan, 1967) p. 9. Also M. E. Chadwick, 'The Role of Redistribution in Making of the Third Reform Act', *Historical Journal*, vol. 19, no. 3, 1976, pp. 665-83.
13. Russell, p. 166.
14. Lloyd, 'Uncontested Seats in British General Elections', pp. 262 and 263.
15. See J. Cornford, 'The Transformation of Conservatism in the Late 19th Century', *Victorian Studies*, vol. 40, no. 7, 1963, p. 55. See also Blewett, *The Peers, the Parties and the People*, pp. 22 and 378.
16. J. P. D. Dunbabin, 'Parliamentary Elections in Great Britain, 1868—1900: A Psephological Note', *English Historical Review*, vol. 81, 1966, p. 91.
17. See Smith, pp. 212—13.

2

The Emergence of British Political Parties

Introduction

By the 1880s the organisational outlines of modern political parties were visible. Both the Liberal and Conservative Parties possessed coherent extra-parliamentary organisations both at national and local level. These organisations were structures primarily designed to mobilise the voters, generate election funds and arrange for the nomination of local candidates. Neither the Liberal nor the Conservative Party organisations were successful in gaining any appreciable influence over the policy-making processes of their parliamentary parties, though the leadership could not entirely ignore the views of their rank and file, particularly in the Liberal Party. Power was to remain firmly in the hands of the parliamentary parties during and after the development of these extra-parliamentary structures.

The Irish Home Rule Party did not differ from the Conservative and Liberal models with regard to this basic power relationship, but it did display, particularly under the leadership of Parnell, a greater degree of parliamentary cohesion, exhibiting fewer of the coalition aspects of the two larger parties.

The Labour Party, founded in 1900, did give indications of being different with regard to the distribution of power. It was the only one of the parties to be formed outside Parliament. The extra-parliamentary organisations of the Conservatives, Liberals and Home Rulers emerged to ensure the continuance of parties already having parliamentary representation. The Labour Party gave its extra-parliamentary wing much more policy-making power. However, in the long term this power was to be no match for the growth in prestige of the parliamentary party.

The new party structures did not represent a complete break with the past. *Ad hoc* committees, especially for the purposes of nominating candidates, and registration societies existed before the extension of the franchise in 1867. The new party structures were built on these and on various groups that emerged to agitate for parliamentary reform in the 1860s. In the two main parties the new structures reflected these diverse origins. These parties were coalitions before and following the emergence of the extra-parliamentary organisations.

Yet it was not merely the extension of the franchise in 1867 and 1884 that facilitated the rise of party organisations. Certainly these reforms were important, and the larger electorates, coupled with the other electoral reforms outlined in Chapter 1, did demand more sophisticated means of conducting elections. But the emergence of these modern parties also owed much to other historical developments. The growth of a national press[1] and the rise of organised Nonconformity were two important factors in the 1860s and 1870s. In the late nineteenth century electoral issues became less community-based and more national. Technological developments, especially in transport, the continued growth in large cities and the decline of agriculture as a source of employment again tended to produce national constituencies. Above all, it was the emergence of class issues, particularly in the 1880s, that helped to polarise British politics, changing the Liberal Party, strengthening the Conservatives, and giving birth to the Labour Party.

Yet again care must be taken to avoid imposing a particular pattern of development on the process of party evolution. Economic cycles, levels of unemployment, the intrusion of special issues such as Ireland and the impact of political personalities such as William Gladstone prevent any historical neatness. Nevertheless, by the beginning of the twentieth century modern political parties in the form we know them today had clearly emerged, and it is this process that we will now examine.

The Liberal Party, 1867–1905

To contemporaries the nineteenth-century Liberal Party appeared to be the pioneer in British party politics. It was the coalition of the left, and was the more radical of the two main parties. It was later to take up the cause of social reform and it was the party of constitutional innovation. (Irish Home Rule and the reform of the Lords are but two examples.) It was the party that was to suffer the biggest split in the period and it was the party that was ultimately to be replaced by the Labour Party. It was also the party which introduced party organisation into British politics at both national and local levels, and it is these organisational innovations that we will examine first.

The Organisation of the Liberal Party

The foundation of the Birmingham Liberal Association in 1865 was to lead to imitations throughout the country and to the establishment of the National Liberal Federation in 1877. This new organisation, disparagingly known as the 'Caucus', had its roots in long-standing political relationships and practices in the city.[2] The weaknesses of working-class organisations in the area made the Birmingham artisans natural allies of the Liberal middle class. With a favourable Nonconformist political culture and with middle-class leadership the Caucus emerged to take advantage of the wider franchise provided by the Second Reform Act.

The Birmingham model was based on forms of direct and indirect democracy. Wards provided the bottom rungs of the organisation and each ward elected representatives to a General Committee which decided the general policy of the Association and selected parliamentary candidates. The general work of the Association was carried out by the Executive Committee, partly elected by the wards and partly nominated by the General Committee. Membership of the

Association was free to all who agreed with the objectives of the Liberal Party.

Local Liberal organisations sprang up in other large towns, though it should be noted that the Liberal Party remained weak in London, partly as a consequence of the weakness of organised Nonconformity there. They emerged from the various *ad hoc* organisations that existed before 1867, and although the Birmingham model was widely copied, especially after the establishment of the National Liberal Federation in 1877, there were important organisational dissimilarities from place to place. Many, like Leeds, depended on the small subscriber, while others, like Manchester, had wealthy members.[3]

The establishment of the national organisation to represent these local caucuses owed much to the Birmingham enthusiast, Francis Schnadhorst. Representatives of ninety-five Liberal associations attended the inaugural meeting in Birmingham in 1877.[4] The National Liberal Federation was essentially a democratically structured organisation with power vested in the annual conference. It was always dominated by the middle-class, radical wing of the party. Yet the extra-parliamentary organisation never dominated the parliamentary wing of the party in spite of its democratic claim to have more influence.

There was another national organisation, the Liberal Central Association, founded in 1874 to replace the older Liberal Registration Society. It was basically controlled by the parliamentary Whips and existed to raise money and to encourage the establishment of constituency organisations to contest elections. At first the relations between the two organisations were strained, but as the National Liberal Federation became more conservative and respectable in the 1890s, so closer co-operation was possible with regard to elections and organisation. Both organisations did share one common weakness: neither found it easy to influence the local associations, particularly in the area of candidate selection.

Local control over candidate selection was to have a major impact on the future of the party. The defection of the Liberal Unionists in 1886 increased its financial difficulties as it lost some of its wealthier subscribers. Moreover, the 1885 seat re-distribution accelerated the movement of the middle classes to the Conservative Party. Thus it was now imperative for the Liberal Party to win greater support from the working-class voter and to begin to harness the power of organised labour. This necessitated the selection of more working-class parliamentary candidates, but the middle-class local associations failed to do this in spite of constant appeals from the parliamentary leadership. One result was the establishment of an independent Labour Party. The agreement between the Liberal and Labour leaders in 1903 limiting election contests between the two parties could be said to have come too late for the future health of the Liberal Party.

To contemporaries, the new political organisations certainly appeared electorally efficient and they must be termed a success in regard to the mobilisation of the vote. Perhaps the claim that the Liberal victory of 1880 was mainly due to the work of the new constituency associations organised on the Birmingham model was exaggerated, but there is clear evidence of their organisational achievements. The Birmingham Liberal Association won all three parliamentary seats in the city immediately after the passing of the Second Reform Bill. This legislation had a minority clause which gave each elector only two votes in a three-seat constituency, and was clearly designed to prevent one party taking all the seats. Yet such was the organising power and influence of the 'Caucus' that this difficulty was overcome by the astute distribution of the Liberal vote.

These successes increased the fears of the critics of the new organisations. These organisations were new, undemocratic and dangerous. In 1902 Ostrogorski wrote that 'the Caucus bids fair to set up government by machine instead of responsible government by human beings'.[5] He saw political power drifting into the hands of professional party bosses, breaking the democratic links between MPs and constituents and encouraging electoral corruption. The Caucus, he claimed, 'warped the representative principle on which parliamentary government reposes',[6] and repressed every attempt at 'independent political thought'. The machines, he continued, attracted the bigot, the enthusiast, while 'the great mass remained outside, sunk in its apathy and its indifference'.[7]

This type of criticism, also levelled at the Conservative

Party, but more mutedly, was to become a familiar charge against political parties in the twentieth century. The claim that unrepresentative party activists undemocratically intruded themselves between the MPs and the voters and distorted the British Constitution is a constant theme in the contemporary Labour Party, and was used, as we shall see later, as a major argument in the constitutional conflicts in the party in the late 1970s.

However, for the Liberal Party, the power of the extra-parliamentary organisations *vis-à-vis* the parliamentary wing was exaggerated. There is no doubt that in regard to policy-making the parliamentary leadership was firmly in control. The radical Newcastle Programme of 1891, adopted by the National Liberal Federation conference, was completely ignored by the Liberal government of 1892—5. Yet it is more difficult to dismiss the charge that the new organisations were internally undemocratic. One view is that the new structures allowed every member of the party to participate in decision-making within the extra-parliamentary organisations. The opposite view maintains that these structures allowed self-elected minorities, unrepresentative of Liberal members and Liberal voters, to dominate the party. Neither view contains the whole truth, and reality lies somewhere between.[8]

The Political Ideas of the Liberal Party.

There is little doubt that throughout its history as one of the two major political parties the Liberal Party remained a coalition.[9] Especially in the second part of the nineteenth century there was not one Liberal creed but a variety of principles, causes and group interests all seeking supremacy. The Liberal Party was more a coalition than was the late nineteenth-century Conservative Party, not least because the Liberal Party was intent, with varying degrees of success, on clearly articulating its views to the electorate. However, the task of disentangling the various strands of Liberalism before 1905 is made difficult by the overlapping nature of these ideological tendencies.

The Whig wing of the party dominated parliamentary representation at the beginning of this period, particularly in the House of Lords. The Whigs constituted the landowning, aristocratic and more conservative element in the Liberal Party. Changing social patterns were not immediately reflected in the structure of representation and parliamentary leadership. The period after 1867 saw an increasing shift of the landed interest towards the Conservative Party. This process was hastened by the Liberal split of 1886, but the Whig element never entirely disappeared in the pre-1905 party: 26 per cent of Liberal MPs were identified as landowners in 1868; this element had dropped to 8 per cent in 1906.[10] The largest element in the party became the industrial and commercial middle classes. It was from this group that the Radical wing of the party drew its strength, and generally this middle-class section provided most of the religious dissenters. The working-class element inside and outside Parliament always remained small, but the Celtic influence was consistently important.

The Radical wing of the party, though never capturing the parliamentary leadership, consistently retained a strong following in the House of Commons and was even more central to the extra-parliamentary organisations. In many ways Radicalism was the most enduring feature of the nineteenth- and early twentieth-century Liberal Party. The Radical creed may be summarised as an individualistic belief in the virtues of *laissez-faire* economics, a suspicion of state power, a hostility to the landed interests and a belief in the need to democratise British political institutions and processes. A moral earnestness based on reason could characterise the basis of Radical action. The Radicals were particularly strong in the National Liberal Federation and in Birmingham, and their most outstanding spokesman before 1886 was Joseph Chamberlain. In 1889 the Radicals attempted to form their own political organisation with their own Whips; but the basic incoherence of Victorian Radicalism, and the inability of the Radicals espousing various political causes to agree on a common programme, ensured its immediate disintegration.[11] The Newcastle Programme of 1891 contained the essence of Liberal Radicalism with proposals for temperance reform, abolition of food taxes, reform of the Lords, disestablishment of the Welsh Church, taxation of land values, leasehold enfranchisement and, of course, Irish Home Rule.

Many of these Radicals represented British Nonconformity in the House of Commons. The degree to which militant Nonconformity was important is sometimes exaggerated, yet Nonconformity was a significant factor in the Liberal Party, especially in galvanising the party into moral crusades. The opposition of the National Education League to the 1870 Education Act is a good example of organised Nonconformity, but it is atypical in the sense that after 1874 Nonconformists tended to work within the party to gain their ends rather than publicly oppose it. There are numerous examples of this strain in the party. There was very strong Nonconformist opposition to the Conservative 1902 Education Act, seen as strengthening Anglican schools from the rates paid by Nonconformists. This issue played an important part in the Liberal victory in the 1906 election, as did the moral indignation at the use of Chinese 'slave labour' in South Africa. The 1906 election saw the last significant gasp of Nonconformity in the Liberal Party. As politics increasingly polarised around class issues, the middle-class leadership of British Nonconformity drifted to the right and the Conservative Party.[12]

Both Radicals and Nonconformists were strongly represented among the 'faddists' of the Liberal Party. These were the Liberals who espoused particular causes, often seeing the success of their cause as the sole aim of political activity. Temperance was the outstanding example throughout the period. Another is the campaign led by Josephine Butler over the Contagious Diseases Act (concerning the regulation of prostitution in garrison towns).

The Liberals also represented the Celtic fringes; Welsh Nonconformity was particularly strong in the party and the campaign to disestablish the Welsh Church was seen to many as being as important as the Second Irish Home Rule Bill in the 1890s. Yet it was the Irish question that impinged most devastatingly on the party, leading to the serious split of 1886. Gladstone's last ministry of 1892–4 was obsessed with Ireland, but the issue temporarily abated after his retirement, until 1910.

Another tendency within the Liberal Party surfaced in the 1890s, that of Liberal imperialism. One historian has described the Liberal imperialists as 'intellectual Whigs'.[13] They centred on the aristocratic personages of Rosebery, Grey and Haldane with opportunist support from Asquith. They distrusted the Little Englanders, such as Morley and Harcourt, rejected the individualism of the Radicals, and wanted a consolidation of Empire based on strong foreign and defence policies. Their approach was based on the yardstick of 'national efficiency'; they judged most domestic issues by the test of whether reforms would be effective in strengthening Britain as a nation. Their reluctance to criticise the Conservative government during the Boer War is an indication of their emphasis on the 'national interest'. The Liberal imperalists, however, were always a less influential element in the party than were the Radicals.[14]

The basic ideological problem for the Liberal Party at the end of the nineteenth century was its relationship to labour. The Party tended to perform badly in the working-class areas of London and Lancashire. We have noted the tendency of middle-class associations to reject working-class candidates. The Lib–Lab tradition was, however, important in the party: working-class representatives had been elected to the House of Commons since the 1870s under the Liberal banner, miners being particularly important in this regard. However, the individualism of the Radicals was quite opposed to 'class representation', and the Radical suspicion of state power did not easily coexist with working-class demands for government intervention. The irony of trade-union representatives often sharing the same constituency with their capitalist masters was not lost on the working-class participants, no matter how enlightened the employer. Often the dominant issues for the Liberal Party, such as temperance, Church disestablishment and Home Rule, seemed irrelevant to labour interests. It was not until the first decade of the twentieth century that the Liberal Party was converted to some degree of social reform and a more flexible attitude in regard to working-class representation in Parliament.

Yet the relationships between these various strands and tendencies within the Liberal Party are highly complex. Working-class MPs could be as individualistic and concerned with temperance as middle-class Radical Nonconformists.

The Welsh Radical could be a 'Little Englander'. But in spite of the divisions in the party, especially during the South African war, no particular tendency succeeded in dominating the party. The emergence of Campbell-Bannerman as leader, then prime minister in 1905, saw the emergence and triumph of an ideological coalition of the centre — a collection of disparate and often conflicting tendencies within the party which he led to a decisive election victory in 1906.

The Conservative Party, 1867–1903

The Conservative Party emerged in the second half of the nineteenth century as a modern national party with a distinctive electoral appeal and a centralised party organisation. Electorally the party was to be the most successful of all in the late nineteenth and in the twentieth centuries. From 1885 to 1980 the Conservative Party formed a single party government with a majority in the House of Commons for forty-six of those years and was faced by a single opposition party having a majority in the Commons in only eighteen of those ninety-five years. In terms of parliamentary representation and government power, the Conservative Party has proved to be the most durable and successful of modern political parties.

As with the other political parties, the Conservative Party reflected the changing social and economic face of Britain and the interrelated impact of political and institutional reform. A measure of the party's response to change can be seen by comparing the relative powerlessness of the party in the large towns in 1868, when it derived its strength from the smaller boroughs and the counties, with the electoral strength of the party in the urban areas, particularly the suburbs, in 1885. In 1885 the Conservative Party won 114 of the 226 English borough seats, as well as maintaining its strength in the rural counties and in industrial Lancashire.

The 1884 Reform Act and the Redistribution of Seats Act of 1885 were important to this new electoral power. The 1885 Act succeeded in splitting the centres of large cities from the more prosperous middle- and lower-middle-class suburbs, and the emergence of a new white-collar class created a firm nucleus of new and old Conservative supporters in these new constituencies: 'Villa Toryism', as it was called, had arrived.[15] Professor Cornford has underlined the political significance of these changes:

> What happened between 1880 and 1885 was not a mass conversion, but the Redistribution Act with its reallocation of seats and its single member constituencies. Where Conservative supporters had formerly been swamped in huge constituencies, they were now high and dry on islands of their own.[16]

Thus the social changes, coupled with boundary changes, helped to compensate for the decline of agricultural prosperity in the 1870s, the loss of the small borough and some county seats in the 1885 Act, and the lower-class enfranchisement of 1884.

Yet in spite of these changes the Conservative Party leadership remained overwhelmingly aristocratic and upper middle class until the second decade of the twentieth century; political decisions in the party were still being made mainly in the country-house circuit of the political and social leaders. It was not the leadership that changed but the political machinery the leadership established and used, coupled with a different emphasis in electoral appeals that changed in the decades after 1867. Yet both the political organisations and the party's electoral programmes had their roots firmly in the years prior to 1867. There was no complete break with the past.

Conservative Party Organisation
After 1832 the Carlton Club was the only central focus of party organisation outside Parliament. Elections were managed by the Whips in conjunction with various firms of solicitors. The degree of electoral co-ordination rested increasingly on the Principal Agent, an appointee of the Whips. After the Second Reform Act the party remained very strong in the rural counties and small towns, and in these constituencies there was no need for strong local organisations. Here the

elections were controlled by the landowners, or in the case of some small boroughs by powerful outsiders. Hanham estimates that in the elections of 1874 there were only forty-four associations in the eighty-two county divisions.[17] The rural counties and the small towns fiercely resisted any attempts by the central organisations in the party to encourage more efficient organisations.

However, the electoral future of the Conservative Party was not to be decided primarily by these constituencies that were to suffer in the political reforms of 1883—5. It was in the larger towns that party organisation was to play such a significant part in deciding elections. Here the party's national bodies encouraged the growth of new local structures.

Partly as a result of the clamour for the 1867 Reform Bill, numerous working men's clubs and associations appeared and became part of the local electoral organisation for the Conservative cause. These new organisations grew alongside older organisations such as the Conservative registration societies and the older working-class groups such as the Operative Conservative Societies of Lancashire and Yorkshire, the products of earlier Tory reform movements. By 1874 there were at least 150 working men's associations in fifty-seven boroughs and five counties,[18] and by 1875 Robert McKenzie estimates that 472 local Conservative associations were affiliated to the National Union.[19] These newer local organisations became more important after 1885 with the greater nationalisation of electoral politics, the larger electorate, and the increasing importance of the party label in winning elections. With this greater impact of local organisation, the role of the central party organs also increased.

The electoral defeat of 1868 and the consequences of the Second Reform Act encouraged more efficient central organisation. The National Union of Conservative and Constitutional Associations was founded in 1867, on a voluntary basis, to co-ordinate the electoral activities of the new working men's clubs and associations. At first it had important rivals in the field of electoral propaganda and management, and in the early 1870s it was not nearly so important as regional electoral organisations such as the Metropolitan Conservative Alliance and the Central Conservative Registration Association.[20] The new organisation came near to collapse in its first two years of existence, with only seven delegates attending its second annual meeting in 1868.[21] However, Disraeli placed J. E. Gorst in charge of the central organisation in 1870. Gorst immediately established the organisation which became the Conservative Central Office and attempted to combine its activities with close liaison and control of the National Union. Thus, already by the early 1870s, the main contours of the modern Conservative Party were discernible: the National Union, concerned with electoral propaganda, was closely linked to the Central Office responsible to the party leader and with important lines of communication to the party whips; local associations with a wide degree of autonomy had the tasks of registering voters, choosing candidates and conducting the elections, co-ordinated through the National Union and, importantly, through the Central Office; finally, and not least, there was the party in Parliament, with unfettered power in the field of policy-making.[22]

Gorst's period as chief party organiser was not always a smooth one for intra-party relations despite its importance for the growth of the party. He constantly quarrelled with the party whips, blaming their interference for the decay of the party organisation after the victory of 1874. The electoral defeat of 1880 led to the recall of Gorst to manage Central Office again for two years. He summarised the main work of the central organisation at this time as that of collecting and distributing information, ensuring the registration of party supporters, propaganda, and the crucial task of stimulating and encouraging the growth of local organisations.[23]

With the growth of local organisations and the National Union, tensions began to appear in the party between the upper-class leadership in Parliament and the more middle-class leadership in the provinces. Party managers such as Gorst wished to democratise the party further and to appeal more directly to the middle classes in the urban constituencies. This movement got caught up with the personal ambitions of Randolph Churchill and the activities of the Fourth Party, but it had little to do with Churchill's demand for 'Tory Democracy' and appeals to the working class.[24] The 1883 Conference of the National Union, orchestrated by Churchill and Gorst, demanded more say in party affairs. The rebellion was soon over; Churchill became reconciled to the party leadership of Lord Salisbury, though he politically overreached himself in 1886 and was cast out into the political wilderness. These events underlined the basic powerlessness of the National Union. It had been created from the top, and had not grown as the National Liberal Federation did from the activities of the constituency rank and file. It resumed once more its permanent role as 'handmaiden' to the party in Parliament and was firmly under the control of Central Office.

In 1885 Captain Middleton became Principal Agent. His period of office to 1903 coincided with a long period of Conservative government. He established good relations with the local associations and the parliamentary leadership and ensured there was to be no democratic challenge to the leadership by the extra-parliamentary organisation. Ostrogorski's thesis had no relevance to the Conservative Party. Middleton's smooth efficiency encouraged the growth in the number of constituency organisations based on uniform models and with the overriding task of returning Conservatives to Parliament. By the time of Middleton's retirement the modern Conservative Party was in existence.

Conservative Party Ideology

In 1867 it could be argued that the Conservative Party had few distinctive ideological differences with the Liberal Party, especially given the consensus on free trade. Lord Salisbury claimed that the mid-century saw no differences of principle between the parties, but merely one of bias: 'the conservative had a prepossession against change, the liberal had a prepossession in its favour'.[25] It cannot be argued that a clear Conservative ideology had emerged by 1900, but the party had by then carved out a distinctive electoral image. In the face of social and political change the party developed a pragmatic acceptance of the new, and when political and electoral realities demanded, the party was even willing to take the initiative.

'Tory Democracy' is a term that indicates the party's willingness to adapt party values to changing political demands. Conservatives were willing to pioneer social and political reform in the face of electoral pressures, but these reforms had to be grafted on to an unchanging power structure. Real political power was to remain in the hands of the propertied classes; the Conservative Party was not to be tainted with political or social egalitarianism.

Disraeli has been consistently praised for his efforts in social reform and his attempts to relieve the economic lot of the lower classes in his 1874–80 administration. The Public Health Act, the Artisans Dwelling Act, the Merchant Shipping Act and his trade-union legislation constitute some of the significant reforms of the period. As one Lib–Lab MP, a contemporary of Disraeli's, said, 'The Conservative party have done more for the working classes in five years than the Liberal party have in fifty.'[26] In his famous Crystal Palace speech of 1872 Disraeli linked social reform with the concept of 'empire', emphasising the need for good health, housing and factory reforms and appearing to give a unity to his romantic image of England as one nation. Yet Disraeli's concern for reform, especially social reform, was vague and superficial; perhaps the Conservative was more paternal than the Liberal. Most reforms in the social sphere before 1900 could have been initiated by either party. There was no clear programme of reform, merely a pragmatic reaction to political realities.[27] Social reform was a theme relatively absent from Conservative government legislation between 1886 and 1905 in spite of the acquisition of the ex-Liberal Radical, Joseph Chamberlain.

However, there was a self-conscious Conservative electoral appeal to the working classes in the late nineteenth century. The party claimed in its election propaganda that it was the Conservative Party not the Liberal Party that had done most to help the lower classes and it called for inter-class unity in the name of patriotism and empire.[28] Nevertheless, the core of the party's strength after 1885 lay with the middle classes, even though electoral victories were impossible without working-class support.

The Conservative themes of authority, hierarchy and the preservation of existing political structures were scarcely changed by the representation of the newer urban classes. The essential aristocratic nature of the party leadership was to last well into the twentieth century. However, there was one important change which has remained the hallmark of the party ever since: it became the national party of patriotism and empire. The imperial policy espoused in the 1870s contrasted sharply with the bulk of the Liberal Party's adherence to 'Little Englandism' and its Gladstonian distaste for the expansion of empire. This new imperial creed was to become linked with the struggle to prevent Home Rule, and, after the end of the Boer War, was to lead to a bitter ideological debate which rocked the party. The retirement of Salisbury in 1902 brought on the intra-party struggle on free trade versus imperial protection.

The Irish Home Rule Party

The Irish Home Rule Party deserves some attention in the study of political parties despite its permanent minority position and its relatively short life. The party was important because the main plank in its platform, that of Home Rule for Ireland obtained by constitutional means, often dominated British politics during this period. The issue effected the important split in the Liberal Party in 1886. In addition, the party held the balance in the House of Commons between 1885 and 1886 and from 1910 until the formation of the Asquith coalition of 1915. An even more crucial reason for the political significance of the party to the student of British political parties is that it pioneered and reflected the rise of centrally dominated political organisations in British politics and the growth of party discipline in the House of Commons. The young Edwardian Labour Party, recognising that a minority position could be compensated by party discipline and parliamentary tactics, sought to emulate the Irish Party.

The Irish Home Rule Party emerged from the political confusion and agrarian agitation in Ireland in the 1860s and 1870s. The Fenians who wanted an independent Ireland to emerge by violent revolution were active in the 1860s, but they did not represent the mainstream of Irish political opinion.[29] However, the Fenians did frighten the more conservative elements in Ireland, particularly the Roman Catholic hierarchy, into greater co-operation with the English Liberal Party. Gladstone, the Liberal leader, was determined to solve Irish problems, and the Liberal cause was strong in the Ireland of the late 1860s. Gladstone did succeed, during the Liberal administration of 1868–74, in disestablishing the Irish Church, but was less successful in regards to education reform, and failed with the all-important land issue, especially that aspect concerning security of tenure. It was out of this failure that the Home Rule Party was born, and the Liberal Party strength in Ireland ebbed.

The Home Rule Party was a conservative party, wanting more self-government within the constitutional structure of the United Kingdom, and its founder and early leader, the amiable Isaac Butt, reinforced this social conservatism; it was difficult to distinguish the party from elements in the Liberal Party. However, with the election of Parnell as leader in 1880, the party began to take on a different complexion. The 'Whig' landlord element was gradually ousted from the party and the leader's control over the parliamentary rank and file became more pronounced. From a loose collection of fifty-seven MPs in 1874 and sixty-one in 1880, the party emerged as the most tightly disciplined of all its contemporaries. The capture of eighty-five seats established the norm that the party was to maintain until 1918.

There were two basic elements in the evolution of the party in these years. First was the organisation within the House of Commons, and second, the party organisation in the constituencies.

Before the election of Parnell as leader the party had engaged in parliamentary guerrilla tactics to force the twin issues of land reform and Home Rule on the attention of the Westminster Parliament. The disruptive effects of these tactics, with one debate in 1881 lasting for forty-two hours, led to the adoption of new procedural rules in the House of Commons. After 1880 Parnell began to stamp his image on the party. He was a conservative, insular man who in spite of his landowning Protestant background had developed an intense dislike for the British ruling classes. He enforced the party pledge by which each member promised to abide by the decisions of the majority, and with a small group of advisers not only dominated the party but ensured that by 1886 all Home Rulers were Parnellites. By 1886 over half of the parliamentary party was receiving financial help from party funds. The degree of party discipline he achieved enabled him to bargain with the two main political parties in the period separating the crucial elections of 1885 and 1886, in the full knowledge of his ability to commit his party.

The Parnellite Irish Home Rule Party also built up political machines in the constituencies that mirrored some of the developments in the contemporary Liberal Party. Before 1880 the Irish Home Rule Party depended on organisations such as the Land League, the Irish Home Rule League, the Home Rule Confederation of Great Britain and on various local clubs with which the clergy dominated the nominating process. It should be noted that at this time the Irish franchise was even more restricted than the franchise in Britain.[30] However, in 1882 the Irish National League was established and dominated by the parliamentary party, and it soon came to control the nominating process. In fact, it was an alliance between the League and the local clergy that assumed control of this process, and it was this alliance, by means of local conventions or selection conferences, that ensured the return of Parnellite candidates. By 1886 there were 1,285 working League branches. The whole process of nomination was effectively controlled by a caucus of the parliamentary party.[31]

Parnell fell from power in 1890; he was cited as co-respondent in a divorce action, a moral lapse which scandalised Gladstone, the Irish Church and conservatives in the Irish Party. His fall temporarily split the Irish Party in the House of Commons, but it was gradually re-united under the leadership of the former Parnell supporter, Redmond. It remained a socially conservative, middle-class, constitutional party until its final annihilation at the polls in the election of 1918. Through its parliamentary discipline and domination of the constituency nominating process, it was to suffer no challenge before 1914. Its pivotal position ensured the passage of the Home Rule Bill through the Commons in 1912, but the outbreak of war and the rapid turn of events in Ireland, particularly after the Easter rising in Dublin in 1916, led to the party's destruction. It managed to return only seven MPs in 1918 and its victorious challengers in the southern part of Ireland refused to attend the House of Commons, establishing their own assembly in Dublin.

The Labour Party before 1903

In the general election of 1900 the Labour Representation Committee (LRC) endorsed fifteen candidates and two, Keir Hardie and Richard Bell, were elected. This was the organisation that was to grow and form the first Labour government in 1924. Before 1880 labour or working-class representation in the House of Commons was sparse; what representation there was was by courtesy of the Liberal Party. After the election of 1880 there were three working men in Parliament, and by 1886 this number had increased to eleven. They were all elected under the Liberal label, being known as 'Lib—Labs'. However, between 1880 and 1900 a genuinely independent working-class party did emerge, with a national organisation and independent parliamentary representation. This party was ultimately to replace the Liberal Party as the main challenger to the Conservative Party in British politics.

It is tempting to view the emergence of the Labour Party as an inevitable process. It could be thought that with the achievement of a wider franchise, the decline of religion, and the growth of trade unions and class politics, the appearance of a working-class party to challenge the parties of capitalism was but a matter of time. Yet the Liberal Party could and did dominate the processes of working-class representation for a long time, and there are strong reasons why it could have continued to do so long into the twentieth century. That it did not was partly a result of its own failings but also of the activities of socialist societies and developments in the trade unions.

The Role of the Liberal Party

The role of the Liberal Party is of crucial importance. It was Ramsay MacDonald, the future Labour leader and first Labour prime minister, who said, in 1895, 'We did not leave the Liberals. They kicked us out and slammed the door in our face.'[32] With the strength of Nonconformity and the personality of Gladstone, the Liberal Party dominated working-class electoral allegiance in the last decades of the nineteenth century. Yet only in the concentrated working-class mining constituencies were the Liberal constituency associations obliged to bow down to the necessity of working-class Liberal candidates, and it was from this type of constituency that the main body of Lib—Lab MPs came. Only in London and in Lancashire did the Liberal Party fail to attract the bulk of the working-class vote.

The Liberal Party succeeded in alienating this working-class support in two ways. First, the emergence of middle-class-dominated caucuses made it more difficult for working-class candidates to get nominated under the auspices of the Liberal Party. (Remember that there was no salary for MPs until 1911.) The best example of this hostility to working-class candidates is to be found in the failure of Keir Hardie, the Scottish miners' nominee, to win Liberal Party backing in Mid-Lanark in 1888; the local Liberals nominated a London barrister instead. Hardie, in spite of his leanings towards Liberalism, was to turn away from the party and ultimately form the Independent Labour Party in 1893. The central Liberal organisations were conscious of the political necessity of winning working-class support and the allegiance of the working-class activists like Hardie, but they were frustrated by the power of the local associations over the selection processes. The national party leaders did finally negotiate the secret deal of 1903 in an attempt to stop the damaging effects of independent labour representation.

Second, the Liberal Party alienated key sections of working-class support before 1900 by ignoring legislative programmes of social and political reform that would benefit the working class. The party was obsessed first with Home Rule and then with House of Lords reform in the 1880s and 1890s and failed to implement the party's own radical Newcastle Programme of 1891 or even the proposal to pay MPs. The party continued to provoke hostility among trade unions by its lack of sympathy to such demands as the shortening of the working day.

The Socialist Societies
Yet these failings of the Liberal Party might have been less

important had it not been for the rise and the political activities of various socialist groups after 1880. Working-class agitation and organisation had not completely collapsed with the death of the Chartist movement in the 1840s, but the 1880s and 1890s witnessed a new blossoming of socialist and working-class organisations outside the ranks of the existing trade-union movement. These groups were to contribute significantly in different ways to the founding of the Labour Party.

The Social Democratic Federation (SDF) was originally founded in 1881 and remained the one avowedly Marxist organisation in British politics in this period. It always remained a sect, but in its nurturing of a Labour leadership and the part it played in raising working-class consciousness it was politically significant. The organisation's numbers were small, but its faith was influential. Yet its weaknesses were manifest. It was weak outside London, its Marxism was narrow and Hyndman's leadership was often a disadvantage. It had too many leaders compared with followers, and was predominantly middle class. Its failure to merge with the ILP in 1893 and 1897 and its early seccession from the newly born LRC in 1901, ensured its relative weakness in terms of working-class representation.

The Fabian Society, founded in 1884, claimed a greater degree of political significance. With some justification, it presented itself as the middle-class political and intellectual powerhouse of the early Labour movement. It was not designed to be a mass party and sought to achieve its ends mainly through a slow permeation of the Liberal Party, detaching itself, before 1900, from all attempts to secure independent working-class representation. Yet although the policy of permeation failed and its claim for intellectual influence was exaggerated, the literary output and research of members such as Sidney and Beatrice Webb provided important justification for working-class political and socio-economic demands. Fabians were to have an important influence on both the organisation and policy directions of the Labour Party before 1918.

However, it was the ILP, founded in Bradford in 1893, that was to represent the mainstream of British socialism and to make the most significant contribution of all the socialist societies to the setting up of the Labour Party. One hundred and twenty delegates, mainly from Lancashire and Yorkshire, founded this essentially provincial organisation. The ILP owed much to the simple political genius of Keir Hardie. He possessed a dogged determination, an organising tact and a socialist faith derived from his early Nonconformity. His 'cloth-cap' entry to the House of Commons in 1892, when he was one of two successful independent working-class MPs, may have been exaggerated,[33] but there is little doubting his zeal in seeking independent working-class representation.

The Trade Unions

Perhaps Hardie's greatest service to the Labour Party was the part he played in persuading the trade unions to support a working-class party. The Trades Union Congress (TUC) had encouraged working-class representation, establishing the Labour Representation League in 1869 and the Labour Electoral Association in 1886. Yet until the turn of the century the trade unions, individually and collectively, were content to seek parliamentary representation through the Liberal Party. The Lib—Labs were strongly organised through the powerful mining and cotton unions, and succeeded in voting down attempts to give TUC support for an independent party in the years before 1899.

There were various contributory causes for the change of attitude among some of the trade unions. We have already mentioned Hardie's tireless diplomacy in the 1890s. The growth of 'new unionism' after 1887 added a degree of militancy to the political outlook of the unions. The 'new unionism' was the movement for organising the unskilled and semi-skilled workers, such as dockers, into trade unions. There was the renewed militant hostility of the employers in certain industries that led to lock-outs and to the establishment of employer organisations on the contemporary American pattern. The employers instigated a number of damaging legal actions against trade unions in the late 1890s which severely restricted the unions' ability to strike, legal actions that were to culminate in the most damaging one of all, the House of Lords' Taff Vale decision of 1901.

All this was taking place against a background of social and economic uncertainty. Cyclical depressions and periods of unemployment reduced the relative living standards of the working class. There was a belief that the lot of the lower classes was deteriorating, especially among the skilled unionised workers, a group from which many of the early Labour Party activists were drawn. This feeling of relative deprivation was intensified by the greater conspicuous consumption of the upper classes that became a feature of late Victorian Britain.

Thus socialist propaganda fell on more receptive ears and it was against this background that the TUC conference of 1899, by a narrow margin, voted for the calling of a conference of all interested bodies with a view to establishing an independent labour party. The socialists had made a significant advance; they were to harness the much-needed financial resources of British trade unionism to the cause of independent working-class representation. Yet the forces working to this end should not be exaggerated. Class consciousness had increased, but many unions steeped in the Lib–Lab tradition were reluctant to cut their links with the Liberal Party. Increased class polarisation did not mean a stronger belief in theories of class conflict, and the strength of 'new unionism' had ebbed somewhat by the mid-1890s. So in many ways the 1899 decision was as surprising as it was important.

The Labour Representation Committee
The political party that emerged from the 1900 conference called by the TUC, the Labour Representation Committee, later to be called the Labour Party, was a strange creature indeed. Organisationally it reflected the federal base of its origins. The conference in February 1900 was attended by 129 representatives of the ILP, the Fabians, the SDF and of over half a million trade unionists. Numerically the trade unionists were overwhelmingly dominant, but the first party executive of twelve gave the trade unions only seven representatives (eight when the SDF left the party a year later). Importantly, Keir Hardie succeeded in getting Ramsay MacDonald, also of the ILP, appointed as party secretary. In the first year of its existence the new party had a trade-union membership of 353,000, while the membership of the socialist societies numbered just over 22,000, which of course dropped

when the SDF left; there were seven constituency parties. In the first election of October 1900, in the unfavourable circumstances of the jingoistic atmosphere of the Boer War, the party had thirty-three pounds to fight the elections, endorsed fifteen candidates, mostly from the ILP, and gained two victories, Hardie in Merthyr Tydfil and Bell in Derby. The membership of the party was to increase dramatically in terms of trade-union membership following the Taff Vale decision. By the end of 1903 the LRC had increased its parliamentary representation to five as a result of by-election victories, though it is important to add that by this time Bell was indistinguishable from the Lib—Labs in the House of Commons.

Ideologically the party reflected its federal framework. It was not a socialist party; the attempt by the SDF to force the party to recognise the 'class war' was defeated at the inaugural conference. The ethical base of nineteenth-century Radicalism was strong, and the gravitational pull of the Liberal Party and support for the various moral causes that Liberalism embraced were still in evidence. The relative parliamentary insignificance of the party forced a greater dependence on the Liberals than was healthy for a new party and there was no immediate guarantee that the party would not be absorbed by the Liberal Party. The secret electoral agreement of 1903, which is discussed in Chapter 3, reflected the weaknesses of both parties, but particularly those of the LRC. Most trade unionists simply regarded the new party as a parliamentary pressure group to protect their interests, and some larger unions, such as the miners, did not join the party for a considerable number of years. There were socialists in the party, but as with the two major parties the LRC was a coalition of many ideas and interests. The one idea that united the majority of its members in the early years was that of independent working-class representation in the House of Commons.

Notes to Chapter 2

1. See J. Vincent, *The Formation of the Liberal Party* (Harmondsworth: Penguin, 1966) pp. 93—101.

50 *The Making of the British Party System, 1867–1922*

2. See T. R. Tholfsen, 'The Origins of the Birmingham Caucus', *Historical Journal*, vol. 2, no. 2, 1959, pp. 161–84. Also P. C. Griffiths, 'The Caucus and the Liberal Party in 1886', *History*, vol. LXI, 1976, pp. 183–97.
3. See H. J. Hanham, *Elections and Party Management in the Time of Gladstone and Disraeli* (London: Longman, 1959) ch. 7.
4. For an account of the setting up of the National Liberal Federation, see F. H. Herrick, 'The Origins of the NLF', *Journal of Modern History*, vol. XVII, 1945, pp. 116–19. See also B. McGill, 'Francis Schnadhorst and the Liberal Party Organisation', *Journal of Modern History*, vol. XXXIV, no. 1, March 1962, pp. 19–39.
5. See M. Ostrogorski, *Democracy and the Organisation of Political Parties*, vol. 1 (Chicago: Quadrangle Books, 1964) p. 304.
6. Ibid, p. 313.
7. Ibid, p. 293.
8. See Hanham, p. 142.
9. See D. A. Hamer, *Liberal Politics in the Age of Gladstone and Rosebery* (Oxford: Clarendon Press, 1972) p. 1.
10. W. L. Guttsman, *The British Political Elite* (London: MacGibbon & Kee, 1965) p. 104.
11. See Hamber, p. 150.
12. See J. F. Glaser, 'English Nonconformity and the Decline of Liberalism', *American Historical Review*, vol. LXIII, no. 2, January 1958, pp. 353–63.
13. H. C. G. Matthew, *The Liberal Imperialists* (Oxford University Press, 1973) p. 290. See also T. Boyle, 'The Liberal Imperialists 1892–1906', *Bulletin of the Institute of Historical Research*, vol. 52, 1979, pp. 48–82.
14. Ibid, p. 289.
15. See Kitson Clarke, *The Making of Victorian England* (London: Methuen, 1962) ch. 8.
16. J. Cornford, 'The Transformation of Conservatism in the Late 19th Century', *Victorian Studies*, vol. 40, no. 7, 1963, p. 58.
17. Hanham, p. 20.
18. Ibid, p. 106.
19. R. T. McKenzie, *British Political Parties*, 2nd edn (London: Heinemann, 1963) p. 159.
20. See E. J. Feuchtwanger, 'J. E. Gorst and the Central Organisation of the Conservative Party, 1870–1882', *Institute of Historical Research Bulletin*, vol. 32, no. 86, November 1959, p. 159.
21. McKenzie, p. 154.
21a. M. Pugh, *The Making of Modern British Politics, 1867–1939* (London: Blackwell) pp. 49–53, stresses the importance of the Primrose League in terms of generating support for the Conservative cause.
22. See list of functions prepared by Gorst in Feuchtwanger, pp. 205–6.

23. The Fourth Party was the title given to the group of four members of the Conservative Party in the House of Commons, Churchill, Wolff, Balfour and Gorst, who from 1880 onwards co-operated with each other virtually independently of the Conservative Party leadership in the Commons. See R. Blake, *The Conservative Party from Peel to Churchill* (London: Eyre & Spottiswoode, 1970) p. 135; and W. S. Churchill, *Lord Randolph Churchill*, 2nd edn (London: Odhams Press, 1951) pp. 104–41. See R. E. Quinalt, 'Lord Randolph Churchill and Tory Democracy 1880–85', *Historical Journal*, vol. 22, no. 2, 1979, pp. 443–54.
24. Quoted in R. B. McDowell, *British Conservatism, 1832–1915* (London: Faber, 1959) p. 61.
25. Quoted in S. Beer, *Modern British Politics*, 2nd edn (London: Faber, 1969) p. 264.
26. See P. Smith, *Disraelian Conservatism and Social Reform* (London: Routledge & Kegan Paul, 1967) pp. 322–3.
27. See R. T. McKenzie and A. Silver, *Angels in Marble* (London: Heinemann, 1968) pp. 42–47, for examples of this propaganda.
28. See E. Norman, *A History of Modern Ireland* (Harmondsworth: Penguin, 1971) p. 155.
29. See Connor Cruise O'Brien, *Parnell and His Party* (Oxford: Clarendon Press, 1964) pp. 39–41.
30. Ibid, pp. 128–33.
31. Quoted in H. Pelling, *The Origins of the Labour Party, 1880–1900*, 2nd edn (Oxford: Clarendon Press, 1964) p. 224.
32. See K. O. Morgan, *Keir Hardie* (London: Weidenfeld & Nicolson, 1975) pp. 54–5, for a discussion of this episode.

3

The Parties in Transition, 1903-22

Introduction

In May 1903 Joseph Chamberlain made a speech in Birmingham calling for the end of free trade in the interest of consolidating the British Empire. The speech was a great sensation and it opened up a wide split in the Conservative Party. In the same year, Captain Middleton, the guiding force behind the Conservative Party organisation since the 1880s, retired. The party was to suffer three consecutive defeats in general elections and would not win an election independently of other parties until 1922. In February 1903 the 'Newcastle Resolution' passed at the Labour Party conference stated that members of the party should not identify themselves with or forward the interests of the Conservative and Liberal Parties. Yet in the same year a secret agreement with the Liberals was a recognition that the Labour Party, for all its independence, would need the co-operation of the Liberal Party to return members to the House of Commons. In January 1906 the Liberal Party scored one of the greatest electoral triumphs in modern times.

Yet in 1922 the Conservative Party, winning the general election with an absolute majority over the other parties, was about to dominate party politics for the next eighteen years. At the same election the Labour Party became the second largest party and the official Opposition in the House of Commons. The Liberal Party, split into two halves, was condemned to third-party status and was to enter a period of decline.

The contrast is stark, yet the outcome not inevitable. The Conservative recovery owed as much to its opponents as it did to its own recuperative powers. The party could have lost its separate identity and merged into an anti-socialist centre party after 1918. It is possible that the Liberal Party could have transformed itself into the permanent majority party of the left, leaving the Labour Party as a small parliamentary pressure group on the flanks of the Liberals. The purpose of this chapter is to analyse the three political parties in turn to discover why neither of these possibilities materialised.

The Conservative Party, 1903—22

The history of the Conservative Party between 1903 and 1922 is only partly dominated by the tariff question; the opposition to the Liberal government's budget of 1909 and the sub-sequent Conservative defence of the House of Lords constitute a second theme. There was also the issue of Irish Home Rule and the party's support for the Protestants in Northern Ireland, support which was to carry the Conservative Party close to the borders of unconstitutionality in the years 1910—14. Again, the experiences as part of the coalition govern-ments from 1915 to 1922 under Asquith and Lloyd George allowed the party to appear in the guise of the national party that was most concerned by the threat of socialism. Finally, to understand the nature of the party in these years, we will have to examine the party leadership and the state of the party organisation.

Free Trade vs Tariff Reform
The origins of the tariff reform movement in the Conservative Party can be found in the alarm felt at the decline of British industry around the turn of the century. In terms of total industrial output, Britain had been overtaken by Germany and the USA; and if the key industries of coal and steel are singled out, the decline was even more pronounced. Britain's share in world trade in industrial goods had also declined

relative to her main competitors, and imports of manufactured goods had increased. As had been the case throughout the nineteenth century Britain maintained a favourable balance of trade by means of invisible exports (shipping, insurance, etc.).

Thus one reason for the imposition of tariffs on imported goods was to protect British industry, but this was only one of the factors in the increased support for tariff reform in the Conservative Party. Joseph Chamberlain's crusade for imperial unity had received further momentum from the shock of the Boer War. The war had heightened the sense of Britain's military vulnerability and political isolation. Preferential treatment for food growers in the Empire would increase imperial unity and ensure a securer outlet for British goods. Imperialism allied to social reform was regarded by Chamberlain's supporters as a sound recipe for ensuring working-class electoral support.[1]

Whatever the causes and origins of the controversy in the party after 1903, there is no doubting the seriousness of the split and the electoral damage it was to cause to the party. The party of political pragmatism was to exhibit an ideological conflict unmatched in the history of the Conservative Party since that time. The party was not only to be ravaged in Parliament but also in the extra-parliamentary sections. Various organisations grew up within and outside the party to marshal support, the most important being the Tariff Reform League and the Free Food League.

The issue split the party in Parliament into three factions: the tariff reformers, the free fooders and the neutrals or fence-sitters centred on Balfour. The tariff reformers constituted the strongest group; by the middle of 1904 they numbered 177 and a year later had increased their total to 245. Proportionately their strength increased after the electoral disaster of 1906, the tariff reformers numbering 79, the Balfourites 49 and the free fooders 31.[2] The free fooders were the supporters of free trade, and were particularly hostile to taxes on food; generally they constituted the conservative wing of the party, preferring the status quo on most matters. They almost completely disappeared from the party in Parliament by 1910 in the face of a lack of protection from the party leadership and a ruthless campaign in the constituencies by the tariff reformers to hound them out of public life.

The position of the neutrals or Balfour faction became increasingly more difficult as the tariff reformers grew in strength. The reformers had captured the support of the National Union, neutralised the pro-Balfour support of the Central Office, and with the help of the Tariff Reform League monopolised the support of the constituency associations. There were hardly any free-food candidates in the Conservative ranks in the January 1910 election. Balfour had begun to make overtures to the dominant tariff-reform faction after the 1906 election and by the first election of 1910 could be regarded as at least a tariff-reform fellow-traveller.

The intense faction fighting within the party between 1903 and 1911 can be seen both as a clash of rival ideologies and a conflict between progressive Conservatives and those whose attitudes were in favour of the status quo. The radicals wanted a link between protectionism, social reform and empire; they tended to be the younger men of the party with industrial/manufacturing backgrounds. Chamberlain, leader of the tariff reformers even after his stroke following the 1906 election, ruthless, impatient of delay, determined to push through his radical policies at all cost, and Balfour, suspicious of change, trying to keep the party united, to some extent symbolised the divisions.

Although the tariff reformers triumphed within the party, their success cost the party dear in general elections. The 'dear-loaf' issue was one of the most important in the 1906 election. The challenge to free trade united a divided Liberal Party and brought out a vastly increased Liberal vote. Issues such as 'Chinese slavery' in South Africa, the controversial 1902 Education Act and the trade-union problem were of great importance in giving the Liberals 400 seats to the Conservatives 157, yet contemporaries pointed to dear food as the central issue.[3]

The same conclusions can be drawn from the January election of 1910. To the Conservative Party, the tariff-reform issue was the most important, yet the party failed to win more seats than the Liberals. The party then retreated from sole concentration on the tariff issue before the December election. Before this second election Balfour agreed that, should the party be successful, the issue of tariff reform would be put to the people in the form of a referendum. After the second defeat for the party in that year, a distinction began to be made between preferential treatment for certain industries and full protectionism. In 1913 the new Conservative leader, Bonar Law, made a promise that, given a Conservative victory in the next election, preferences on food would wait until a further intervening election.

The 1909 Budget and the House of Lords

The action by the House of Lords in rejecting Lloyd George's 1909 Budget threw Britain into a serious constitutional crisis and polarised the political parties to a dangerous degree. It immediately led to the first election of 1910, proposals to limit the power of the House of Lords in the Parliament Bill of April 1910 and to unsuccessful constitutional conferences between the parties to resolve the crisis. The Lords did finally pass the controversial Budget in the April, but neither that nor the constitutional and political complications of Edward VIII's death in May could prevent a second election. Before this second election the new king, George V, promised to create enough Liberal peers in the event of a Liberal electoral victory to swamp the Conservative majority in the Lords and ensure the passage of the Parliament Bill. The narrow government victory in the election secured the passage of legislation through the Commons and, amid great excitement and political tension, the Lords finally passed the Bill in the summer of 1911.

The role of the Conservative Party in these events was both dangerous and self-defeating. The party emerged from them as further divided and was plunged into a crisis of party leadership. Since the 1906 electoral humiliation, the party had begun to recover in terms of by-elections, and the party in the House of Lords had been only rejecting Liberal legislation not tied directly to working-class interests. Thus, while the Education Bill, the Licensing Bill and a measure on plural voting had been defeated, the Upper House had passed the Trade Disputes Act, the Old Age Pensions Act and the Bill dealing with the Eight Hours Day. Yet the party came out totally opposed to Lloyd George's 'People's Budget' of 1909.

There is little doubt that one of the main reasons behind the Budget was Lloyd George's desire to revive the flagging fortunes of the Liberal Party and to tempt the Conservatives into outright opposition. The style of presentation was as dramatic as the contents. The Budget, with its land taxes, liquor tax, mineral rights tax, plus provocative justification, offended every Conservative vested interest. Landowners, brewers, the City of London, tariff reformers, the House of Lords, and both the party in the Commons and the extra-parliamentary organisation, were united in their opposition, and Balfour, falling in with the rest of his party, recommended the dangerous course of House of Lords rejection.

The House of Lords crisis coincided with the fiscal dispute in the party, a period of weakened party leadership, and the party's frustration at its parliamentary impotence. All served to intensify the inter- and intra-party conflict. Conservatives felt that the Liberals did not have enough votes in the House of Commons to introduce important constitutional changes — they did not have a mandate from the people. The Liberals, they believed, were acting unconstitutionally. Above all there was the fear that the Liberal government was leading Britain in the direction of socialism at home and military weakness abroad. The fierce reaction of the Conservatives reflected the degree of polarisation of Edwardian politics. The party came out of the crisis leaderless, divided, electorally rejected twice, having lost on both the Budget and on House of Lords reform. The bitterness of these defeats was in no small measure responsible for the dangerous Irish policies of the party before 1914.

The Conservative Party and Ireland, 1910—14

The dependence of the Liberal government on Irish support in the Commons after the elections of 1910 was bound to bring the Irish question back to the fore in British politics. A Home Rule Bill was introduced into the Commons in 1912, and under the rules of the 1911 Parliament Act shuffled back and forwards from Lords to Commons for two years, being seriously diluted by Asquith in the process. It became law in

September 1914, but was not implemented because of the outbreak of war with Germany.

The Conservative Party had a consistent policy towards the Irish question. It recognised that the Home Rule movement sprang in part from the social and economic ills of Ireland but insisted on the preservation of the Union. Thus before 1905 Conservative governments had tried to 'kill Home Rule with kindness'; the Land Act of 1903 is an example of this approach. However, the atmosphere of crisis that pervaded the Irish question after 1911 was not conducive to party moderation. The determination of the predominantly Protestant North to resist Home Rule, the drilling of volunteers by both Protestants and Catholics and the continual gun-running activities of both sides brought Ireland to the brink of civil war before 1914.

In this heated political atmosphere the Conservative Party adopted attitudes and policies that could only be viewed as unconstitutionally encouraging Ulster Protestant armed resistance. Deprived of a majority in the House of Commons, the party, particularly the flamboyant Carson, urged Protestant Ulster to resist the British government by force. Bonar Law, the Conservative leader, had few doubts as to the constitutional illegality of his party's stance on the issue. In March 1914, demanding an immediate election, he said this:

> I said to the Prime Minister: Make certain — and surely in the face of all this trouble it is worthwhile making certain — that you have the country behind you, and so far as the Unionist party are concerned we will absolutely cease all unconstitutional opposition to the carrying of your measure.[4]

It was from this dangerous course that the First World War rescued the Conservative Party.

The First World War and the Problems of Coalition
The First World War rescued the Conservative Party from its own internal divisions and its unconstitutional tactics and allowed it to pose as the party representing the national interest.[5] In May 1915 the Conservatives joined the Asquith

coalition, which was replaced by the coalition led by Lloyd George in December 1916. The Lloyd George coalition of a section of the Liberals and the Conservative Party lasted until October 1922, having successfully waged the 1918 election gaining 478 of the 707 seats. The questions for students of the Conservative Party are why the party joined and maintained the coalition governments for so long and why the party ended them in 1922.

The first reason why the party joined and maintained the coalitions is that it came to regard itself as the party of the national interest, transcending party conflict. In 1914 the party readily agreed to the electoral truce which ended by-election contests between the parties, including the Labour and Irish parties, for the duration of the war. It joined the Asquith coalition because it felt that national unity and a Conservative contribution to government would be to the benefit of all; the party even accepted a smaller proportion of government posts than its parliamentary size would have reasonably entitled it to. Bonar Law's support for Lloyd George's replacement of Asquith in 1916 could be defended on similar grounds. Asquith had patently failed as a war leader and therefore the party should support the more effective and dynamic leadership of Lloyd George, the only realistic alternative. This time, however, the party did rather better than in 1915 in the distribution of government posts, though Lloyd George's Liberals still had the same number of War Cabinet posts as the Conservatives even though the Liberal Party was now split.

A second reason for the support and the perpetuation of coalition government until 1922 was the fear of socialism. Labour troubles during the war, the Russian revolutions in 1917, the electoral successes of Labour after 1918 and the continuation of industrial conflict after the war created within sections of the Conservative Party, and indeed in parts of both halves of the Liberal Party, a desire for a strong centre party that would stem the tide of socialist advance. The fear of Labour was one motive behind the 1920 discussions between the Conservative Party and the Lloyd George Liberals with a view to fusing the two organisations.[6] The prospect faded and the Conservative Party ultimately broke with Lloyd

George and was to adopt a much more flexible and realistic approach to the growing Labour Party.

The third reason for the Conservative Party's attitude to coalition government in these years was that of narrow party interest. In 1915 the party gained what had eluded it for three successive general elections since 1905, a share in government. In the early years of the war the party did not shrink from capitalising on the mistakes of, and the divisions in, the Liberal Party. The support for Lloyd George in 1916 ensured the downfall of Asquith. The 1918 general election completed this destruction, and the electoral success of the coalition was a vindication of the Conservative view that Lloyd George had to be captured by the party in view of his enormous popularity as 'the man who had won the war'. In some ways the coalition of 1918–22 can be viewed as the Lloyd George–Conservative Party coalition. When the party no longer saw any advantage for itself in maintaining the government, Lloyd George fell from power.

The fall of the coalition in 1922 was the result of various, interrelated factors. The arrangement was always one of mutual convenience; Lloyd George, leader of a diminishing band of coalition Liberals without a grass-roots organisation, needed the Conservatives in 1922 more than they needed him. The mistakes of the government ensured that the marriage of convenience would not last long. Yet the Conservative Party was divided; prominent leaders such as Austen Chamberlain, Balfour and Birkenhead remained firm in their support for the prime minister. At the famous Carlton Club meeting of 1922 the Conservative coalition supporters could still muster 88 to the anti-coalitionists 185 in spite of the government's disastrous record.

A most important consideration shaping attitudes to the coalition was the future of the Conservative Party. Bonar Law stayed out of the government in 1921–2 in order to maintain the integrity of the party, and his prime consideration was party unity. When Younger and other party managers reported that if the Conservatives went into the next election on a coalition ticket, the party could lose up to a hundred seats, for Bonar Law the issue was almost decided. The need to protect the party and the dislike of Lloyd George personally by many Conservatives fused in the famous speech by the party's future leader, Stanley Baldwin, to the Carlton Club meeting:

> It is owing to that dynamic force, and that remarkable personality, that the Liberal Party, to which he formerly belonged, has been smashed to pieces; and it is my firm conviction that, in time, the same thing will happen to our party . . . I think that if the present association is continued, and if this meeting agrees that it should be continued, you will see some more breaking up, and I believe the process must go on inevitably until the old Conservative Party is smashed to atoms and lost in ruins.[7]

Lloyd George resigned the same day as the adverse vote in the Conservative Party meeting. Bonar Law became prime minister and the Conservative Party won 345 seats out of 615 in the November 1922 election.

Party Leadership and Party Organisation

Against the background of intra-party conflict and intense partisanship among the political parties, the role and the position of the party leader became of the utmost importance. Balfour smoothly succeeded Lord Salisbury in 1902 as prime minister and consequently was unanimously elected leader of the party. The position of leader was not always distinct; there had been two leaders after Disraeli retired in 1881, one in the Commons and one in the Lords, and Salisbury only became party leader in 1885 after he had been appointed prime minister. Since the party leader was in the Lords, Balfour had been leader in the Commons since 1891.

Yet however smooth his accession, the leadership of Balfour was far from unchallenged. He was an intellectual aristocrat, detached, rational, able, but not always capable of seeing the electoral consequences of his actions. He presided over a very troubled period in party history and his tenure of office was perhaps prolonged by the fact that his chief adversary, Joseph Chamberlain, was a Liberal Unionist who was physically incapacitated in 1906. The weakness of Balfour's position can be seen in his movement towards the tariff reformers' policies after 1906 and in his agreement with Chamberlain in order to avoid a confrontation before their respective followers. Balfour was no party democrat, and he did not want party policy decided by a party meeting of MPs. The extremism of attitudes over the House of Lords issue in the party finally led to his resignation in 1911; the Ditchers — those adamantly opposed to change, especially with regard to the House of Lords — could not forgive his moderation. His negative concept of opposition in the Commons and the fact that he had committed the worst sin of a Conservative Party leader — he had led the party to three successive election defeats — left him relatively isolated by 1911, and he was driven out of the party leadership.

His successor, Bonar Law, was a different character. He was dour, energetic, with a formidable bluntness of approach. He came from a Presbyterian industrial background and his determination to keep the party united — 'I am their leader. I must follow them'[8] — partly explains his forays into unconstitutional extremism in regard to Ireland. His selection in 1911 throws some light on the nature of the procedural processes of leadership selection. The two front-runners as successors to Balfour, Walter Long and Austen Chamberlain, decided to withdraw, believing that their competition was exacerbating the divisions in the party, and Bonar Law went forward as the only candidate even though he was relatively unknown. Yet he was only elected leader of the party in the House of Commons; Lord Landsdowne continued to lead the party in the Lords. (It is interesting to note that the election of the new leader in 1911 was hurried to avoid the National Union conference claiming the right of participation.)[9] In fact, when Bonar Law was invited to become prime minister after Lloyd George's resignation in 1922, he would only accept the invitation after he had been elected leader of the party, and thus did not become prime minister until his leadership of the party had been approved by MPs, peers and prospective parliamentary candidates. When Bonar Law retired in 1923 because of ill-health, Baldwin was elected leader after he had been appointed prime minister.

The reluctance of the party to appoint a leader who was not prime minister is illustrated by the case of Austen

Chamberlain. When Bonar Law stepped down in March 1921, he only left vacant the position of Conservative leader in the House of Commons; it was to that post that Chamberlain was elected by the Conservatives in the House of Commons, and it was that post that he resigned when his pro-coalition policy was defeated at the Carlton Club in October 1922.

In all political parties it is common to blame the party organisation for election defeats and nowhere more so than in the Conservative Party. The three successive defeats of 1906 and 1910 (twice) led to not unjustified criticism of the party's electoral machine and to measures of reform. The extra-parliamentary organisation had begun to decay before the retirement of the legendary Captain Middleton in 1903, but with his retirement the fusion of the National Union and Central Office that had lasted since 1885 came to an end. The organisational problems were further complicated by the fact that the Conservative Party was in electoral harness with the Liberal Unionists, who until 1912 had their own parliamentary Whips and a separate party organisation.

There is little doubt that the state of the party organisation was responsible for the poor electoral record before 1914.[10] Criticism was made of the poor co-ordination between the centre, especially Central Office, and the constituency parties. The party agents were generally regarded as ageing and inefficient. Constituency parties were in a poor state of repair, often depending on the energy and, more importantly, the financial contributions of the party candidate, though there were notable exceptions, such as Alderman Salvidge's political machine in the Conservative Party-dominated City of Liverpool. The top echelons of the party came in for particularly savage criticism; first Wells and then Hughes were inadequate successors to Middleton, and the Chief Whip from 1902 to 1912, Acland Hood, had deficiencies fully recognised by his friends and himself.

However, much of the responsibility for the poor state of the party's electoral machine can be laid at the door of the bitter internal conflict between the tariff reformers and the free fooders. The tariff reformers had seized control of the National Union and had won support of most of the constituency parties before the 1906 election and were quite ruthless in ousting candidates opposed to their own fiscal views. The large number of changes and retirements immediately before the election did nothing to increase party morale. But the tariff reformers could not capture control of the Central Office or the Whips Office; thus a harmful dualism developed within the party machine. The reformers attempted to democratise the party in the same way that Churchill had tried to do in the 1880s in his bid for the party leadership, and the reforms of 1906 increased the responsibilities of the National Union, particularly in the field of propaganda.

The disastrous electoral consequences of this organisational strife and confusion led to the setting up of a committee to inquire into the party's organisation in 1911. The reforms that resulted ended the bid to democratise the party through increasing the power of the National Union; it was merged once again with the Central Office. Schemes were introduced to improve local parties and, importantly, two new posts were created, a treasurer and a party chairman, the latter to be of Cabinet rank. Balfour, who was once alleged to have said that he would rather take advice from his valet than a Conservative Party conference,[11] at least had the satisfaction at the time of his repudiation of seeing the leadership fully reassert its control over the party machine.

The Labour Party, 1903–22

The Electoral Advances of the Party

The secret agreement negotiated with the Liberals in 1903 established the cornerstone of the electoral efforts of the Labour Party in the elections before 1914. The LRC negotiators, MacDonald and Hardie, had both been rejected by local Liberal parties in the past and both were firmly committed to Labour independence, yet both felt that Labour would not make a sufficient breakthrough in the electoral arena without some form of co-operation with the Liberals at constituency level. Such co-operation had helped Hardie and Bell to get elected in 1900 and gave Shackleton a free run against the Conservatives in Clitheroe in 1903. For the Liberals the attraction of a limited electoral understanding with the LRC stemmed from various considerations. First, there was the harm that triangular contests might do to the Liberal Party in the next election, with the possibility of splits in the 'progressive vote' and the handing over of seats to the Conservative Party. Second, there was no doubt that the Liberal leadership was impressed by the power of the new party; Henderson's success in Barnard Castle over both of the major parties in 1903 and the Labour gain in Woolwich earlier in the same year was evidence of this power. Third, the LRC election fund could be used to relieve hard-pressed Liberals of financial pressures in certain constituencies. Fourth, the Labour Party might succeed where the Liberals had failed in winning working-class seats from the Conservative Party, particularly in London and parts of Lancashire.

The electoral understanding was to be limited to one election only, but in fact its principles dominated Labour—Liberal electoral relations until 1914. The Liberal Party guaranteed no Liberal opposition to Labour candidates in thirty constituencies and in return the LRC was to 'demonstrate friendliness' to the Liberal Party in other constituencies. It was not a formal alliance and it was to remain secret.[12] The fruits of the agreement and its importance to the Labour Party were underlined by the election results of 1906: the LRC put up fifty candidates and thirty-two of these were allowed straight fights with Conservative candidates; only in three of the seventeen seats in which Labour and Liberal opposed each other was the seat 'lost' to the Conservatives; but most importantly, in the thirty seats won by the LRC (twenty-nine plus a Durham miner who declared his allegiance to the party after the election) twenty-seven of these were won without Liberal Party opposition or in two-member constituencies. It should be noted that the inter-party co-operation did not always run smoothly. There were numerous constituencies in which the attempts to enforce the spirit of the agreement caused friction within and between the two parties.

The size of the Liberal majority after the election prevented the Labour Party (it officially changed its name from the LRC in 1906) from exerting great pressure on the new Liberal government, though Labour did have some influence in the drafting of the Trade Disputes Bill that reversed the Taff Vale decision and in the Eight Hour Day legislation. It was difficult for the smaller party to distinguish itself clearly from the Liberals in Parliament given the presence of many Lib—Labs and the complete agreement of many Labour MPs with the Liberal government's programme. The Labour MPs did, however, establish themselves on the opposition benches to emphasise their independence of the Liberals.

The party narrowly elected Hardie as chairman of the parliamentary group in preference to the more Liberal-inclined Shackleton, and in 1907 the party conference gave the parliamentary party a degree of discretion in decision-making without impairing the theoretical sovereignty of the party conference itself. The most significant step in the party's growth after the 1906 election was the Miners' Federation's decision in 1908 to affiliate to the party. The party gained over half a million new members as well as the financial support of this important union. Before affiliation the Labour Party could only claim the allegiance of three of the sixteen representatives of the miners' unions. Yet MPs for mining constituencies in the Labour Party did not all settle happily in the party before 1918 and many continued to hanker after the old alliance with the Liberal Party. Complete loyalty was, however, just a matter of time and the miners' affiliation brought the last of the major unions into the Labour Party.

The years 1909—14 saw a slackening of the momentum for the Labour Party's progress. There were three major reasons for its relative failures in Parliament and in electoral fortunes in these years. First, the political issues of the 1909 Budget, House of Lords reform and the tariff issue tied the party closer to the Liberals, a dependence made worse by the lack of an over-all majority for the Liberals after the 1910 elections. Second, the House of Lords' decision in the Osborne case in 1909 effectively limited the unions' financial contributions to the Labour Party. The judgement was not as devastating to the party as is commonly believed, but it did retard growth. However, the payment of members in 1911 and the repeal of the Osborne judgement in 1913 on more favourable terms for the Labour Party (although this was not realised at the time) ensured that the detrimental effects of 1909 were not long-lasting.[13]

The third factor retarding Labour's growth was the more hostile and aggressive attitude of the Liberal Party in regards to electoral co-operation. In the two elections of 1910 the Liberal Party was unwilling to bargain with the Labour Party to increase the number of Labour seats. In January all twenty-seven Labour candidates in three-cornered contests were unsuccessful. The Liberals gained three seats by attacking ones held by the Labour Party. In twenty-three of the twenty-seven seats in which there was competition from the Liberals, the Labour candidate finished bottom of the poll. A similar pattern emerged in the December election; the party fought fewer seats, and although it had two successes in straight fights with Liberals, it could be strongly argued that the electoral advance of the Labour Party had been halted.[14]

By-elections between 1910 and 1914 have been analysed to support this picture of the containment of Labour; the party lost all four of the seats it was defending in the period, and never finished higher than third in any by-election.[15] However, it has been argued that these by-elections give a false picture of the party's electoral strength in this period since all four losses were in unrepresentative seats, while other contests were also in seats generally unfavourable to the party. In this view party electoral support was growing, and an examination of local election results for the same years, while not over-flattering to Labour, illustrates underlying Liberal weaknesses and the Liberal tendency to seek electoral alliances with the Conservatives at local level to compensate for these weaknesses.[16]

The Labour Party agreed to the electoral truce of August 1914 and Labour's only wartime loss was that of Keir Hardie's old seat of Merthyr Tydfil to a jingoistic Labour independent in 1915. It was not until June 1918 that the party conference voted for the ending of the truce. The war did bring some benefits to the prestige and strength of the party: the trade unions increased in membership and financial strength and they were now consulted by governments (Henderson and others entered the coalition governments after 1915). Indeed, the collectivist attitudes adopted by all wartime governments were generally in tune with Labour ideology. However, the party was seriously harmed by the war; MacDonald resigned as chairman and both the anti-war and pacifist wings of the party became unpopular, as illustrated by the defeats of Labour leaders in the 1918 election. The critics of the war were unpopular in the party, especially those critics in the ILP, and in 1917 the trade unions tried to oust the socialist societies from the Labour Party itself. Events during the war, particularly the industrial unrest on Clydeside and in South Wales, led the unions to a greater emphasis on industrial as opposed to political action, an emphasis that was to last until 1921. It was a pattern that was seriously to weaken the Labour Party.

The party was not successful in the 1918 election; it nominated 361 candidates and only sixty-three won, mainly in Northern constituencies. Most of the successful candidates were nominated by the trade unions and had little parliamentary experience; former parliamentary leaders such as MacDonald, Henderson and Snowden were defeated. Thus the parliamentary party appeared to have been seriously weakened. Certainly its performance from 1918 to 1922 was disappointing and the Labour movement as a whole concentrated more on industrial militancy and tended to neglect the political wing.

Yet these aspects of the Labour Party's performance belied the basic strength of the party. The 1918 Reform Act finally allowed Labour to make the electoral gains in votes and seats that were impossible with the pre-1918 restricted franchise and registration procedures.[17] Its own 1918 Constitution equipped the Labour Party with a structure that allowed it to exploit the new electorate. In addition, the Liberal Party was temporarily split, and the Labour Party, despite its small size, became the largest opposition party in the House of Commons. The spectacular by-election success at Spen Valley in 1919 that so impressed contemporaries was one indication of the pattern that was to emerge. The Labour Party concentrated its electoral fire on the divided Liberal Party and rejected any Liberal requests for electoral co-operation. The 1922 election confirmed Labour's position, the party gaining more seats and votes than both parts of the Liberal Party combined.

Labour Party Organisation, 1903–22

Unlike the other two major parties, the greatest strength of the Labour Party was in its extra-parliamentary organisation. The successes of the Labour Party were in no small measure due to the evolution of an organisation and an increasing membership reflecting the greater involvement of the trade unions. The growth of membership in these years is impressive: from 376,000 in 1901 to 1,072,000 in 1907; it had reached 1,572,000 in 1914. The growth of trade-union membership during the war was reflected in a total Labour Party membership of 2,960,000 by 1918. When the Labour government took office in 1924, the party membership stood at 3,194,000.[18] These membership totals reflected trade-union affiliation, while individual membership through the socialist societies remained relatively small.

The party established in 1900, in fact, did not allow for individual membership or the establishment of local constituency parties, but the pattern of growth before the establishment of the 1918 party constitution did encourage both direct individual membership and the emergence of affiliated local parties, which were formally permitted after 1905. There were many variations in local party organisation before 1918 and Head Office would take into account local factors in the encouragement and approval of the various types of local structures. Basically, the local constituency organisations conformed to four patterns and types:

(1) Local parties affiliated to the Labour Party with individual members paying fees to the local party. Woolwich is the best example of this 'model' party which was to become the norm after 1918.

(2) The trades councils in the area representing the various trade unions would perform the role, often inadequately, of a local party and attempt to co-ordinate the electoral efforts on behalf of a Labour candidate. At first the trades councils formed the majority of the local organisations and their slow replacement by other types of organisation, especially during the war, led to many conflicts as to which local organisation was entitled to affiliate to the Labour Party.

(3) The trades council type of organisation was often indistinguishable from federal local Labour Representation Committees. These consisted of representatives of trade unions and socialist societies in the constituency on the pattern of the central party.

(4) In some areas, especially in the early years, the local socialist society, particularly the ILP, would form the basis of the local party organisation, as was the case with MacDonald's constituency at Leicester.

There were many variations in the above pattern, especially where constituency boundaries did not conform to the area of competence of particular local bodies. The absence of uniform local labour organisations before 1914 gave rise to such incidents as the famous election of Victor Grayson for Colne Valley in 1907. Grayson was supported by various local labour groups and was encouraged by several national leaders of the party, but for various reasons he was denied the official backing of the party. But whatever the type of local electoral organisation, the number of local affiliated organisations continued to rise during the whole period with the exception of the years 1909–13 when the Osborne judgement was having its effect.

The central structure of the party did not change greatly between 1900 and 1918. The party remained a federal party with a sovereign annual conference and a National Executive responsible to and elected by the conference, reflecting the federal nature of the party. Thus in 1910 the National Executive Council (NEC) consisted of fifteen members, of whom eleven were elected by and represented the trade unions, three were elected by the socialist societies and one represented the trades councils. In 1912 there was an additional member of the NEC, the party treasurer elected by the whole conference and therefore, in effect, the choice of the trade unions.

The Labour Party differed from the other two parties in that its parliamentary leadership played an active role in the administration and direction of the party. The two chief figures in the early history of the party who between them did most to ensure its eventual success, MacDonald and

Henderson, occupied at various times the important posts of chairman of the parliamentary party, party secretary and party treasurer before 1914. They held some of these posts simultaneously. The importance of the two men to the early organisational history of the party is more easily forgotten because of the events of 1931 in MacDonald's case and in that of Henderson because he did not appear to play a strong, public, political role. The administrative ability and tireless zeal of both men, with their contrasting personal characteristics, gradually built up a national party.

Henderson was the key figure in the establishment of a new party constitution in 1918. There were several reasons for the need for constitutional changes: the stronger position of the trade unions; the new importance of the party in national politics; the need for a clear break with the Liberals; the inadequacies of the existing structure given the electoral reforms of 1917—18. The main provisions of the new constitution were:

(1) The establishment of the constituency parties as the basic units of local organisation.
(2) The full acceptance of individual membership through local parties alongside indirect membership through trade unions and socialist societies.
(3) All members of the NEC were to be elected by the whole conference instead of the constituent sections.
(4) The NEC was to consist of thirteen representatives from affiliated bodies, five from local parties, four women and a treasurer. (Henderson first proposed eleven union places on the NEC, but he was forced to increase the number to thirteen and eliminate the representative of the trades councils, which were suspected by the conservative unions of harbouring zealots.)
(5) By Clause IV of the new constitution, the party was equipped with a 'socialist' goal.

Party Ideology, 1900—22
There was no overt set of ideological goals established when the LRC was formed in 1900 but Clause IV of the 1918 Constitution reads:

To secure for the producers by hand or by brain the full
fruits of their industry, and the most equitable distribution
thereof that may be possible, upon the basis of the
common ownership of production, and the best obtainable
system of popular administration and control of each
industry or service.

A later conference of the Labour Party in the same year
proceeded to adopt a policy document called *Labour and the
New Social Order,* which gave the party an election programme on broad socialist lines. However, it has been argued
that far from making the Labour Party a socialist party, the
ideological elements in the constitution were introduced as a
'sop to the professional bourgeoisie',[19] and to ensure a clear
distinction between the Labour Party and the Liberal Party.
The wording, in any case, was sufficiently vague to ensure
support from all sections of the party, including the trade
unions, which were still suspicious of the wartime activities
of the socialist societies.

It is in fact difficult to establish whether the Labour Party
had any clear ideological base between 1900 and 1922. The
LRC was formed on the basis of the pragmatism of the trade
unions and the moral zeal of several socialist societies. The
platform that united all parts of the party was the need for
independent working-class representation. The party had its
origins and built its strength on British working-class consciousness and class loyalties, not on the basis of any particular brand of socialism, though the umbrella of the party
embraced many socialists. Many of the early Labour Party
leaders were anxious to establish an independent Labour party
not because they fundamentally disagreed with Liberal goals,
but because they had been rejected by Liberal caucuses.
They saw the Labour Party as a pressure group on the Liberal
flanks, and not as a party destined ultimately to replace the
Liberal Party. The emotional flamboyance of, say, Victor
Grayson's socialism in the House of Commons between 1907
and 1910 was a great embarrassment to many sections of the
Labour Party in Parliament. Shackleton, who always had great
sympathy for the Lib–Lab position, very nearly became
chairman of the parliamentary party in 1906.

Certainly there were critics of this ideological pragmatism. Many of the critics were in the ILP, but the ILP itself had no united coherent socialist view. MacDonald was conscious of this ideological vacuum; in 1905 he said, 'Everytime I go abroad and see on the bookstalls evidence of intellectual and imaginative activity amongst foreign socialists, I am ashamed of our English movement.'[20] Keir Hardie's biographer sees Hardie's 'utter ignorance of socialist theory, especially of Marxism' as a source of strength.[21] The early Labour Party produced no figure of intellectual importance in the tradition of the European socialist parties. Ideology was subservient to the important tasks of organising electoral success. It was perhaps this empiricism that was the party's greatest strength in replacing the Liberal Party. The need to maintain the active support of the trade unions took precedence over ideological purity, and the collectivism of the trade unions was not necessarily an ideological stance. As one historian of the Labour Party in this period has remarked, 'If it is objected that it [the Labour Party] has not served the cause of socialism or even the "true" interests of the working-classes the answer is that it was never designed to.'[22]

The Liberal Party, 1905—22

The Liberals in Power, 1905—15
In December 1905 Campbell-Bannerman formed a minority Liberal government when Balfour resigned. In the election of January 1906 the Liberal Party and its allies scored one of the greatest electoral victories in modern times. Yet within twenty years the party was condemned to a permanent minority position in British politics.

The victory of 1906 cannot be seen as a victory for reform. In fact, it was the Conservative Party that played the more radical role, especially with regard to tariff reform. The Liberal Party was defending free trade and trade-union rights threatened by Taff Vale. It was attacking the Conservative 1902 Education Act and leading the protest against the previous government's South African policy, especially with regard to Chinese labour there. The Liberal Party did not win the election on a positive reform platform; it won by attacking the policies and mistakes of the former Conservative government: 'The prevailing impression of the General Election of 1906 is that it was a sweeping victory for social reform. In fact, nothing could be further from the truth.'[23]

Yet the Liberal administration, partly spurred on by the threat of Labour, did achieve a number of impressive reforms before 1914.[24] It immediately remedied Taff Vale with the Trade Disputes Act, in the eyes of contemporaries giving generous legal immunities to trade unions; and when the Osborne judgement of 1909 threatened the political funds of trade unions, the government partly reversed the decision with its legislation of 1913. The Liberals passed legislation on wages boards, labour exchanges and old-age pensions and finally achieved payment for MPs. Furthermore, the 1909 Budget was seen as an attempt to redistribute income by increasing the taxes of the rich, while the National Insurance Act of 1911 still provides the basis of the modern system. Finally, the government after two general elections and a prolonged constitutional crisis succeeded in enacting the 1911 Parliament Act to reduce the powers of the House of Lords.

There is no doubt where the failures of the Liberal government lay. The House of Lords before and after the Parliament Act sabotaged a great deal of legislation, such as the Education Bill, the plural voting measures and Welsh Disestablishment. The Irish Home Rule legislation was never implemented despite enormous dilutions it suffered before 1914. Besides the constitutional crisis of 1909—11, the government was unable to deal adequately with the militant suffragettes or with the industrial troubles on the eve of war. It presided over the drift to civil war in Ireland between 1910 and 1914, and its foreign policy contributed to the outbreak of the First World War in 1914. In the elections of 1910 the party lost many of the 1906 gains, particularly in the South, and by-election results after 1910 lead to the conclusion that there would have been a Conservative election victory in 1915 if the election had not been postponed until 1918.[25]

This is not to criticise the Liberal Party as such or to claim that there were not circumstances beyond the control of the government; nor is it to neglect the contributions of other political actors. Yet the achievements and failures of the last Liberal administration are important and pertinent to a discussion of the reasons for the party's decline.

Whatever the difficulties faced by the Liberal government before 1914, the government's direction of the war did not enhance its reputation. At first the war united the party behind the leadership in spite of the problems caused to liberal consciences.[26] However, wartime problems erupted with the resignation of Fisher as First Sea Lord and the crisis over the shortage of shells. Bonar Law could not hold back Conservative criticisms of the government, and Asquith, in the interests of national unity, was forced to form a coalition government in May 1915. Wilson called the change of government, 'not merely a Liberal retreat. It was a triumph in party warfare for the Conservatives.'[27]

The setting up of the coalition, reluctantly accepted by many Liberal MPs, did not improve Asquith's political position. Military reverses brought his war leadership increasingly into question and compulsory military service not only led to Liberal revolts in the Cabinet and on the floor of the House of Commons but also succeeded in bringing the struggle between Lloyd George and Asquith out into the open. In December 1916 Asquith resigned and Lloyd George, with the support of Bonar Law and the Conservative Party, became prime minister. The Liberal Party was in effect split into two main factions and was not to experience any form of reunion until 1923. There are many arguments concerning the nature of the conflict between Lloyd George and Asquith which was so damaging to the party. There is no doubt that Lloyd George's political ambitions and his contempt for Asquith's handling of the war were the most important factors; the part played by the Conservatives was also crucial. From the point of view of the political fortunes of the Liberal Party, the short-term reasons for Asquith's resignation — whether he was pushed, whether he chose to go, or whether it was all a political accident — are less important than the split it caused. It is difficult to see, in the light of Lloyd George's ambitions and the role of Bonar Law, any chance of Asquith's survival.[28]

The Divided Party, 1916–22

Lloyd George became prime minister of a government that was heavily dependent on Conservative support. Asquith and all the senior Liberals sat on the Opposition benches, and although for the remaining years of the war there was no sustained opposition to the government from the Asquithian Liberals, the division lobbies increasingly found Liberals on opposite sides. In December 1918, a month after the end of the war, Lloyd George called an election and threw in his lot with the Conservative Party. He secured 159 constituencies in which his 'couponed' Coalition Liberals would not be faced by Conservative opponents, and given his refusal to moderate the general crude dishonesty of the election campaign there was no option but for the two wings of the Liberal Party to attack each other. In the long term the election was a total disaster for the Liberal Party as a whole and a sweeping success for the Conservative Party. The Asquith Liberals put up 253 candidates, 28 of whom were elected, and although the Coalition Liberals were seemingly successful with 133 victories out of 159 contests, these Liberals were elected with Conservative support and often in industrial constituencies that were to make them consequently vulnerable to Labour Party attacks.[29]

The period after 1918 was one of perpetual decline for the Liberal Party. The bitter Leamington Conference of 1920 cemented the split, and Lloyd George formally established his declining group of Liberals as the National Liberal Party in January 1922. The major barrier to any form of reunion was the attitude of Lloyd George himself; as prime minister until the fall of the coalition, he became increasingly a prisoner of his Conservative partners. He constantly hankered after the setting up of a centre party consisting of the Conservatives and his own Liberals as a means of combating the strength of Labour and perpetuating his own power, but it was his own Liberals who thwarted this project in 1920. Yet even after the fall of his government Lloyd George still attempted to keep lines of communication open with sections of the Conservative Party, and his behaviour during the 1922 election was ambivalent in his refusal to attack his former Conservative friends wholeheartedly and in his lack of co-operation with Independent Liberals. Also, of course, his record as prime minister neither improved the Liberal electoral image nor assisted Liberal unity. His handling of the troubled industrial situation gave him the reputation for anti-labourism and increased his fame for political unreliability and Machiavellianism, while his conduct of the civil war in Ireland, especially his notorious pacification programme, united all radicals inside and outside the Liberal Party against him.

Yet all the troubles of the Liberal Party cannot be heaped on the shoulders of Lloyd George. Asquith was an indecisive and politically inept leader of the Independent Liberals; the party was ideologically in confusion, having no strategy to carve out a distinct stance between the Conservative Party and the advancing Labour Party. The Conservatives contemptuously tossed aside the requests for co-operation from the Coalition Liberals in the 1922 election, while after 1918 the Labour Party consistently refused all Liberal overtures for electoral co-operation, much to the bewilderment of those Liberals who looked back nostalgically to Liberal—Labour co-operation before 1914. Now Labour treated the Liberal Party with the same patronising indifference that it itself had experienced from the Liberals after 1910.

The electoral record of both halves of the Liberal Party after 1918 was dismal. The Coalition Liberals lost ten out of twenty-five seats in by-elections and gained none; the Labour victory in Spen Valley in December 1919 was a minority vote victory with the Liberal vote split between two candidates. Yet the electoral malaise went deeper than the party divisions. Both wings of the party consistently lost industrial seats to Labour, and it was this trend that underlined the decline of the party. The record of the Liberals in local elections in these years reflected the national electoral pattern, and in both national and local elections Liberals ceased to contest many seats. In the 1922 election the National Liberals won only 62 of the 162 contests and Asquith's Liberals 54 of 328 contests. Most of the Liberal losses went to Labour, which emerged clearly as the second major party to the Conservatives.

Liberal Party Organisation, 1905—22
During the years of the last Liberal administrations, the party

was organisationally in good shape, at least at the national level. The years before 1914 saw a strengthening of the central organisations at the expense of the local associations. Particularly important here was the centre's control of and the constituencies' need for money; the Chief Whip, through the agency of the Central Association, was able to obtain greater political leverage, especially in terms of candidate selection, through the control of these funds. The party as a whole was not in a more disadvantaged position regarding finance than the Conservative Party, and Liberal governments were equally willing to sell honours to augment party funds.[30]

The Liberal Party was fortunate compared with its main electoral rival in having an able party secretary at this time. Hudson combined the posts of secretary to the National Liberal Federation with that of secretary to the Liberal Central Association, thus ensuring a greater degree of co-ordination between the national organisation for the constituency parties and the parliamentary wing of the party (and, further, ensuring the primacy of the latter). The establishment of regional organisations, Liberal Federations, from 1908, further eroded the power of the local organisations. The setting up of these new organisations certainly took some power from the central bodies but also relieved the Chief Whip's Office of a great deal of work, especially in terms of fund-raising. The Liberal Federations were more susceptible to central influence and their establishment must be seen as a further strengthening of the centre *vis-à-vis* the localities.

Nationally, therefore, the party, faced by a divided Conservative Party before 1914, seemed to possess a cohesive, efficient organisation. An examination of the three elections of 1906 and 1910 appear to give no indication of the future collapse of the party; for example, only 13 Conservatives were returned unopposed in 1906 compared with 163 in 1900, and although the number slightly increased to 19 in January 1910, there was no dramatic fall in the number of Liberal candidates (they only fell by 23 between 1906 and 1910 and there were still a hundred more Liberal candidates in 1910 than there had been in 1900). Although these figures are open to many interpretations and there were problems of clear identification owing to the vagaries of party labelling, they all point on the surface to an improved level of national electoral activity by the Liberals.[31]

However, these national examples may be misleading; the health of local organisations in terms of local electioneering gives a less rosy view. We have already noted that Liberals were seeking local alliances with Conservatives to ward off the Labour challenge in local elections before 1914, and this trend increased after 1918. Thompson has analysed the local organisational weaknesses of the party in London before 1914 and sees these as basically damaging to the Liberal cause.[32] The war, the split of 1916, and the emergence of two Liberal Parties after 1918, demoralised both the central and the local organisations. Lloyd George's Coalition Liberals may have failed to establish any real organisation outside Wales at constituency level, but their electoral activities were very damaging to confused constituency organisations. The reunion in 1923 came too late in the face of the advance of the Labour Party and many Liberal organisations had already withered away. Ideological confusion and lack of direction of the party(ies) after 1918 added further disincentives to the perpetuation of sound Liberal organisation.

The 'New Liberalism'

The Liberal Party achieved its overwhelming victory of 1906 mainly because of mistakes and lack of electoral appeal of the Conservative Party. The election manifesto and the themes echoed by Liberal leaders outlined no new policy departures. Campbell-Bannerman was content to restate the traditional radical tenets of Gladstonian Liberalism. The Liberal Party that won the election was an ideological coalition and it was, on the surface, the traditional Liberal ideological coalition, offering no new departures in the direction of social and economic reform.

Yet the 1906 administration, especially after 1908, is correctly seen as a strong reforming government, most strikingly in social welfare and with state interventionism in the social and economic spheres. It was this new ideological dimension that was given the name 'the new liberalism'.

The impact of 'new liberalism' can be seen in the reform measures of the Liberal governments. The 'new liberalism' emphasised the need for state action to redress blatant social and economic inequalities — to make the state primarily responsible for the relief of poverty. It recognised that economic misfortune was not necessarily the result of individual moral weakness and that collectivist action was necessary to remedy social evils. True, the reforms were sometimes justified on the grounds that they would increase national efficiency or that healthier individuals were more productive individuals; nowhere was this type of approach better illustrated than in the defence for feeding children school meals. Nevertheless, this jump to a recognition of the state as an interested and responsible participant in forms of social reconstruction is ideologically a very important one.

The ideas underlying the 'new liberalism' were not entirely an echo of nineteenth-century social and economic reforms with regulatory and moral emphasis (yet neither were they a revolutionary break). They had been germinating in the latter years of the nineteenth century; they were a response to the recognition of certain social and economic ills, a recognition that had stimulated the revival of English socialism in the 1880s. But it is important to stress the interrelatedness of the reform proposals of 'new liberalism'. They were not merely an electoral response to the Labour Party; far from being piecemeal, they were the consequence of a comprehensive view of British society and they could be seen as a natural progression of nineteenth-century Liberal thought.[33]

The 'new liberalism' was part of the Liberal Party's adjustment to the collectivist demands of the twentieth century. The Labour movement was similarly affected, but ironically part of Labour's process of adjustment was the slow abandonment of the Lib–Lab tradition. Of course, the Liberal Party saw electoral advantages in the new policies; it desperately needed to ensure the support of the working-class vote and to counter the challenge of the Labour Party. The advocates of the 'new liberalism' were certainly stronger in terms of parliamentary representation after 1906. Between 1892 and 1910 the number of businessmen in the party in Parliament decreased, while the number of professional men, especially journalists, increased: a change that would make the party more sympathetic than before to social reform.[34]

Yet one should not exaggerate the changes in Liberal representation. The party in the Commons did not radically differ from the Conservative Party in terms of social composition. The chief differences lay in the landed interest and Anglican strength in the Conservative Party. The advocates of the 'new liberalism' always remained a minority in the party in Parliament, and the business interest, the group most suspicious of the new departures in policy, still remained the largest group in the Liberal coalition. The social radicals suffered worst in the election losses in 1910. They were never a homogeneous group, espousing with varying degrees of enthusiasm the many strands that constituted the 'new liberalism'.

The new creed did not capture all the reformist enthusiasm of the party. Constitutional issues such as the Lords, Ireland and plural voting were important, if necessary, distractions from the themes of social reform. If the traditional middle-class themes of education and temperance had waned in emphasis, Welsh Disestablishment was still there, and the new issue of land reform can only be put under the banner of 'new liberalism' with difficulty.

Because 'new liberalism' was a product of various themes in traditional liberalism, it was more concerned with ameliorating social ills than with any structural attack on the causes of those ills. The social radicals had no wish to alter the fundamental economic relationships in society; they accepted competition as inevitable but wished to remedy its harsher consequences in capitalist society. They did not come to terms with the increasing importance of class in British society. They were certainly not social egalitarians. The Liberals were attempting to be the party of social reform with a classless base, yet in its need to counter the advance of the Labour Party with social reforms the party risked alienating its own middle-class supporters.

Here was a fundamental weakness of the social radicals. They may have been influential at the parliamentary level, but the 'new liberalism' failed to take hold at the constituency level. The middle-class caucuses rejected the new creed just as they rejected working-class representation. There is no evidence of the social radicals responding to grass-roots pressure in the party; on the contrary, local Liberals were more enthusiastic in allying themselves with local Conservatives to fight the working-class menace of Labour. It was the failure to carry the party in the country with them that constituted the greatest weakness of the social radicals. There was some degree of harmony in Parliament, but 'beyond Westminster Liberal adaptability was seriously impeded by the legacy of historical development and the traditional loyalties of class and occupation'.[35]

The Debate on the Decline of the Liberal Party

The debate on the decline of the party has continued unabated; most of the general contours of the discussion have already been touched upon. There are two central questions in the historical controversy: what were the chief factors causing the decline; and whether the decline was 'inevitable'. The evidence is wide-ranging and complex but, at the risk of oversimplification, we can distinguish the following main arguments in the debate:

(1) There are those who emphasise the changing political, social and economic backcloth of Edwardian England and suggest that the Liberal Party could not survive and/or adapt to the crises and changes of the period. George Dangerfield offers the most colourful thesis, claiming that the constitutional crisis over the House of Lords, the industrial disputes, militant suffragettes and above all the Irish question 'slowly undermined England's parliamentary structure until, but for the providential intervention of a world war, it would have certainly collapsed'.[36] These problems, argues Dangerfield, coupled with the rise of the Labour Party, ensured the demise of the Liberal Party before 1914.[37]

Dangerfield's model has been dismissed as a 'literary confection, which does not attempt serious analysis',[38] yet there is no denying the crisis of stability in Edwardian Britain which did not leave the Liberal Party unaffected. The problem Dangerfield does not solve is whether, despite the intensity of the crises it faced, the Liberal Party was fit to survive them. The orthodox reply is that the Liberal Party was incapable of doing so. For example, Pelling argues that the decline of Liberalism 'was the result of long-term social and economic changes which were simultaneously uniting Britain geographically and dividing her inhabitants in terms of class'.[39] He goes on to develop the argument that the Labour Party was in a far more advantageous position to benefit from these changes in the long term.

(2) The interpretations that stress the positive attributes of the Labour Party claim that although the Labour Party suffered electoral setbacks, particularly in the period before 1914, the erosion of the electoral agreements with the Liberals was harming the latter even more. This view emphasises the growing constituency organisations of the Labour Party, and increased support from the trade unions, particularly the change of the miners' allegiance, so electorally important in 1918. The Labour Party was a centralised party with its strength in the extra-parliamentary organisations. In terms of parliamentary representation it had accommodated itself to the politics of class. To argue that there was little ideological difference between the two parties and that therefore the replacement of one party by the other was not necessarily inevitable, is, it is argued, to miss the reasons for the rise of the Labour Party. The Labour Party was less concerned with socialism than with class representation, and it was here that Liberalism failed.[40]

(3) There are a collection of counter-arguments which accept the importance of the socio-economic changes but maintain the Liberal Party (a) was in the process of successfully accommodating itself to these changes, (b) had successfully blunted the rise of the Labour Party, and (c) would have survived as a major party if the effects of war and consequent splits in the leadership had been avoided. Clarke, in his study of pre-war Liberalism in the north-west of England, has strongly argued the 'accommodation' thesis. Through this ideological adaptation, argues Clarke, the Liberal Party was able to make decisive electoral gains in 1906, and to hold them in the 1910 elections; the 'new liberalism' was 'viable', he claims. Furthermore, the party had successfully contained the Labour Party after its initial successes in 1906.[41] In neither ideology nor electoral success could the Labour Party be seen as replacing the Liberal Party before 1914. Thus the war was crucial:

The Liberal party can be compared to an individual who, after a period of robust health and great exertion, experienced symptoms of illness (Ireland, Labour unrest, the suffragettes). Before a thorough diagnosis could be made, he was involved in an encounter with a rampant omnibus (the First World War), which mounted the pavement and ran him over. After lingering painfully, he expired.[42]

(4) However, the problems with these counter-arguments are many. Clarke himself raises the point as to whether generalisations can be made from Lancashire Liberalism, and it may be that, as Pelling suggests, Liberal successes there were more the consequences of the older tariff question. We have already examined the weaknesses of the 'new liberalism'. The Labour Party suffered wartime splits and loss of electoral popularity in the nationalistic fervour of the post-war period. It can also be observed that the Liberals had suffered a severe split in 1886 and yet survived. But the fundamental problem with these views of Liberalism's ability to accommodate itself to change is why did it not similarly accommodate itself to the demands of war? In view of this failure between 1914 and 1918, it is unlikely that the 'new liberalism' would have rescued the Liberal Party from political decline.[43]

Notes to Chapter 3

1. See P. Cain, 'Political Economy in Edwardian England: The "Tariff Reform Controversy" ', in *The Edwardian Age: Conflict and Stability, 1900—1914*, ed. A. O'Day (London: Macmillan, 1979) p. 52.

2. First set of figures from J. Ramsden, *The Age of Balfour and Baldwin, 1902—1940* (London: Longman, 1979) p. 15; the second set of figures from N. Blewett, 'Free Fooders, Balfourites, Whole Hoggers: Factionalism Within the Unionist Party, 1906—10', *Historical Journal*, vol. XI, no. 1, 1968, p. 96. See also A. Sykes, *Tariff Reform in British Politics* (Oxford: Clarendon Press, 1979).

3. See A. K. Russell, *The Liberal Landslide* (Newton Abbot: David & Charles, 1973) pp. 172—82.

4. Quoted in Ramsden, p. 79.

5. There is some conflict on how much the war was to the Conservative Party's advantage. T. Wilson, *The Downfall of the Liberal Party, 1914—35* (London: Collins, 1966) p. 28, represents the view that the party gained from the war. Ramsden, p. 110, offers some qualifications.

6. For a discussion of the various motives behind the 'fusion' moves, see K. O. Morgan, *Consensus and Unity: The Lloyd George Coalition Government, 1918—1922* (Oxford: Clarendon Press, 1979) pp. 174—91.

7. Quoted in K. Middlemas and J. Barnes, *Baldwin* (London: Weidenfeld & Nicolson, 1969) p. 123.

8. Quoted in Ramsden, p. 67.

9. R. T. McKenzie, *British Political Parties*, 2nd edn (London: Heinemann, 1963) p. 29.

10. See Russell, pp. 51—63, for comments on the 1906 election; and N. Blewett, *The Peers, the Parties and the People* (London: Macmillan, 1972) pp. 265—76, for comments on the state of the party organisation in the 1910 elections.

11. McKenzie, p. 82.

12. For details of the agreement and discussion of events leading up to it, see F. Bealey and H. Pelling, *Labour and Politics, 1900—1906* (London: Macmillan, 1958) ch. 6.

13. See A. J. P. Taylor, *English History, 1914—1945* (Oxford: Clarendon Press, 1965) pp. 114—15, for the argument that a separate political fund necessitated by the 1913 Act, far from harming the Labour Party, guaranteed it a regular income from the unions and increased the amount received from that source.

14. See Blewett, pp. 234—65. Also R. I. McKibbin, 'James Ramsay McDonald and the Problem of the Independence of the Labour Party 1910—14', *Journal of Modern History*, vol. 42, no. 2, 1970, pp. 216—235.

15. See R. Douglas, 'Labour in Decline', in *Essays in Anti-Labour History*, ed. K. D. Brown (London: Macmillan, 1974) pp. 105—25.

16. See R. McKibbin, *The Evolution of the Labour Party, 1910—1924* (Oxford University Press, 1974) pp. 20—8. For local election results, see C. Cook, 'Labour and the Downfall of the Liberal Party, 1906—14', in *Crisis and Controversy: Essays in Honour of A. J. P. Taylor*, ed. A. Sked and C. Cook (London: Macmillan, 1976) pp. 38—65.

17. See note 5 to Chapter 1 (p. 24).

18. D. Butler and A. Sloman, *British Political Facts, 1900—79* (London: Macmillan, 1980) p. 142.

19. McKibbin, p. 97.

20. Quoted in D. Marquand, *Ramsay MacDonald* (London: Cape, 1977) p. 88.

21. K. O. Morgan, *Keir Hardie* (London: Weidenfeld & Nicolson, 1975) p. 289.

22. McKibbin, p. 247. See also S. Beer, *Modern British Politics*, 2nd edn (London: Faber, 1969) pp. 137—52.

23. Bealey and Pelling, p. 265.

24. See pp. 79—82 for a discussion of the reasons for the Liberals' new policy departures.

25. M. Pugh, *The Making of Modern British Politics 1867—1939* (London: Blackwell) p. 152, disputes the claim of a possible Conservative victory in 1915.

26. See Wilson, pp. 23–7 and 30–8, for a discussion of the effects of the war on various members of the Liberal Party.
27. Ibid, p. 53.
28. For different views of the crisis, see ibid, pp. 65–97; Taylor, pp. 64–70; and C. Hazlehurst, 'The Conspiracy Myth', in *Lloyd George*, ed. M. Gilbert (Englewood Cliffs, N.J.: Prentice-Hall, 1968) pp. 148–57.
29. See Wilson for a full description of the 'coupon election'. See also E. David, 'The Liberal Party Divided, 1916–18', *Historical Journal*, vol. XIII, no. 3, 1970, pp. 509–33.
30. See Blewett, p. 289.
31. See Russell, p. 59, and Blewett, pp. 209–21.
32. P. Thompson, *Socialists, Liberals and Labour: The Struggle for London, 1885–1914* (London: Routledge & Kegan Paul, 1967) pp. 176–9.
33. For a discussion of these social and economic themes of the 'new liberalism', see H. V. Emy, *Liberals, Radicals and Social Politics 1892–1914* (Cambridge University Press, 1973); P. F. Clarke, *Lancashire and the New Liberalism* (Cambridge University Press, 1971); and M. Freeden, *The New Liberalism* (Oxford University Press, 1978), who states that 'Liberalism was by 1906 intellectually better equipped than any other ideological force to handle the pressing social problems that had at last secured the political lime-light' (p. 255).
34. See Emy, pp. 94–103.
35. M. Petter, 'The Progressive Alliance', *History*, vol. 58, 1973, p. 58. Freeden, p. 148, echoes the view that 'the majority of the Liberal Party did not and could not keep up with the developments in Liberal thought'.
36. G. Dangerfield, *The Strange Death of Liberal England* (London: Paladin, 1966) p. 75.
37. 'With the election of fifty-three Labour representatives, the death of Liberalism was pronounced; it was no longer the Left' (ibid, p. 24).
38. McKibbin, p. 236.
39. H. Pelling, *Popular Politics and Society in Late Victorian Britain*, 2nd edn (London: Macmillan, 1979) p. 120.
40. See McKibbin, pp. 240–4; Pelling, pp. 101–20; and Freeden, p. 149.
41. P. F. Clarke, 'The Electoral Position of the Liberal and Labour Parties 1910–14', *English Historical Review*, vol. 90, no. 358, October 1975. For support of these arguments, see also Douglas, 'Labour in Decline', pp. 105–25.
42. Wilson, p. 18.
43. For a hostile comment on Clarke's thesis, see J. White, 'A Panegyric on Edwardian Liberalism', *Journal of British Studies*, vol. 16, 1977, pp. 143–53, particularly for the comment on p. 51: 'It was not "the war" but *the political response to the war* that was decisive, and in the crucial moment Progressivism was found wanting.'

PART TWO

The Interwar Party System, 1922–40

Introduction: The British Party System, 1922-40

The fall of the Lloyd George coalition in 1922 marked the beginning of a new period in British party politics. The eighteen years between 1922 and the establishment of the Churchill coalition in May 1940 were characterised by four features. First, the Conservatives dominated British politics; there was either a Conservative government (October 1922 to January 1924 and November 1924 to June 1929) or a Conservative-dominated National government (October 1931 to May 1940). Second, this was a period when politicians of relative mediocrity were in the ascendancy, with men like Baldwin, Chamberlain and MacDonald fearing the dynamism and radical proposals of men such as Lloyd George, and even such a maverick as Mosley. Third, it was a time when the labour movement was politically and industrially on the defensive: the unions, despite their constitutional caution, were defeated in the General Strike of 1926, and suffered even more in the economic depression of the 1930s; the Labour Party, despite its determination to follow the road of respectable moderation, produced such unlamented administrations as those of 1924 and 1929–31 and was reduced almost to political insignificance in the election of 1931. Fourth, the period witnessed the continuing decline of the Liberals. The way was being prepared for the post-1945 emergence of a firm two-party system.

The backcloth to these party conflicts was indeed dismal. Unemployment remained high throughout, particularly after the economic crisis of 1931, rising from 10 per cent in 1928 to 22 per cent in 1932 and never dropping below 11 per cent until the outbreak of war. The economic and social miseries of the period, especially the 1930s, are well reflected in the writings of Orwell, the dramatic 'murder' of Jarrow and the hunger marches. The older industries in the north of England, in South Wales and in Scotland declined, producing a marked contrast to the relative prosperity of the South and South-East of England. The history of the 1930s was in retrospect made even more miserable by the failures of British foreign policy; Britain neither averted a war nor was fully prepared for a war, and the appeasement policies of successive British governments produced delay rather than prevention. These failures in economic policy and foreign policy were to have a significant impact on the party system.

After the fall of Lloyd George, Bonar Law won the ensuing November election handsomely, but the major element of this election result was the clear success of the Labour Party over the Liberals:

Conservatives	345 seats with 38% of the vote
Labour	142 seats with 29.5% of the vote
National Liberal (Lloyd George)	62 seats with 11.6% of the vote
Independent Liberal (Asquith)	54 seats with 17.5% of the vote

The party system was still in a most confused state; not only were there three main parties but one of the parties, the Liberals, was split. The complexities of the party system were not made any easier when Baldwin, Bonar Law's successor, suddenly called a surprise election in December 1923 on the issue of tariff reform. This had two main consequences: it allowed the Liberal Party to reunite and fight the election on its ancient strength, free trade, and second it threw the Conservative Party into temporary disarray. The results of the election reflected both aspects:

Conservatives	258 seats with 38.1% of the vote
Labour	191 seats with 30.5% of the vote
Liberal	159 seats with 29.6% of the vote

The chief result of this indecisive election, indecisive in that the government was defeated but still had a simple majority in the Commons, was a display of vacillation by Asquith, disastrous to the Liberals, and the short-lived Labour government of 1924 under Ramsay MacDonald. This first Labour government, cautious and respectable, depending on, yet contemptuous of, tacit Liberal support in the House of Commons, was finally defeated after ten months over a relatively insignificant issue.[1] The ensuing election became notorious for the use of the Zinoviev letter, later shown to be a forgery, but believed by some at the time to be instructions from the Soviet government concerning the encouragement of political unrest. The letter did not decide the election result but its use did underline the suspicions of the Labour Party as a party of socialism and the willingness of Labour's opponents to deny it political legitimacy. The election results were a triumph for the Conservatives and a catastrophe for the Liberals:

Conservatives	419 seats with 48.3% of the vote
Labour	151 seats with 33.0% of the vote
Liberal	40 seats with 17.6% of the vote

Even these returns hide the fact that many Liberals were re-elected with Conservative support and that the Liberal Party did worse in direct confrontation with Labour. *The Economist* claimed in May 1928 that 'The three-party system has come to stay and we have got to learn to live with it', but in fact the 1924 election sounded the death-knell of the Liberals as a major force in British politics. However, the party took an uncommonly long time to sink finally into oblivion.

Baldwin was now the political master. His soft flexibility sought to unite the country and mitigate what he saw as the evils of party conflict across the class divide. However, when challenged, the Conservatives under Baldwin proved able and uncompromising. The defeat of the trade unions in the 1926 General Strike and the harsh Trade Disputes Act which hit trade-union membership of the Labour Party badly may suffice to illustrate this aspect of Conservatism.

The 1929 election gave the Labour Party a simple majority in the House of Commons:

Conservatives	260 seats with 38.2% of the vote
Labour	288 seats with 37.1% of the vote
Liberal	59 seats with 23.4% of the vote

Unlike 1923, the Liberals were in no position to dictate which party formed the next government given the Labour majority over the Conservatives, and the Liberal decline continued. The Labour government trod the same timid path of 1924, but the 1931 economic crisis and the inability of the government to deal with the problems, or even agree on the policies that should be followed, resulted in the establishment of the National Government under MacDonald, including Conservatives and Liberals but with the bulk of the Parliamentary Labour Party in opposition. This government was seen as a temporary expedient, but, much to the political advantage of the Conservative Party and to the detriment of the others, the government decided to extend its life and to fight an election in October 1931. The decision hardened the splits in the other parties, and allowed the Conservative Party to pose as a national party, not a sectional party. The Conservative Party never faced more favourable circumstances in any of its twentieth-century electoral campaigns and it has never won so many seats, even disregarding the successes of its dependent coalition partners:

Conservatives	473 seats with	55.2% of the vote
Liberal and Labour (coalition)	48 seats with	5.3% of the vote
Liberal (Samuel)	33 seats with	6.5% of the vote
National Government	554 seats with	67.0% of the vote
Labour	52 seats with	30.6% of the vote
Liberal (Lloyd George)	4 seats with	0.5% of the vote

It was a most bitter election contest and the split in the Labour Party added to the degree of invective used in the campaign. The Labour Party felt it had been betrayed by its former leaders, MacDonald, Snowden and Thomas, and the latter replied with accusations that the party that they had recently abandoned was rife with Marxists. Ralph Miliband has provided this verdict on the 1931 election:

> Even if account is taken of the General Elections of 1918 and 1924, there can be no good ground for disagreement

with the *Manchester Guardian*'s view voiced at the time, that the campaign of 1931 was 'the most fraudulent campaign of modern times'. Given the manner in which the 'National' government was formed, its composition and programme, it had to be.[2]

The National Government, lasting in theory until 1940, increasingly became purely a Conservative administration; Baldwin became prime minister before the 1935 election with the retirement of the ailing MacDonald. The 1930s was the Conservative decade. Labour made a slight recovery in the 1935 election:

Conservatives	432 seats with 53.7% of the vote
Labour	154 seats with 37.9% of the vote
Liberal	20 seats with 6.4% of the vote[2a]

The large discrepancy in votes between the two major parties underlined the large difference in seats. Many left intellectuals increasingly looked outside the trade-union-led Labour Party, and against the background of the Spanish Civil War and continuing fascist aggression flirted with the Communist Party. The British Union of Fascists increasingly took to street-fighting in the absence of any real political power.

The political influence of the Labour Party was not helped by the accession of Neville Chamberlain to the leadership of the Conservative Party. Chamberlain lacked Baldwin's magnanimity to the weak Labour Party, and inter-party relationships soured. The outbreak of war in 1939 put a premium on Labour's co-operation, but Chamberlain paid for his contempt with Labour's unwillingness to serve under him. His failures as war leader paved the way for the coalition of all parties under Churchill in May 1940. Paul Addison has stressed the importance of the events of May 1940 for the British party system:

The Coalition was formed in a particular fashion . . . In fact it resulted from the public shipwreck of a Conservative administration, and the corollary was that Labour were not *given* office: they broke in and took it, on terms of moral equality.[3]

Notes to the Introduction to Part Two

1. The issue was the non-prosecution of the acting editor of a communist newspaper, the *Workers' Weekly*. See A. J. P. Taylor, *English History, 1914—1945* (Oxford: Clarendon Press, 1965) p. 225, for details of the incident.

2. R. Miliband, *Parliamentary Socialism*, 2nd edn (London: Merlin Press, 1972) p. 189.

2a. For a detailed account of the 1935 election, see C. T. Stannage *Baldwin Thwarts the Opposition. The British General Election of 1935* (London: Croom Helm, 1980).

3. P. Addison, *The Road to 1945* (London: Jonathan Cape, 1975) p. 62.

4

Conservative Party Dominance, 1922-40

Party Leadership

Between 1922 and 1940 the Conservative Party dominated British party politics, only once losing the position of the largest party in the House of Commons, and only for two short periods being denied at least a share in government. Yet Conservative Party historians find it difficult to regard the period with pride; the achievements of the Conservative and Conservative-dominated administrations have, in retrospect, been regarded as poor. Nevertheless, the period in terms of the development of the party is an important one. The party was in a process of adapting to new electoral and political pressures; the expanding electorate, the period's economic difficulties and the importance of foreign and imperial policy provided the backcloth to the party's move away from inflexible Conservatism to a more pragmatic, electorally conscious approach. During this period the party was dominated by the rotund figure of Stanley Baldwin, and to understand the changing nature of Conservatism and the pattern of power distribution within the party, the emergence, the tribulations and the ultimate triumph of this Conservative leader are important.

Baldwin emerged as Conservative leader almost by accident. Bonar Law's illness that forced him to resign in May 1923 was too sudden for the pro-coalition faction in the party, a group that included such prominent figures as Austen Chamberlain and Birkenhead, to work their way back to positions of power within the party after their defeat at the Carlton Club meeting in 1922. There were only two contenders for the positions that Bonar Law had suddenly left vacant: Stanley Baldwin and Lord Curzon. Baldwin was the junior aspirant. He had entered government only in 1917 as Financial Secretary to the Treasury, but did not enter the Cabinet until 1921, first at the Board of Trade, and then, under Bonar Law, he was second choice for the Exchequer. Curzon, on the other hand, had had a glittering political career, holding most of the prestigious offices of state; he had a gilded aristocratic background and a natural arrogance and belief that he would be preferred over the insignificant Baldwin. In fact, Bonar Law, while possibly preferring Baldwin, fully expected Curzon to emerge victorious.

Yet it was Bonar Law's reluctance to advise George V on his successor as prime minister that led to the leadership dispute. Stamfordham, the King's private secretary, began sounding out opinion in the party and found that influential figures supported both candidates; Salisbury, for example, favoured Curzon, and the ex-leader Balfour was an advocate for Baldwin. The extra-parliamentary party expressed pro-Baldwin feelings through the new party chairman, Jackson. There is some dispute as to the influence of a memorandum from Davidson, Bonar Law's secretary, delivered to Stamfordham and claimed by some to represent Bonar Law's preference for Baldwin, yet there is no disputing the fact that the basic reason for George V sending for Baldwin was the latter's membership of the House of Commons and Curzon's confinement to the Lords. Baldwin was unanimously elected as leader of the Conservative Party after his appointment as prime minister.[1]

Baldwin uncharacteristically, and to the puzzlement of many then and since, rushed the party into an immediate election on the issue of free trade versus protection. He neglected either to make soundings within the party or to educate the party or the nation as to the issues involved. The subsequent loss of the Conservative over-all majority and the installation of the first Labour government was a salutary lesson to him; it reinforced his customary political caution and 'never again was he to rush his fences'.[2] Baldwin's period of Conservative leadership is full of such contradictions. He must be separated from his image, partly self-propagated, of a slow, unintelligent, lazy politician, not always in control of his subordinates, yet expressing the desires of the British people at a time of political, economic and social stress, giving the nation the pragmatically based security so desired and which the more dynamic leaders, such as Lloyd George and Churchill, could not provide.

Part of this image bears some resemblance to reality; he was patriotic, uninterested in foreign affairs, centrist in his policies and adverse to change whether it was suggested by the left or the right, and therein may lie the answer to the accusations of policy failure. But this picture ignores the ruthlessness in Baldwin's character. This aspect was clearly illustrated by his conduct and direction of his government during the General Strike of 1926; contrary to many views, Baldwin was in firm control, not directed by his subordinates.[3] His firmness was fully illustrated years later when he secured the abdication of Edward VIII. Yet Baldwin's main claim to fame is his role as party leader. His main aim was the protection of the interests of his party. Before becoming leader he was one of the main factors in the rescue of the party from the clutches of Lloyd George in 1922; he was not too perturbed by the accession to power of Labour in 1924, seeing Asquith dig the Liberals' electoral grave much to the advantage of the Conservative Party; he was ultimately convinced of the need to make either the Labour Party or the Labour leadership responsible for the harsh economic cuts after the 1931 crisis; he risked the accusation of putting party before country in his refusal to re-arm with full vigour in the 1930s.[4] His strength as party leader resulted partly from a warm personality and partly from a lack of extreme partisanship. His greatest claim to fame was that in spite of losing two elections as party leader he maintained his leadership and he chose his moment to retire accompanied by the fulsome praise of his followers.

Baldwin maintained his leadership by employing the same ruthlessness he displayed as prime minister. His greatest test of his control of the party came in the years 1930–1 when a strong attack on Baldwin's leadership developed within the party. The reasons for the attack are many and complex and not necessarily interrelated. First, Baldwin had lost the 1929 election, a not uncommon reason in the Conservative Party for expressing doubts concerning the abilities of the leadership. Second, the issue of Dominion status for India had antagonised the diehards in the party and finally brought Churchill into open opposition to the party's imperial policy. Third, Baldwin was blamed for such dangerous innovations as the enfranchisement of women over the age of 30 and the reform of the Poor Law; at the same time he was earning the criticism of MPs from industrial constituencies of not being sufficiently radical for winning working-class support. Fourth, the organisation of the party came in for heavy criticism; Davidson was regarded as a liability as party chairman because he had not been in the Cabinet and because he immersed himself in the details of party organisation instead of concerning himself with general electoral strategy (probably the real reason here was that Davidson had personally antagonised many influential people in the party). Fifth, Baldwin came in for personal criticism in that he was too detached and failed to provide more dynamic leadership: 'He did not appeal so much to the Party man, as although he was a good Tory, he wasn't really a partisan Tory', is the view of one of his admirers.[5] Finally, however, the issue that caused the main attacks during this period was the perennial one: protection versus free trade.

In January 1930 the Rothermere Press, spearheaded by the *Daily Mail*, launched a campaign against Baldwin and entered into a fragile alliance with Beaverbrook and his Express newspapers to convert the Conservative Party into a party of protection. Both men were prepared to break up the Conservative Party to achieve their aims and greater bitterness was added to the campaign by Rothermere's personal dislike of Baldwin. They launched the United Empire Party, supported by their immense media resources, and began to oppose pro-Baldwin or anti-Empire Free Trade candidates at by-elections. The official Conservative only just beat off the unofficial Beaverbrook nominee at Bromley in August 1930, and in the following February the intervention of a Beaverbrook candidate lost the Conservatives the Islington East seat. Moreover, the threat to intervene in other seats, the rumours that sitting MPs would resign to fight again as Empire Free Trade candidates and the difficulty of finding official party candidates demoralised Central Office. As Beaverbrook himself remarked of the by-election that was to be so important in the leadership struggle, that of St George's, Westminster, in March 1931: 'The primary issue of the by-election will be the leadership of the Conservative Party', and later added, 'If we win this fight the Conservatives will select a new leader and take up our policy and we'll all live happily ever after.'[6]

Baldwin's opponents claimed the scalp of Davidson as early as May 1930; Neville Chamberlain replaced him as chairman. It is difficult to measure the extent of feeling against Baldwin in the House of Commons during these troubled fifteen months, but the Principal Agent, Sir Robert Topping, did express strong doubts as to Baldwin's ability to lead the party to victory at the next election. Baldwin himself thought he would not survive the onslaught and in the October of 1930 he was expected to resign.[7]

Baldwin employed various weapons in his fight for survival. He did suggest at one time that the party might hold a mini-election, with four MPs resigning their seats to test the level of support for Empire Free Trade on a regional basis. He followed the 1911 precedent of calling for a referendum, an initiative that likewise failed to materialise. He was even driven to the lengths of being prepared to fight the St George's by-election with himself as the candidate, an idea which fortunately for the authority of the leadership came to nothing. All through the months of victories and setbacks he continued to negotiate with his main opponents, using Neville Chamberlain as his main means of communication. He consistently played for time, giving the opposition the impression that he was moving to their policy positions. He even called for what amounted to a vote of confidence from the party when he summoned a meeting at the Caxton Hall in October 1930, probably his lowest period, of MPs, peers and candidates, winning by 462 votes to 116. At no time could it be said that Baldwin was masterminding a victory campaign; he existed from day to day, his pessimism interrupted by bouts of enthusiasm. Yet when aroused he proved a formidable opponent. It was the lukewarm attitudes of support from Neville Chamberlain and Lord Hailsham, coupled with the request from Austen Chamberlain for the release of his brother, Neville, from the party chairmanship (presumably to be in a better position to challenge the party leader), that drove Baldwin into furious fighting stances. He threw himself wholeheartedly into the St George's election in support of Duff Cooper, and it was this campaign that produced his most aggressive speech castigating the power of the press magnates: 'What the proprietorship of these papers is aiming at is power, and power without responsibility – the prerogative of the harlot throughout the ages.'[8]

If the by-election victory proved the turning-point in Baldwin's fight for political survival, the basic reasons for his survival lie elsewhere. Certainly his renewed vigour and determination are important factors and he was fortunate in being able to turn the last stages of the intra-party struggle into one of the legitimate party leadership against extra-party press interference. Yet the keys to his victory lie elsewhere. First, his many opponents inside and outside the party never joined forces; the Empire Free Trade enthusiasts did not align themselves clearly with the critics of Baldwin's India policy and there was a great deal of personal suspicion between his opponents in the various opposition camps; Beaverbrook's suspicion of Rothermere is one example. More importantly, Chamberlain, the likely successor in the event of leadership changes, played an ambivalent role. He fully expected that Baldwin would be ousted, but as party chairman he loyally put the party organisation behind the leader. He was critical of Baldwin in private, yet his failure to act directly in any way to bring Baldwin down was the major reason for Baldwin's eventual triumph. Chamberlain summed up his own dilemma of wanting the party leadership and at the same time being forced to show loyalty: 'I cannot see my way out. I am the one person who might bring about S.B.'s retirement, but I cannot act when my action might put me in his place.'[9]

The Rise and Fall of Chamberlain, 1937–40

There was no succession crisis when Baldwin finally stepped

down as prime minister and party leader in May 1937. Chamberlain earned his reward for long service to the party and for his fragile loyalty during the leadership crisis of 1930–1. He belonged, like his father and half-brother, to the Liberal Unionist strand of the party, and in domestic policies he was more progressive in terms of paternalistic social reform than most of his followers. He proved to be a more dynamic leader than Baldwin, both in terms of party management and government policy, yet his vision was narrower. He was reluctant to delegate, was suspicious of his subordinates, and he was very confident of his own abilities. His contempt for the Labour Party, and especially for its parliamentary leadership, was never hidden: a mutual dislike that was to prove of great significance in his struggle to survive in 1940.

His period as prime minister was short, though he did remain titular party leader for a short while longer. It is interesting to note that the leaders of the party in the twentieth century who had least difficulty in reaching the leadership, Balfour, Chamberlain and Eden, were all forced to resign after a difficult period in office. The turning-point in Chamberlain's tenure of office was the Munich Agreement of September 1938. Whatever the military justification of the need to reach an agreement with Germany, it was ultimately to discredit the prime minister when the policy upon which it was based failed. Although Chamberlain succeeded almost to the end in securing the support of the majority of his party, there was a slow erosion of support, especially after the outbreak of war. Even during the 'phoney-war' period from September 1939 to May 1940, Chamberlain continued to believe that full-scale war with Germany could be averted, and as late as April 1940 he could claim that Hitler had 'missed the bus'. These failures were compounded by his reluctance to put the country on a clear war footing. He ignored pleas to institute the same type of War Cabinet as that set up by Lloyd George in 1916, and furthermore, he insisted on retaining in his government those men who had been most discredited by the defence failures.

There were two further elements that led to his final downfall. First, by including Churchill in his reconstituted government he had strengthened one of his main critics, and although

Churchill was to remain loyal to his leader until Chamberlain resigned, his image as the man who was determined to wage an all-out war was constantly strengthened. Second, Chamberlain's disdain for the Labour Party remained unabated. There was a growing recognition after the outbreak of war that a coalition of all parties should be formed and that the full support of all sections of the labour movement should be harnessed to the war effort. Chamberlain did not resign immediately after the dramatic fall in the size of his majority in the Norwegian Campaign debate in the Commons in May 1940; the decision to resign was made inevitable afterwards when the Labour Party again refused to join his government.

The result of the May debate in the Commons was not inevitable; Chamberlain still had strong party support in spite of the failure of the British military expedition to Norway. However, Chamberlain and his party managers misjudged the intensity of feelings among his critics within the party. There were a series of effective speeches scorning Chamberlain's position, particularly from Amery, Lloyd George and Keyes. The prime minister mistakenly appealed to the loyalty of 'his friends', and in spite of Churchill's support his majority in the Commons slumped from the normal 200 down to 81: eighty of his supporters voted against him or abstained.

On 10 May Chamberlain and the Chief Whip called both Winston Churchill and Lord Halifax to a meeting to settle the succession. Both the prime minister and the Chief Whip appeared to favour Halifax, as did many leaders in the Labour Party. However, when at the crucial moment Chamberlain asked Churchill or Halifax to speak, there was a pause and then Halifax said that he would be willing to serve under Churchill, adding that his membership of the House of Lords was a disadvantage. In his memoirs Churchill says of this moment when power passed to him: 'As I remained silent a very long pause ensued. It certainly seemed longer than the two minutes which one observes in the commemoration of Armistice Day. Then at last Halifax spoke.'[10] Chamberlain preferred Halifax, but all knew that Halifax could not form a government without Churchill's co-operation; the period of silence cast doubt on Churchill's willingness to serve under

Halifax. Churchill was able to become prime minister because by now he had sufficient support in the Conservative Party as well as in the other parliamentary parties. Yet Chamberlain remained an influential and popular figure in the party. In fact, Churchill did not become leader of the Conservative Party until 9 October 1940, when ill-health forced Chamberlain to retire completely. A Liberal Unionist had been replaced by a party leader who had been a Liberal minister, an independent MP, a Conservative minister and then, throughout the 1930s, a constant critic of Conservative administrations.

The Organisation of the Conservative Party between the Wars

There were no fundamental changes in the organisational structure of the party during this period, and neither was the power balance between the parliamentary and extra-parliamentary wings of the party disturbed. As usual there were inquests after the election defeats of 1923 and 1929, but these investigations did not lead to changes comparable with those following the 1945 defeat. The Fourth Reform Act increased the size of the electorate and brought women into greater prominence. It abolished the need for parties to concentrate on the registration of voters; thus the Conservative Party, especially at the local level, could concentrate on fund-raising and recruitment, which in turn led to an emphasis on social activities. Some of the confusion regarding names was removed, at least at the national level, by the decision in 1925 to revert to the title 'Conservative' instead of giving prominence to the name 'Unionist'. The party had added the title 'Unionist' to its party label after the Liberal Unionists split with the Liberals in 1886 and became almost indistinguishable from the Conservatives. As the Conservative Party and the Liberal Unionists had formally merged in 1912, the 1925 decision had little significance for the organisation of the party.

There were changes that increased the organisational efficiency of the party. Agents became more professional, improved their status and increased their pay. The party became more conscious of the need to raise money, and

Davidson, the party chairman between 1926 and 1930, was particularly successful in this regard. Although some of the blatant methods of the Lloyd George period were abandoned, the party continued to raise funds through the sale of honours.[11] Davidson has also thrown interesting light on the party's intelligence services or spy network, or what would be called in the USA during the Watergate scandal the 'dirty tricks department':

> With Joseph Ball I ran a little intelligence service of our own, quite separate from the Party organisation. We had agents in certain key centres and we also had agents actually in the Labour Party Headquarters, with the result that we got their reports on political feeling in the country as well as our own. We also got advance 'pulls' of their literature. This we arranged with Odhams Press, who did most of the Labour Party printing, with the result that we frequently received copies of their leaflets and pamphlets before they reached Transport House. This was of enormous value to us because we were able to study the Labour Party policy in advance, and in the case of leaflets we could produce a reply to appear simultaneously with their production.[12]

However, Davidson did legitimately improve the output and the quality of party publicity and propaganda, and rightly claimed responsibility for the establishment of the Conservative Research Department in 1929. There were other organisational changes at the top at this time: the post of chairman of the party organisation was finally separated from that of chairman of the executive committee of the National Union, giving the latter post more formal autonomy; in 1931 the post of Principal Agent was converted into that of General Director. Yet the importance of these posts depended on the quality of the incumbents, and after a few disastrous appointments the calibre improved with the appointment of first Blain and then Topping, the latter holding the newly named position of General Director until the end of the war.

The period also saw a democratisation of the party at its constituency base. The increasing power of women and the continuing influx of the middle class made local parties more sensitive to the main areas of electoral support. MPs and candidates were less and less expected to support the local party out of their own pockets; Baldwin, for example, ended his payments to his constituency party in 1928. Thus the independence and democratic aspects of local parties were enhanced.

Of course, there were still many problems in terms of organisation. The party organisation was justly criticised for the cautious approach to the 1929 election and the concentration of electoral fire on the Liberal Party. Personality clashes were a feature of these years, as of any others, and Davidson's quarrels with Blain and the campaign against the party chairman in 1929–30 are but two examples. The degree of democracy within the party was qualified by the fact that although the middle class and the business elements were gradually replacing the upper class and aristocratic strain,[13] the party still basically closed the door against working-class representation at most levels within the party despite the importance of the working-class vote. Furthermore, no matter how democratic the lower echelons of the party were, the extra-parliamentary wing of the party was still denied a voice in the direction of party policy. Certainly, the National Union helped to bring down the coalition in 1922, and, as we have seen (p. 60), Younger's advice on party opinion in the extra-parliamentary party was quite crucial. The leadership narrowly escaped defeat at the hands of the National Union on Ireland in 1921 and on India in 1933–4, yet all attempts to force the parliamentary leadership to reform the House of Lords were unavailing. The plaintive cry of a speaker at the Conservative conference of 1929 aptly sums up the distribution of power within the party: 'The party was very democratic until it reached the top.'[14]

The Changing Nature of Conservatism, 1922–40

Baldwin's pragmatic approach to Conservatism dominates the interwar period. He attempted to project an image of 'English' common sense which produced a cautious inactive approach to the role of government and a suspicion of men of action and theory such as Lloyd George or Keynes. His anti-theoretical approach to political problems would have accepted that 'The mind, when it is allowed to indulge in speculative thought, is an ambitious, organising and dictatorial instrument. It is drawn to absolutes and systems. It seeks to impose rational order upon natural disorder.'[15] His dislike of socialism was based on the view that it was an imported foreign system, but his political sense allowed him to be indulgent towards the Labour Party and to recognise its moral, English basis.

Baldwin's slow-moving, political pragmatism was exemplified in the type of election campaign he waged in 1929 with its emphasis on 'Safety First'. There is an absence of support for any form of egalitarianism, and Baldwin would have shared Leo Amery's view of British democracy as 'government of the people, for the people, with, but not by, the people'.[16] Baldwin emphasised the responsible paternalist strand of modern Conservatism, while the vindictiveness of the 1927 Trades Disputes Act showed the teeth of Conservatism when that paternalism was challenged.

Although Baldwin was not interested in social reform, this was not true of Neville Chamberlain. While Minister of Health in 1924, Chamberlain planned twenty-five Bills, of which twenty-one reached the statute book,[17] and this interest in aspects of social reform continued throughout his political career, emphasising the Liberal Unionist strand in interwar Conservatism. He legislated on housing, health insurance, unemployment insurance, factories, and the Poor Law, with an aggressive administrative confidence that would have entitled him to membership of the Fabian Society.

However, it was the changing Conservative attitude to the government's role in the management of the economy that exemplified the most significant change in interwar Conservatism. Baldwin was generally opposed to government interference in trade and industry, though here, as elsewhere, his pragmatism overrode any theoretical preferences. There were examples of nationalisation during the 1920s, such as the BBC and electricity generation, but it was the return of the Gold Standard that clearly illustrated Baldwin's economic orthodoxy. Yet the demands of economic crisis after 1930 were to force new directions on the Conservative Party. True, the party did not yet embrace Keynesian economics, but there was a gradual abandonment of *laissez-faire* doctrines; the swift abandonment of the Gold Standard and the culmination of the long drawn-out struggle to adopt protective tariffs are the clearest indications of the new economic approaches in Conservative policies. This was the start of an approach to collectivism that was not to be challenged seriously in the party until the 1970s. Beer claims that it was the Conservative-dominated National government which laid the foundations of the modern managed economy.[18]

In spite of this pragmatism before and after the Great Depression, we should recall that the Conservative Party remained what it has always been, an ideological coalition. Certainly, the intense debates and struggles that harmed the party's electoral chances before 1914 disappeared, but the reactionary elements in the party continued to fight over Ireland before 1922 and over India in the 1930s. It was fortunate that the defence and foreign policy debates of the late 1930s cut across left—right divisions in the party and so did not widen differences already present. There was still a radical left, albeit small, symbolising the patrician concern with the working classes that could not be mirrored by the municipal, cold, bureaucratic efficiency of a Chamberlain. Harold Macmillan best exemplified this older tradition with his book, *The Middle Way,* published in 1938. Macmillan, representing a Northern industrial constituency (a constituency unrepresentative of the main Conservative strongholds), advocated Keynesian economics, greater state interference and a greater emphasis on the provision of welfare. It was Macmillan's ideas that were to seize hold of the Conservative Party during and after the Second World War.

Notes to Chapter 4

1. The dispute over whether Davidson's memorandum was seen as an expression of Bonar Law's views is partly obscured by our ignorance of Stamfordham's reaction to the document he had asked Davidson to submit. The King's secretary favoured Curzon, yet, Davidson's courier, the unreliable Waterhouse, did not know, according to

Davidson, the contents of the memorandum. It is probable that Stamfordham accepted the memorandum as expressing the opinions of Davidson alone, and even if this is in doubt it is unlikely that the memorandum alone would have decided the succession issue. See R. Rhodes James, *Memoirs of a Conservative: J. C. C. Davidson's Memoirs and Papers, 1910–37* (London: Weidenfeld & Nicolson, 1969) pp. 150–66; K. Middlemas and J. Barnes, *Baldwin* (London: Weidenfeld & Nicolson, 1969) pp. 161–7; R. Blake, *The Unknown Prime Minister: The Life and Times of Andrew Bonar Law, 1858–1923* (London: Eyre & Spottiswoode, 1955) pp. 516–28.

2. Middlemas and Barnes, p. 248.
3. Ibid, pp. 378–417.
4. In November 1936 Baldwin said: 'Supposing I had gone to the country and said that Germany was re-arming and we must re-arm . . . I cannot think of anything that would have made the loss of the election from my point of view more certain.' Quoted in G. M. Young, *Stanley Baldwin* (London: Rupert Hart-Davis, 1952) p. 229.
5. Rhodes James, p. 171.
6. Quoted in A. J. P. Taylor, *Beaverbrook* (Harmondsworth: Penguin, 1974) p. 400.
7. See Middlemas and Barnes, pp. 578 and 586.
8. Ibid, pp. 599–600. There is the odd curiosity that Duff Cooper had previously sent a telegram of congratulation to Beaverbrook when Beaverbrook's candidate beat the official Conservative at South Paddington in October 1930. See Taylor, p. 390.
9. K. G. Feiling, *The Life of Neville Chamberlain* (London: Macmillan, 1946) p. 185.
10. W. S. Churchill, *The Second World War: Vol 1 The Gathering Storm* (London: Cassell, 1948) p. 529.
11. Davidson claims that he ended the sale of honours completely, but Ramsden has pointed out that the sale was simply done more discreetly. See Rhodes James, pp. 278–90; and J. Ramsden, *The Age of Balfour and Baldwin* (London: Longman, 1978) pp. 221–4.
12. Rhodes James, p. 272.
13. See Ramsden, p. 361, for a survey of the changing occupational backgrounds of Conservative MPs between 1914 and 1939.
14. Quoted in R. T. McKenzie, *British Political Parties*, 2nd edn (London: Heinemann, 1963) p. 181.
15. I. Gilmour, *Inside Right: A Study of Conservatism* (London: Hutchinson, 1977) p. 113.
16. Quoted in S. Beer, *Modern British Politics* (London: Faber, 1969) p. 95.
17. Feiling, p. 129.
18. Beer, pp. 278–301.

5

The Labour Party in Turmoil, 1922-40

The Labour Party, 1922–31

When the Labour Party became the official Opposition in the House of Commons after the election of 1922 it introduced a significant change regarding the party leadership. Ramsay MacDonald, who had been elected chairman of the parliamentary party in place of Clynes, was referred to as 'Chairman and Leader'. This titular change represented an important shift of power in the Labour Party; as a potential government, the PLP now began to emphasise its greater independence of the extra-parliamentary party, and as potential prime minister the leader of the PLP was increasing his power both at the expense of the party outside Parliament and within the PLP itself. Since 1906 the party had changed its chairman no less than six times and the post had never won the power and status accredited to the leader in the Conservative and Liberal Parties. After 1922 the Labour Party more clearly conformed to the practices of British parliamentary government, and in spite of opposition to the leadership concept within the party inside and outside Parliament the period from 1922 to the establishment of the National government in 1931 was a period of the undoubted domination of MacDonald over all sections of the party.

Evidence of the power of the leader may be found in an examination of the short experience of the minority Labour government from January to October 1924. There were discussions in all sections of the party concerning the advisability of taking office as a result of the inconclusive 1923 election. MacDonald himself was clearly eager to take up the challenge. Above all, MacDonald, with his gradualist view of parliamentary politics, wanted to show that Labour could govern competently and with moderation, thus enabling the party to win more middle-class support and finally lay to rest the myth that the Labour Party wished the establishment of a Soviet-style system in Britain. His latest biographer comments: 'MacDonald had not become prime minister to devise a new economic policy, but to prove that Labour could form a presentable government and to drive the Liberals out of the middle ground of politics.'[1]

In forming his government MacDonald consulted no one. Discussions within the party centred on the precedents established by the Australian Labour Party for a greater party say in the composition and balance of a Labour government, but MacDonald swept any doubts aside. He formed his minority government with the same degree of independence from party control as any previous Liberal or Conservative prime minister. McKenzie has underlined the significance of this moment in Labour Party history:

> MacDonald conformed to the usual British parliamentary practice and as far as is publicly known no attempt was made by his immediate colleagues or by the PLP to impose any other system on him. By accepting all the customary parliamentary practices with regard to both the Prime Minister and the Cabinet, the Labour Party moved in one great stride towards the full acceptance of the leadership principle which had been operative throughout the modern history of the Conservative and Liberal Parties. Thereafter, even when the Labour Party returned to opposition, it could not seriously be pretended that the Chairman of the PLP was merely an ordinary member of the parliamentary party who happened to be chosen to serve for a year as spokesman for his colleagues.[2]

After the fall of the Labour government in October 1924, in spite of widespread disappointment in the party over the failure of the government to achieve or even strive for what could be called socialist objectives, the prestige and power of MacDonald remained intact. Ernest Bevin, leader of the recently formed Transport Workers' Union, led an attempt to put curbs on the leadership as regards its freedom to form minority governments in the future, but the attempt was easily defeated at the 1925 conference. In 1924 and 1925 all conference motions attempting to impose stricter party control over the PLP and a Labour Cabinet were likewise defeated.[3] It is true that MacDonald was prepared to discuss Cabinet-making with his senior colleagues when he formed his second minority government in 1929, and there is evidence that he was reluctantly forced to agree to Henderson becoming Foreign Secretary.[4] However, the basic principles established in 1924 were adhered to: the Labour leader had the same political freedom as other party leaders. When the government resigned in the midst of the August crisis of 1931 and MacDonald left to form the National government, he was not immediately expelled from the party, and loyalty to him, even in this moment of crisis, was surprisingly very high.

Part of the explanation for the ascendancy of the leadership in this period lies in the character and personality of MacDonald. He was a complex man, sensitive, touchy, moody and often suspicious of others' motives, fearing conspiracies against his leadership; surprisingly his belief that others were plotting against him even brought him to suspect the unambitious and loyal Henderson. He was accused of social climbing and snobbery, preferring the company of titled ladies such as Lady Londonderry to the basic camaraderie of the Labour Party that Henderson revelled in. Philip Snowden relates the following story concerning the establishment of the National government in 1931: 'I remarked to him [MacDonald] that he would now find himself very popular in strange quarters. He replied, gleefully rubbing his hands: "Yes, tomorrow every Duchess in London will be wanting to kiss me".'[5] His low estimation of his colleagues, whether well founded or not, led him to assume too much responsibility himself, with consequent overwork. He was reluctant to delegate; in 1924 he was both prime minister and foreign secretary. There is little doubt of the dislike and contempt he aroused in the party and trade-union leadership in the 1920s; the Webbs' hostility is well known, and even Snowden, who followed him into the National government, found it hard to hide his distaste for him. The opposition of trade unionists such as Bevin was there before the 'desertion' of 1931.

The alleged betrayal of 1931 retained a very important place in the myths of the Labour Party. The inability of the Cabinet to agree on economic cuts in the midst of the financial crisis and the opposition of the General Council of the TUC to the proposed cuts in unemployment pay left MacDonald with no option but to submit the resignation of the government. However, instead of taking his party into opposition or even resigning both as prime minister and party leader, he chose on the advice of the King and the leaders of the other parties to remain as prime minister of a National government. Yet this fact alone is not the basis of subsequent party hatred. After splitting the party, he chose to extend the life of the new government and even lead it into an election campaign which developed into a virulent attack on his former party and produced a Labour representation of only fifty-two in the House of Commons.

The ensuing hatred for MacDonald and suspicion of 'strong leadership' was not in fact a consequence of policy disputes between MacDonald and his followers. The basic issue was one central to the Labour Party's tradition — loyalty. As Skidelsky has correctly pointed out in his account of the second Labour government: 'MacDonald broke with his colleagues not over policy but over primary loyalty. As Prime Minister he considered his first duty was to the *national interest* as it was universally conceived; the Labour Party saw its first duty to its own people.'[6] Henderson was the antithesis of MacDonald; his primary loyalty was to the party and to the class it represented. It was no surprise that he was elected leader after MacDonald's departure even though he again failed to win a parliamentary seat.

Yet with these failings MacDonald kept the support of the majority inside and outside Parliament until the very end, exercising his powerful attraction on such prominent Labour leaders as Herbert Morrison even after setting up his National government. The reasons for his ascendancy are fourfold: his personality; his history of service to the party; the lack of an alternative leader; and the trends in the development and organisation of the party that were strengthening the centre, particularly the PLP.

MacDonald had a powerful personality. He had a magnificent speaking voice and in his parliamentary performances he towered over his contemporaries in the PLP. He was a handsome man, a romantic and a visionary, and with his oratory he was said by contemporaries to have a 'presence'. Certainly without his voice his speeches translated to the written page seem empty of content and meaning. His generalities could make him all things to all men and the imprecision of his political thought gave most sections of the Labour Party the impression that he was fighting their particular cause. His narrow victory over Clynes for the party leadership in 1922 was clearly gained by wooing the left of the party with promises that were never to be realised; his closest colleagues, who knew him best, did not support him. Churchill called him a 'boneless wonder' during a Commons debate in 1924, a jibe which does succeed in conveying the nature of his often empty rhetoric. Beatrice Webb perhaps best sums up his appeal with characteristic acerbity, claiming that he may not have been a real leader but he was a magnificent substitute for one.[7]

There is no doubting MacDonald's service to the party. His early days as secretary and then as chairman of the party before the First World War were important to the successful establishment of the party's independence. His record of opposition to the war, albeit not on a pacifist platform, endeared him to the left, especially the ILP. His parliamentary performances, while open to many criticisms for their content, did give a political respectability to the party, especially as he was often surrounded by trade-union-nominated mediocrities. Henderson's service to the party was equal to that of MacDonald's, but the latter had an electoral appeal denied the former.

An important reason for MacDonald's ascendancy before 1931 lies in his woolly ideology. He was a gradualist and his socialism was tinged with that scientific, peculiarly biological optimism fashionable at the turn of the century. He believed in the parliamentary road to socialism, and the history of his governments clearly shows his adherence to all the conventions and practices of British parliamentary government. An insight into his political thinking can be found in the Labour Party policy statement of 1927 (*Labour and the Nation*) which replaced the 1918 manifesto. His biographer says of it: 'it consisted in essence of a high-minded, if sometimes prosy, statement of the moral case for gradualist socialism heavily flavoured with the scientific optimism of the day'.[8] Amid the mounting crisis of the second Labour government, MacDonald had little to offer; his knowledge of economics was minimal, and politically he could not rid himself of the Labour apostle of *laissez-faire* economics, Snowden, the Chancellor of the Exchequer, even if he had wanted to. The government had been elected to cure unemployment; it failed dismally. The Liberals under Lloyd George offered a far more radical challenge to the problems of unemployment than did the MacDonald government. Yet MacDonald was fully representative of his party; he and the majority of his parliamentary colleagues had no policy alternatives to offer.

There were ideological challenges to his leadership. The ILP presented one such set of ideological alternatives. The ILP in the 1920s was not a collection of wild revolutionaries; its chief difference with MacDonald (who was a member) stemmed from the ILP view of Parliament 'as territory occupied by the enemy'.[9] The ILP approach can be seen in the policy proposals *Socialism in Our Time*, rejected by the Labour Party as a whole. These 1926 proposals bore the imprint of the ex-Liberal, J. A. Hobson, whose theories stressed underconsumption as the main cause of unemployment. Thus there was a need for a 'living wage' with family allowances to increase the purchasing power of the mass of people. These measures would be accompanied by public control of the banking system, credit controls and import controls. These proposals stand up very well in comparison with the platitudes of *Labour and the Nation,* but the ILP had little political support within the party. It suffered from the image of being a party within a party; on paper it had many members on the Labour benches, but for most of these ILP MPs their first loyalty was to the Labour Party, not the

ILP. It also suffered from the establishment of constituency parties and from the growth of the Communist Party, especially when the latter expanded under the impact of the depression. After 1929 most of the ILP MPs were from Scottish constituencies. The ILP was drawn into greater and greater opposition to the policies of the Labour government and almost inevitably it ended its long association with the Labour Party by disaffiliating in 1932.

The only other important ideological challenge to the supremacy of MacDonald orthodoxy came from Oswald Mosley during the life of the second Labour government. Mosley had switched to the Labour Party in the 1920s. His experiences during and after the First World War made him impatient to realise the dream of a 'land fit for heroes'. There is little doubt as to his ability, but his tactics within the PLP were not very well thought out. His suggestions for the amelioration of the economic effects of the depression were contained in his famous memorandum, his policy document submitted to the Cabinet in February 1930; he wanted administrative reforms of the government machine and put forward plans for long- and short-term economic regeneration and proposals regarding credit and financial reform. Whatever their merits, these proposals were certainly more radical than those of his leader. His ministerial resignation speech in May 1930 made a powerful impression on the Labour Party in the House; yet the opposing forces within the PLP and the Cabinet were too powerful and he offered little threat, though some embarrassment, to MacDonald. Snowden dismissed Mosley with his usual acidity: 'I never had any faith in the sincerity of Mosley's professions of Socialism. I was always suspicious of a rich man who came into the Socialist Movement and at once became more Socialist than the Socialists.'[10]

MacDonald's ability easily to fend off these attacks on the policy directions of the party was partly a consequence of the changes that had been taking place in the organisation of the party in the 1920s. The 1918 reforms had led to the building up of Constituency Labour Parties (CLPs) at the expense of the socialist societies. Model plans for local party organisation were drawn up in 1925 accompanied by a membership drive. The Trade Disputes Act of 1927, while hurting the party in terms of trade-union contributions (a quarter of total income from affiliation fees was lost in the two years following the legislation) and in terms of membership (a drop from 3,388,000 in 1926 to 2,292,000 in 1928), did benefit the local parties in that more candidates were nominated by the CLPs. In the election of 1929 the number of trade-union MPs increased from 88 to 114 and those from the socialist societies and the Co-operative Party went up from 37 to 46, yet the spectacular increase was in MPs nominated by the CLPs; the increase in this section was from 25 to 128.[11] The ILP, though increasing its membership in the 1920s, suffered a loss of power within the party, and its attempt to discipline its own MPs during the second Labour government was a failure. When it broke away from the Labour Party in 1932, it had only five MPs.

The Labour Party conference offered no challenge to the leadership at this time. The combination of MacDonald's oratory and Henderson's management made it quite amenable to the parliamentary leadership. Between 1922 and 1925 the communists, as individual members or as trade-union delegates, were ousted. The conference willingly endorsed *Labour and the Nation* in 1928 and the procedural changes at the 1929 conference further freed the hands of the leadership from extra-parliamentary control.[12] When the ILP apologetically refused to nominate MacDonald as party treasurer in 1927 to ensure him a place on the National Executive, the 1929 conference made the leader *ex officio* a member of the Executive.

The Labour Party after 1931

The collapse of the Labour government in 1931 and the consequent trauma of the general election had profound consequences for the party. The events bred a deep distrust of leadership, the trade-union leadership virtually took control of the PLP and the prestige and the power of the extra-parliamentary party increased.

That the leadership issue aroused strong emotions is attested by the various resolutions and speeches at the party conferences of 1932 and 1933. The 1933 conference passed resolutions that put clear limits on a future Labour prime minister's freedom of action in Cabinet-making and on his ability to dissolve Parliament.[13] Attlee was to ignore these restrictions when he came to form his government in 1945, but their passage illustrates the mood of the party at the time. It was perhaps no accident that the three successors of MacDonald, Henderson until 1933, Lansbury until 1935 and then Attlee, did not seek to lead the party in the style of MacDonald. Henderson had a record of service to the party that was well known, and he resigned voluntarily because of his international commitments. Lansbury, a more nonconformist figure, realised that his pacifism was increasingly at odds with the perceived need of the Labour Party to take a stance in opposing the international aggression of Italy, Germany and Japan. He was prepared to resign in 1934, and the adoption of a resolution opposing Italian aggression in Abyssinia plus a brutal attack on him by Bevin (for 'placing the Executive and the Movement in an absolutely wrong position to be taking your conscience round from body to body asking to be told what you ought to do with it')[14] at the 1935 conference forced him out.

Like Lansbury, Attlee was one of the few with experience of government office who survived the electoral massacre of 1931. After Lansbury's resignation he was elected as temporary leader, and after the 1935 election he defeated Herbert Morrison and Arthur Greenwood in the leadership contest. It could be argued that he was reaffirmed because of his modest approach to the leadership; Morrison believed he himself was unsuccessful because he would have made too dominant a leader.[15] More likely, Attlee's success was the product of his work as deputy and then leader before the election, coupled with the fact that Morrison only returned to the Commons in 1935 and moreover had incurred the intense dislike of certain union leaders such as Bevin.

Before 1940 Attlee was never completely secure. In 1939, for example, there were at one time four nominations opposing him for the leadership; however, the four names were withdrawn to give an unopposed return. Before joining the government in 1940, Attlee referred the question to the NEC and the General Council of the TUC as well as having a favourable resolution passed at the annual conference. He similarly consulted various sections of the party before withdrawing from the coalition government in 1945.

Whether by chance or design. Attlee's style of leadership perfectly suited the party in the period following MacDonald's exodus. His quiet unassuming competence certainly hid the steel beneath, and that toughness was to exert itself more openly in the period after 1945. Yet in most respects he was the apotheosis of MacDonald. His years as Opposition leader and then deputy prime minister after 1940 were the perfect prelude for a full resumption of all the powers of party leadership that MacDonald had enjoyed; it was the style, not the power of leadership that constituted the difference.

Another consequence of the 1931 debacle was that the General Council of the TUC immediately took control of the PLP. It is important not to underestimate the power of Bevin of the Transport Workers' Union and Citrine as General Secretary of the TUC over the whole party throughout the 1930s. The National Joint Council was revived, with half its members being General Council nominees; it was to act as a liaison body between the PLP and the TUC. Soon it was meeting once a month, and although in theory only consultative, it exercised great authority.[16] Of course, the degree of union control was aided by the small size of the PLP; when the PLP is small, the number of union-sponsored MPs is always proportionately larger because of the number of safer seats that the unions contest.

TUC influence in this period can be measured by the successful resistance to left-wing influence in the party and the maintenance of a gradualist approach through Parliament to achieve party objectives. The party continued its policy of rejecting requests by the Communist Party for affiliation; it refused to give support to Communist-dominated movements such as the National Unemployed Workers' Movement; it consistently refused to participate in any form of National or Popular Front movements, whether proposed by the Communists, the ILP or the left within the party itself.

The issues of unemployment, at its peak of over three million between 1931 and 1933, the increasing threats from fascist dictatorships, the issues of the Spanish Civil War from 1936 to 1939, the problems of rearmament and appeasement, all resulted in a radicalisation of various sections of the labour movement in this 'terrible decade'.[17] This radicalisation manifested itself in many guises. Its chief expression in the Labour Party was through the Socialist League, founded in 1932 and operating in a similar fashion to the ILP in the 1920s. Like the Left Book Club, founded in 1936, it expressed the left's frustration with the TUC-controlled party and underlined the dilemma of the British left, that no democratic progress could be made outside the party, a point well illustrated by the dwindling influence of the ILP after it left the party in 1932. Yet all the attempts by the Socialist League and its supporters failed against union majorities at Labour Party conferences. The League was finally dissolved in 1937 after threats to proscribe its members. The party also reorganised its youth wing, the Labour League of Youth, that same year as a result of its ideologically troublesome activities. The final blow struck in the defence of Labour orthodoxy was the expulsion of Sir Stafford Cripps, long a dissenter on the left, for circulating proposals for a Popular Front and refusing to withdraw them. Cripps's dismissal in January 1939 was followed by others when Trevelyan, Bevan and Strauss were expelled in March.

The trade-union hold over the party was sufficiently secure for the unions to agree to allow a constitutional change in 1937 by which the CLP representation on the NEC was increased from five to seven and these were to be elected directly by the constituency section, not by the whole conference, which of course was dominated by union votes.[18] Certainly the prestige of the Labour Party conference improved in the 1930s; there was no return to PLP dominance; even the Party Secretary was forbidden to be an MP after the retirement of Henderson from the position in 1933. In fact, in spite of the challenges from the left, there was little conflict between the parliamentary and extra-parliamentary wings throughout this whole period.

Notes to Chapter 5

1. D. Marquand, *Ramsay MacDonald* (London: Jonathan Cape, 1977) p. 328.
2. R. T. McKenzie, *British Political Parties*, 2nd edn (London: Heinemann, 1963) p. 309. Also W. L. Guttsman, *The British Political Elite* (London: MacGibbon & Kee, 1965) pp. 256—8.
3. See G. D. H. Cole, *A History of the Labour Party from 1914* (London: Routledge & Kegan Paul, 1948) pp. 175—7; McKenzie, pp. 427—8.
4. See P. Snowden, *An Autobiography*, vol. 2 (London: Nicholson & Watson, 1934) pp. 757—61.
5. Ibid, p. 957.
6. R. Skidelsky, *Politicians and the Slump: The Labour Government of 1929—31* (London: Macmillan, 1967) p.387. For a discussion of the importance of party loyalty, see H. M. Drucker, *Doctrine and Ethos in the Labour Party* (London: Allen & Unwin, 1979) pp. 12—14.
7. See F. Williams, *A Pattern of Rulers* (London: Longman, 1965) p. 75.
8. Marquand, p. 479. For the contents see Cole, pp. 205—9.
9. R. A. Dowse, *Left in Centre: The ILP 1893—1940* (London: Longman, 1966) p. 93.
10. Snowden, p. 876. For an account of Mosley's proposals and his speech see R. Skidelsky, *Oswald Mosley* (London: Macmillan, 1975) pp. 199—200.
11. See Cole, pp. 220—1. The Co-operative Party, founded in 1917, was not affiliated nationally to the Labour Party, but MPs elected under the 'Co-operative and Labour' label by joint agreement were indistinguishable from other Labour MPs.
12. See L. Minkin, *The Labour Party Conference* rev. edn (Manchester University Press, 1980) p. 16.
13. 1933 Labour Annual Conference *Report*, pp. 8—10.
14. See McKenzie, pp. 381—2.
15. B. Donoughue and G. W. Jones, *Herbert Morrison* (London: Weidenfeld & Nicolson, 1973) p. 241. See also, K. Harris, *Atlee* (London: Weidenfeld & Nicolson, 1982) p. 120, B. Pimlott, *Hugh Dalton* (London: Cape, 1985) pp. 231—2.
16. See H. Pelling, *A Short History of the Labour Party*, 4th edn (London: Macmillan, 1972) p. 77.
17. The description is Ralph Miliband's. See *Parliamentary Socialism*, 2nd edn (London: Merlin Press, 1972) p. 192. See pp. 193—271 for a powerful indictment of the Labour Party in this period. See also a criticism of attempts to present the 1930s in a less gloomy light: A. Howkins and J. Saville, 'The Nineteen Thirties: A Revisionist History', in *The Socialist Register 1979*, ed. R. Miliband and J. Saville (London: Merlin Press, 1979) pp. 89—100.
18. B. Pimlott, *Labour and the Left in the 1930s* (Cambridge University Press, 1977) p. 129, gives credit for this change to the activities of the Constituency Parties' Association.

6

Third Parties and British Politics, 1922-40

The Liberal Party in Decline

The emergence of the Labour Party in 1922 as the second largest political party and as the alternative to the Conservative Party marked the end of the period of genuine political significance of the once great Liberal Party. The interwar years provide a chronicle of increasing decline and political irrelevance, a process hastened by the fact that the respectable proportion of the votes won by the Liberals was not reflected in the seats gained, an important factor in the 1920s. Liberals dominated the War Cabinets of the First World War, yet the party was not offered even one War Cabinet place in Churchill's new administration in 1940. We have already discussed the basic reasons for the party's decline, and these reasons lie in the years before 1922; the ensuing years only witnessed the party's despairing last convulsions.

Ironically, the year 1923 appeared to promise a new dawn for the party. In that year both the Asquith and Lloyd George wings of the party were united to fight Baldwin's surprise election of December. At first glance the election results showed great improvement for the party. The united Liberals won 159 seats out of the 453 it contested; its share of the vote rose from 17.5 per cent in 1922 to 29.6 per cent in 1923, only marginally below that gained by the Labour Party. The Liberals had a net gain of forty-two seats over the previous year.

However, these successes must be treated cautiously for several reasons:

(1) The circumstances of the 1923 election were unusually favourable to the Liberals and were not to occur again. The issue of free trade was the one issue that could unite the party; its conservative adherence to orthodox economic positions had served the party well in 1906, and seventeen years later it produced electoral rewards, especially in Lancashire.

(2) A closer look at the election details unearths several factors unfavourable for the long-term health of the party. The Liberals did only marginally worse than Labour in the over-all percentage vote, but they made only two gains in Labour seats. Mainly, for this reason, Wilson argues that the disastrous Liberal result in 1924 was the norm and the 1923 result was the consequence of fortuitous circumstances. He points out that in 1924 Labour contested fifty-one Liberal seats not contested in 1923, and the Liberals lost forty-six of them.[1] After 1924 there was no distinct Liberal stronghold and the party was being pushed more and more into greater reliance on its Scottish and Welsh seats. The Liberal Party could sometimes win seats, but unlike the two major parties it could not hold on to its gains.

(3) The Liberal Party was being forced into greater dependence on the Conservative Party given Labour's unwillingness to have any electoral deals with the Liberals. This dependence was clearly evident from the 1924 results: of the twenty-one seats the Liberals gained or held in England, fifteen had no Conservative opposition. The Conservatives, recognising the value of the Liberal Party campaign against the Labour Party, were particularly unwilling to oppose Liberal leaders. As C. P. Scott, editor of the *Manchester Guardian*, observed bitterly:

> The more I think of it the more I dislike the [electoral] deal with the Tories. I don't know how far it has gone, but both Asquith and Simon are certainly compromised. Both, without Tory support, would probably lose their seats.[2]

(4) The Liberal revival of 1923 left the party in the unenviable position of being unable to co-operate with the defeated Baldwin government, while it put the Labour Party in office

without securing any concessions in return. The Liberals suffered the continual disdain of MacDonald's government and then it was manoeuvred by Baldwin into defeating the government and precipitating an election in 1924 which it did not want. Thus Asquith was blamed by the right for installing a Labour government and by the left for its defeat, and the Liberals had nothing tangible to show. Douglas argues that the party was bound to lose in supporting either of the two main parties. 'Asquith,' he said, 'rejected the idea of playing for a Liberal administration. Why he did so must always remain a mystery; and it is arguable that this decision was the most disastrous single action ever performed by a Liberal towards his Party.'[3]

The history of the Liberal Party after 1924 is one of almost continual gloom. There are two main interrelated set of factors: first the problem of leadership and party splits, and second the difficulties of organisation and finance, with only flashes of inspired policy to lighten the darkness.

The problem of conflict between the parliamentary leaders reappeared immediately after the 1924 electoral defeat. Lloyd George was elected chairman of the parliamentary Liberals, but Asquith refused to step down from the leadership of the party. Lloyd George refused to surrender his important political fund to an Asquith-controlled party and attempted to use its political weight as the only major source of party money to force the party to accept his land proposals. The splits in the leadership forced their way into the open during the General Strike. Lloyd George wanted the party to criticise both the strikers and the government, but many in the party, particularly Simon, wanted the party to train its guns only on the trade unionists.

Even with the retirement of Asquith in 1926, with power in the party passing in practice to Lloyd George, divisions in the party remained quite open, and dislike of Lloyd George by many leading Liberals was evidenced by the setting up of the Liberal Council, the ineffective home of his parliamentary critics. The slight improvement in the party's position between 1927 and 1929 and the high optimism that accompanied this improvement were dashed by the poor electoral performance in 1929. The consequence was more vigorous faction-fighting and splits within the party. The basic problem was whether the party should be more sympathetic to the minority Labour government in the hope of influencing it and making gains for the Liberal Party (Lloyd George's position), or should it put on its anti-socialist mask and join with the Conservatives to bring the government down (Simon's position)? One leading Liberal, Jowitt, was soon lost to Labour, and by the summer of 1931 Simon had given up the Liberal Whip and formally started the process of taking his National Liberals over to permanent alliance with the Conservatives, a road well trodden by the Liberal Unionists after 1886.

Lloyd George's policy of co-operation seemed to have some chance of success; at least the Labour Chancellor, Snowden, was fully committed to free trade, and the government included electoral-reform proposals in the 1930 King's Speech. Again misfortune and bad judgement were to worsen the Liberal position. In the crucial days of August 1931 Lloyd George was seriously ill, and Samuel, later supported by Lloyd George, advised George V to propose the establishment of a National government. The Liberals had fallen into the Conservative trap. When the Conservatives agitated for an October election, contrary to intentions expressed in August, Samuel and his official Liberals did not resign, a failure roundly criticised by Lloyd George, whose alienation from both wings of the party was now complete.

The 1931 election was an unmitigated disaster for the Liberals. It returned with seventy-two seats but only gained less than 11 per cent of the vote. Of the seventy-two seats only ten had been contested by official Conservative candidates, and the party emerged in three distinct and separate parts: there were the thirty-one Official Liberals under Samuel, thirty-seven National Liberals under Simon, and four in the Lloyd George section. The Samuelites were to remain in the National government for a year, with the suspension of the convention of Cabinet collective responsibility enabling them to live with the protectionist policies of the government. Finally, with pressure from rank-and-file Liberals, ten Samuelites left the government, while the Simonites stayed in and merged with the Conservative Party.

The splits in the party were accompanied and compounded

in this period by the mounting difficulties of organisation and finance. The reunion of 1923 did not put the Lloyd George fund at the disposal of the party. The year 1925 saw the failure of the 'Liberal Million Fund' in spite of its innovating features.[4] Liberals refused to donate money when they could see Lloyd George's reluctance to give the party the full benefit of the fund. Consequently, Liberal headquarters could give no help to local associations or to area organisations. Constituency organisations decayed at a faster rate, agents could not be paid and disappeared, and there were real difficulties in getting candidates to stand.

The improvements before 1929 were mainly due to the return of Herbert Samuel to reorganise the party machine. He certainly improved party morale, albeit for a short period. There were even by-election victories, though in March 1929 the party was to make its last by-election gain until 1958. The calamitous results of the 1929 election, besides undermining morale, ensured that contributions from Lloyd George were to cease altogether after 1930. In 1936 the organisation underwent major surgery as a result of the Meston Report: the Liberal Party Organisation was created to unite the party organisation and replace the long-established NLF; the ancient LCA was untouched. Basically, the reforms strengthened the parliamentary wing as against the national party, but the reforms could do little to help the chronically ailing constituency associations.

Amidst this decline, the Liberal Party still managed to produce the most imaginative and radical ideas of the 1920s. The Liberal Summer Schools were attended by the most innovative people of the time such as Keynes, Walter Layton and H. D. Henderson. Liberal Party reports on land and coal in 1924—5 were far in advance of much contemporary thinking in the other two parties. In 1928 the party produced its 'Yellow Book' — *Britain's Industrial Future* — and this helped to prepare the ground for Lloyd George's important and striking policy proposals that formed the basis of the 1929 election manifesto — 'We Can Conquer Unemployment'. These radical proposals were firmly placed in the bedrock of Keynesian economics. The 1929 defeat put an end to this most imaginative few years.

A measure of the decline of the party can be seen in a brief glance at municipal elections of the period; the percentage of local elections contested by Liberal candidates dropped from 18 per cent in 1922, to 12.5 per cent in 1929 and to 5.6 per cent in 1938.[5] The 1935 general election results confirmed this trend at national level, only twenty-one successes out of 161 contests, and the share of the total vote dropping to under 6 per cent. The party henceforth was to retain only marginal political importance until the excitement of its by-election gains of the late 1950s and early 1960s. The party could not decide whether it wanted to be a progressive or anti-socialist party and the electoral system assisted this ideological squeeze between the two main parties. Many factors external to the party reduced it to this parlous position, but the history of the party between the wars shows that the Liberal Party was eager to hasten its own funeral.

The Political Irrelevance of the Communist Party

In 1920 a new political party made its appearance on the British political stage. The British Communist Party was formed from existing political groups such as the British Socialist Party (formerly the SDF) and the Socialist Labour Party, which was mainly based in Scotland. The inspiration came from the success of the Bolshevik Revolution in Russia; the Comintern, the Soviet-dominated international organisation of Communist parties, was particularly active in encouraging and sorting out some of the organisational teething troubles of the new party.

The Communist Party introduced two new factors into British politics not characteristic of the older parties. First, the party was heavily influenced by the Soviet Union. While this was important for its financial resources, this dependence produced sudden twisting and turning in policy, irrespective of the necessities of British politics; these policy and tactical changes were to cost the party dearly in terms of any success. Thus relations with the Labour Party were distorted through a Kremlin prism without reference to events in British politics. In the early 1920s and the mid-1930s there were applications to affiliate with the Labour Party, but between these dates the Communists attacked the Labour Party as the enemy of the working class. In the 1930s the needs of Soviet foreign policy produced demands for a Popular Front in view of Hitler's rise to power and the British Communist Party only contested two seats in the 1935 election to avoid antagonising Labour. The Nazi–Soviet Pact of 1939 led the Communists to oppose the war and the coalition government; the German attack on the Soviet Union in 1941 turned this opposition into a wholesale endorsement of the Churchill government's war effort.

The Communist Party also introduced a degree of party discipline and ideological rigidity unknown in the existing parties. The party expelled offenders, and its demands for ideological conformity helped to produce considerable turnover in members. The party was never strong enough to reproduce the classic cell type of organisation, and it basically operated as a branch party along the lines of the Labour and Conservative parties, seeking to widen its membership to create a mass party.

There are three ways of measuring the political effectiveness and strength of the Communist Party between the wars: membership, electoral success, and influence within other organisations, particularly the Labour Party. On all three counts the Communist Party failed to make an impact on British politics.

Party membership always remained small measured against Communist parties in other European countries and against the membership of the Labour Party. By 1921 membership probably stood at 2,500, not the 10,000 claimed by the party itself.[6] Its membership did rise to 10,000 at the time of the General Strike but fell to below 3,000 by 1930. There was quite a marked rise in the 1930s as Communists seemed the most active and successful opponents of European fascism; and with the prestige gained from the role of Communists in the Spanish Civil War, membership rose to 17,000. Obviously there was a correlation between the level of unemployment and the level of recruitment.[7] However, what is surprising about the British Communist Party in the 1930s is not the increase in membership but how small that increase was, given the general economic conditions. The party was not too successful in recruiting the working class, though it was reasonably successful in the recruitment of the middle-class intelligentsia, who constituted its main claim to some political influence.[8] Yet a general weakness in membership was the large turnover in membership.

The electoral success of the party between the wars was small. In 1922 two out of seven candidates were elected; but this was before the Labour Party banned individual Communist Party members, and one of the successes was an official Labour Party candidate. Of the eight candidates who stood in 1923, none succeeded, and only two won their contests in 1924. The number of seats fought by the party increased in 1929 and 1931 to twenty-five and twenty-six respectively but there were no victories to record, and the party's total share of the vote was identical to that of the 1924 election. In 1935, seeking unity with Labour, the party only nominated two candidates, of whom one was elected.

It could be argued that the party was not seeking the electoral road to political power, but sought rather to infiltrate other working-class organisations such as the Labour Party or the trade unions. Certainly the party failed completely to influence the Labour Party. It often sought affiliation, but was always rebuffed, and in 1924 the Labour Party ruled that a member of the Communist Party could not be an individual member of the Labour Party. The question of Communist membership through the trade unions was a more difficult one for the Labour Party and it remained unresolved, yet Communist influence has always been weak in the larger unions. The Labour Party did not hesitate to expel members felt to be arguing a line similar to that of the Communist Party.

The party did have more visible success in various front organisations at the height of the Depression, particularly the National Unemployed Workers' Movement led by Wal Hannington. It was in the forefront of demonstrations and meetings that often ended in violent clashes with either the police or the fascists or with both. The existence of a clearly visible enemy on the streets in the shape of the British Union of Fascists was valuable to the party, and it rightly claimed to be the main opponent of British fascism. Yet in the final analysis, the Communist Party remained irrelevant to the mainstream of British party politics in the period.

The Political Insignificance of the British Union of Fascists

Oswald Mosley's New Party, later the British Union of Fascists, was not merely a challenge to the existing political parties but a challenge to the British liberal democratic concept of representation through political parties. Yet the radicalism of that challenge loses its impact when considered alongside its failure.

Mosley, at first a Conservative MP until 1922, became a member of the Labour Party and was a government minister in the second Labour government. However, despite his undoubted ability and his radical approach to social and economic problems, he was unable to sustain his campaigns within the confines of an orthodox political party. His popularity in the Labour Party was at its highest when he resigned from the government in May 1930 and when he finally left the party early in the following year. Mosley's proposals for public works, government intervention and controls, pensions, and the general application of Keynesian economics were both radical and capable of winning a great deal of support within the party. But Mosley lacked the political patience necessary for success and he completely underestimated the degree of loyalty that a party such as the Labour Party could engender. He did not understand the nature of British party politics.

He founded the New Party in February 1931 with a mixed group of supporters, Strachey, Harold Nicolson and the philosopher Joad being the most prominent. His decision to form a new party and his hopes for its political success lie firmly in the British political tradition that great men decide the course of events; followers and organisation come later. John Strachey was to claim that 'The New Party was carefully planned',[9] but Strachey was speaking more of the intrigues at Westminster. The New Party never in fact had an organisational structure, and with its confused aims it was difficult to classify it as a political party. Skidelsky says of it in

September 1931: 'On the one hand it was a political party organised to seek power in elections; on the other hand it was a para-military force organised to fight communism in a revolutionary situation.'[10] It was not always clear whether Mosley by this time had completely rejected the party game or was seeking to create a party to counter the existing parties.

The New Party failed electorally. Six weeks after its foundation Mosley decided to fight the by-election at Ashton-under-Lyne with Allan Young as the candidate. In spite of the difficulties, the party collected a creditable 16 per cent of the votes cast; but that was its high point. In the general election of 1931, despite a promise to field over 400 candidates, only twenty-four stood and all but two lost their deposits. By then Strachey had left the party together with Joad. The Party's Youth Movement was a foretaste of the fascism to come. The left supporters in the party were alienated by the influx of the middle-class right, and in the spring of 1932 Nicolson left remarking, 'The difficulty about the New Party is that it is no longer new and no longer a party.'[11]

In 1932 the New Party was converted into the British Union of Fascists. It became a political movement more than a political party. It had a military wing and rejected orthodox forms of political action. Its main impact was on the streets, thus underlining its lack of political influence. By 1934 the violence of its tactics had alienated many of its influential supporters; it probably contributed to the break from Mosley of Lord Rothermere, whose newspapers, especially the *Daily Mail,* had previously given enthusiastic support. It won little working-class support and its middle-class members were alienated from the prevailing political system, consisting more and more of men with military backgrounds. There is some dispute about its membership,[12] but it is clear that Mosley's movement failed to attract influential individuals or groups in the British political system.

The BUF decided not to contest any of the constituencies in the 1935 election, underlining both its rejection of the ordinary methods of political action and its political weakness. After 1934 the movement had assumed more pronounced forms of anti-semitism and violence, and although it constituted a threat to civil order, it had little relevance for British politics, and the 1936 Public Order Act was to weaken its impact on the streets.

Notes to Chapter 6

1. T. Wilson, *The Downfall of the Liberal Party, 1914–35* (London: Collins, 1966) p. 307. See also C. Cook, *The Age of Alignment: Electoral Politics in Britain, 1922–29* (London: Macmillan, 1975) pp. 156–79 and 310–33, for analyses of the 1923 and 1924 elections.
2. T. Wilson (ed.), *The Political Diaries of C. P. Scott, 1911–28* (London: Collins, 1970) p. 466.
3. R. Douglas, *A History of the Liberal Party 1895–1970* (London: Sidgwick & Jackson, 1971) p. 175.
4. Ibid, p. 190.
5. Figures from C. Cook, *A Short History of the Liberal Party* (London: Macmillan, 1976) p. 124.
6. See H. Pelling, *The British Communist Party* (London: A. & C. Black, 1958) p. 15.
7. Ibid, appendix A. Also K. Newton, *The Sociology of British Communism* (London: Allen Lane, 1969) p. 33, and L. J. Macfarlane, *The British Communist Party: Its Origins and Development Until 1929* (London: MacGibbon & Kee, 1966) p. 302.
8. John Strachey is but one example, and his attempts to join the Communist Party after his split with Mosley give a rather comic view of the party's unstable relationship with this type of middle-class member. See H. Thomas, *John Strachey* (London: Eyre Methuen, 1973) pp. 109–28.
9. Ibid, p. 96.
10. R. Skidelsky, *Oswald Mosley* (London: Macmillan, 1975) p. 270.
11. *Harold Nicolson's Diaries and Letters 1930–39*, ed. N. Nicolson (London: Collins, 1970) p. 111.
12. See Skidelsky, pp. 331–2.

PART THREE

The Party System and Consensus Politics, 1940-64

7

Party Politics in War, 1940-5[1]

The Changing Political Climate

The establishment of the Coalition government in 1940 marked a turning-point in British party politics. The impact of total war, the involvement of the civilian population, the necessity for sacrifice and the acceptance of wide government powers regarding military conscription, job designation, security, rationing and controls over property, were but some of the factors that were to have profound social and political consequences for Britain. The government adopted sweeping powers regarding the direction of the economy; the war underlined the poverty of the welfare and health services, and total mobilisation could not but affect people's attitudes to the British class system.

The war was the chief factor in ending the chronic unemployment problem of the 1930s, and the unwillingness to contemplate a return to the pre-war level of unemployment became a dominant wartime theme. But the 1930s provided another theme of political import before and after 1945: a distrust of the political leaders that had allowed Britain to enter the war in such a state of military unpreparedness. Books such as *Guilty Men* had an immense impact and struck chords of resentment and anger which took long to subside. The new demands, added to these memories of the 1930s, led to the creation of a new political and social climate. If Britain were fighting fascist dictatorships, the aim of military victory was not enough; equality of sacrifice demanded a more just society after the armed struggle had ended. Every level of British society began to embrace this growing consensus for social reform.

The reception of the Beveridge Report in late 1942, a report which in itself was not notably radical in the context of British social development, provides ample evidence of this new mood. The Report proposed a universal social security scheme based on the 1911 social insurance legislation; it proposed family allowances and improved old-age pensions and stressed the need for a comprehensive health service. Furthermore, Beveridge based his proposals on the fundamental need to avoid the mass unemployment of the 1930s.

The impact of this detailed report was immense; contemporary surveys of opinion illustrated widespread support and enthusiasm for the recommendations, in spite of the hesitant attitude of the prime minister and some members of his government. The debate in the House of Commons in February 1943 was to provoke the first official Labour Party attack on the government, and Churchill was forced to adopt a warmer approach to questions of social reform.

The Beveridge Report was only one indication of the changing political scene. Earlier in the year the Scott and the Uthwatt Reports on land use and urban planning were published; early in 1943 a Ministry of Town and Country Planning was set up. In November 1943 the government established the Ministry of Reconstruction and 1944 saw a succession of White Papers dealing with health, employment and social insurance proposals. A Family Allowances Act was passed through Parliament early in 1945. The major piece of domestic legislation, Butler's Education Act of 1944, reflects both the demand for and the limits to social reform. The Act was an important piece of social legislation. It was to establish the pattern of English and Welsh education for many years, but it was far from egalitarian, reflecting an elitist approach to the organisation of schools, though it did establish a more efficient and fairer system of education.

The mood after 1940 had repercussions for the party system. It certainly strengthened the left, though it was not wholly expressed in party political terms. It ensured that the

Labour Party would win the 1945 election, yet the Labour Party leadership was cautious; there is strong evidence that neither Attlee nor Churchill appreciated how far popular attitudes had changed. Nevertheless, the changes were politically far more beneficial to Labour.

The Conservative Party lost ground because, whatever the attitudes of the Labour Party before 1940, the Conservatives were saddled with the responsibility for all the economic, social and military ills of that decade. The party showed itself more hostile to plans for social reform during the war than the Labour Party, and in spite of the huge popularity of Churchill as war leader there was widespread suspicion that a post-war Conservative government would have social reform low down on the list of priorities. Yet there were movements in the party to approach social issues with more sympathy. The existence of the Tory Reform Committee after 1943 with a small following in the House of Commons is evidence of a revival of some aspects of the theme of Tory Democracy, and this was to point the way for the party after 1945, but the Conservative Party remained basically unconvinced until the electoral realities were to force changes after 1945.

The Coalition, 1940–5

Churchill established his Coalition along party lines, the Cabinet consisting of fifteen Conservatives, four Labour and one Liberal. The balance was to change as the war progressed, but Churchill, whether through political expediency or personal generosity or both, never politically punished the old 'appeasers' in the Conservative Party, nor did he fully reward his small band of pre-1939 political supporters. Yet the influence of the Conservatives on the domestic level within the Cabinet and its sub-committees was to decline before 1945, with Labour leaders forcing the pace and reaping the political rewards, while Churchill further illustrated his relative lack of partisanship during the war with the inclusion of party outsiders: Bevin as Minister of Labour in 1940 provides a good illustration of this aspect of Churchill's government.

The problem for the Conservative Party was that Churchill did not see himself primarily as a party leader; he was a national leader who wanted to dominate and concentrate on grand strategy. It was Beaverbrook who forced Churchill to realise the importance of the party leadership when it became vacant with Chamberlain's retirement in October 1940.[2] This is not to say that Churchill was in any way innocent in the field of party politics. He respected the House of Commons, recognising it as the political base for his security. Nevertheless, Churchill's maverick history ensured that he would be a different party leader from a Baldwin or a Chamberlain. He certainly did not want to restart party hostilities when the war was ended, and he envisaged the survival of the Coalition for at least four years afterwards to deal with the post-war problems. It was the attitude of the Labour Party, particularly its rank and file, that was to force him into the narrower role of Conservative Party leader in 1945.

Throughout the war Churchill's government never experienced the difficulties of governments during the First World War. There was always a great deal of unity in his government, and this consensus was reflected in the House of Commons. Churchill's strength ebbed and flowed according to the fortunes of the war. In the dark days of the collapse of France, the Dunkirk evacuation and the Battle of Britain in the summer and autumn of 1940, all but a few political outsiders such as the Communist Party rallied to his leadership. The German air attacks on British cities, reaching their height in the winter and spring of 1941, and the perilous Battle of the Atlantic which raged until 1943, increased the need for political solidarity. Even the Chamberlainites gradually offered more vocal support for their new leader. Churchill's reputation as a war leader survived the evacuation of Greece in April 1941; and when the Germans attacked the Soviet Union in the June of that year and the Japanese attacked the American fleet at Pearl Harbor in the following December, Churchill's confidence of victory increased. Yet the military reverses in 1942 brought the government to its lowest point; the loss of Singapore in February and the subsequent defeats in Burma with the threat to India were compounded in the summer of 1942 by Rommel's victories over the British in North Africa and the fall of Tobruk. Fortunately, this was the nadir of Churchill's fortunes, and his reputation (never below 78 per cent approval on opinion polls) increased with the Soviet defence of Stalingrad and the victory over Rommel at El Alamein in November 1942. This victory represented not only a military but a political turning-point in the war. While Churchill was never politically safe, members of his government felt there should now be greater emphasis on post-war planning in the wake of the Beveridge Report. As Churchill's own political security increased, his government displayed more disunity. Russian victories in the East, American victories in the Pacific, the elimination of Italy and ultimately the invasion of Northern France in July 1944 ensured military victory, and so the perceived need for political solidarity and the absence of political conflict lessened.

Throughout the war years the leaders of the political parties saw the electoral truce agreed to in 1939 as a political truce. They wanted the almost complete cessation of party conflict inside and outside Parliament. Generally in the House of Commons there was support for the government, especially in the early years of the war, with critics such as Bevan, Shinwell and Winterton seen as irritating exceptions. There was the passing threat to Churchill of Cripps's surprisingly popular reputation in 1942, but he had little political support, and his resignation from the Cabinet at the end of 1942 hardly caused a political ripple. Both main parties settled the issue of who constituted His Majesty's Loyal Opposition by appointing as leader the Labour veteran Lees-Smith, whose official duties included asking questions and dealing with parliamentary formalities. Lees-Smith's qualities for the post were, according to Hugh Dalton, that he was 'very calm, sensible, loyal, experienced, and, no disadvantage in his proposed new duties, a little slow'.[3]

Churchill wanted as few domestic distractions from the war as possible. When the government was at its most vulnerable in 1942, with the military reverses, 'the Government kept Parliament in recess as much as possible during this anxious session'.[4] The government certainly did not contemplate either a general election or contested by-elections, and the electoral register was purposely kept out of date for most of the war, while the life of Parliament was extended. In protesting against the lack of new electoral registers, Acland made the pertinent comment: 'if you can register people for chocolates, if you can register them for fire-watching, you can certainly register them for democracy'.[5]

Thus there were really no threats to Winston Churchill or his government during the war years. There were occasional revolts, but there was general unanimity on the conduct of the war. The one possible threat, the censure motion tabled by Sir Roger Keyes and Wardlaw-Milne in July 1942, collapsed with only twenty-five supporters and some abstentions. It was not helped by Wardlaw-Milne's suggestion that the King's brother, the Duke of Gloucester, should be made Commander-in-Chief.

Extra-parliamentary Political Activity

If opposition to the government in Parliament and within the government itself were minimal, this was not true in the country at large, and the failure of the political leaders to interpret correctly the political signs was to make the 1945 election results so surprising to them. The changing climate of political opinion could be seen, first, within the political parties, particularly the Labour Party; second, by-elections during the war gave early warning signs of what was to come; third, opinion polls clearly charted political opinion, but were ignored.

Following the pattern of the First World War, the three main political parties agreed on 26 September 1939 to an electoral truce, the agreement being signed by the three Chief Whips. The agreement read as follows:

We jointly agree, as representing the Conservative, Labour and Liberal Parties, as follows:

(a) Not to nominate Candidates for the Parliamentary vacancies that now exist, or may occur, against the Candidate nominated by the Party holding the seat at the time of the vacancy occurring.

(b) The Agreement shall hold good during the War, or until determined on notice given by any one of the three Parties signatories hereto.[6]

The problem for electoral politics in subsequent years was that although the agreement was clearly an electoral truce, it was often interpreted by the parliamentary leaders and by the Conservative Party as a political truce: Sir Ivor Jennings held that in the first nine months of the war, for example, there was a 'truce in the normal party conflict, and not a mere agreement not to contest by-elections'.[7] Problems of interpretation became more acute after the establishment of the Coalition in May 1940, and when the tide of war changed in favour of Britain and her allies at the end of 1942 enforcing the truce became more difficult. In one sense post-war politics began at the start of 1943. However, problems of enforcement never seriously threatened the unity of the dominance of the two main political parties, despite the appearance of the Common Wealth Party and the inevitable talk of the need for all good men to join together in the perennial centre party.[8]

The Conservative Party wholeheartedly accepted the truce and wanted its scope widened to make it a political truce. Before the establishment of the Coalition, the National Union stated, 'The present truce between the political parties should not be confined to by-elections',[9] and after May 1940 the party was even more emphatic: 'party warfare has been entirely subordinated to making common cause in the stern fight that lies before us. In face of the danger that threatens all alike internal political differences are suspended.' But the party added, 'it is considered of the greatest importance that the constituency organisations should be kept in being'.[10]

The truce suited the Conservative as a party more than it did Labour. The Conservative Party moved on to the defensive as political attitudes changed during the war years. It was defending the huge majority that had been won in the 1935 election. The party did not hold party conferences between 1939 and 1943, but in face of electoral challenges it was increasingly forced to defend itself. In March 1942 the new chairman of the Party Organisation, Major Dugdale, took a far more aggressive line in urging the party to protect itself despite trying to uphold the 'political' truce. The problem for the party is shown in the following appeal: 'I say to you, therefore: hold public meetings to be addressed by Members of Parliament, candidates or other speakers. Keep the flag of Conservatism flying, but do nothing to revive the old Party dog fight.'[11] The Conservative Party was to claim that one of the reasons for losing the 1945 election was that it neglected its organisation, but there is no real basis for this claim. Admittedly, party membership dropped as in other parties, but the organisation was not neglected, constituencies did not disappear, and the party entered the election with more electoral agents than Labour.

The leadership of the Labour Party was enthusiastic in its support of the truce, but the rank and file gradually became more restive; the leadership won a narrow victory to uphold the truce at the 1942 party conference, and the party had to lean quite heavily on constituency parties that did not observe the truce.[12] By 1942, Attlee had started the unusual practice of issuing letters in support of Conservative candidates.[13] In October 1944 the Labour NEC stated categorically that the party would fight the next election as an independent party; there was to be no repeat of the sordid 'coupon' election of 1918.

Yet it was the contested by-elections that provided most of the political excitement and gave clear indications of the way the political wind was blowing. The early contests were unimportant and mostly contested by independent mavericks of the right-wing variety. Noel Pemberton Billing arose from the by-election past, for example, and fought in one of his guises as a 'Bomb Berlin' candidate. But by 1942 there was more relevant activity. In March the Conservatives lost Grantham. In April three-party official support and a red flag over the committee rooms were not enough to save the Conservatives at Wallasey, where the independent won over 60 per cent of the vote, and on the same day the Conservatives lost Rugby. Between 1942 and 1945 the majority of by-elections were contested — forty-seven out of sixty-six (not including Northern Ireland) — and throughout the war twelve seats changed hands, in spite of the truce. Significantly, the Labour Party only lost one seat — to the SNP in Mother-well.

The major challenges to the truce in later years of the war came from the Common Wealth Party, 'more a revivalist movement than a political party'.[14] In one sense the Common Wealth Party was the Labour substitute before the 1945 election. It incorporated social idealism of Labour with a heavy emphasis on political morality. Its membership, never more than 15,000, was drawn mainly from the professional middle classes, but during its election campaigns the party gained enthusiastic support from Labour activists, frustrated by the electoral truce. The Common Wealth Party fought twelve elections and won three; it averaged 36.6 per cent of the vote, in spite of the out-of-date register. The party was to disappear after the 1945 election, but it did indicate the amount of electoral support that Labour was to gain in 1945.

The final pointer to the changing nature of party support was the opinion polls. Polls before 1943 did not refer to party allegiance but throughout the war they did show a swing to the left in terms of political opinions. From 1943, when voting intentions were measured, the Labour Party never lost its lead over the Conservative Party and all the polls appear to support the political conclusions that could have been drawn from the by-election results.[15] Yet, as we have seen, the political leaders tended to ignore opinion polls and to dismiss each lost by-election as a freak result.

The General Election of 1945

Winston Churchill did not want the 1945 election to take place. He was in favour of extending the life of the existing Parliament, the consent to be sought in a referendum, at least until the end of the war with Japan. He was not apprehensive of electoral defeat but possibly wished to subordinate the tiresome details of domestic party politics to the more important claims of world diplomacy. Attlee and Bevin were inclined to agree to the extension of the Coalition government, but the NEC and the Labour Party Conference meeting in May insisted that the party withdraw in preparation for a general election. The government resigned on 23 May and Churchill headed a Conservative caretaker government until the election results were known. Labour wanted the election to take place in the autumn, to allow for the new register, but Churchill, rather taken aback by Labour's withdrawal, believed that a July election would benefit the Conservative Party. Few expected the Conservatives to lose the election. Churchill told the King that he expected a majority of between thirty and eighty in the new Parliament.[16] Even the *News Chronicle,* which carried regular reports of opinion polls, did not heed their message. The Labour victory was a surprise; the size of the victory unimagined. Labour won 394 seats, and this number was increased with ILP and Common Wealth victories. The Conservatives and their allies won only 212 seats, and the Liberals were reduced to twelve. The difference in votes was not as impressive as the difference in seats between the two main parties, but none the less this was one of the largest Conservative defeats in history. Labour gained 227 seats and the Conservatives lost 172.

The Conservative Party advanced two main causes of their defeat: poor party organisation and continual left-wing propaganda throughout the war by such institutions as the BBC and the Army Bureau of Current Affairs. R. A. Butler's comments are fairly representative of Conservative attitudes:

> Our organisation up and down the country was in parlous condition, much harder hit than our opponents by the absence of agents and organisers on war service [and] The Forces vote, in particular, had been virtually won over by the left wing influence of the Army Bureau of Current Affairs.[17]

However, there is no evidence that the Conservative electoral machine was in worse shape than Labour's, if one uses the indicators of the number of agents and the amount of money spent. Half the electors in the armed forces did not vote.

Far more important in explaining Labour's triumph was the Conservative campaign. The manifestos of the two parties did not greatly differ, but the campaign emphasis on the implementation of those policies did. It seems the electorate believed that Labour would secure full employment, introduce a National Health Service, implement the Beveridge Report and, most importantly, provide more houses. The nationalisation proposals of Labour were not important to the election. Labour's policies were far from the socialist blue-print of the Conservative imagination. Within the consensus engendered during the war years they were essentially conservative proposals made by political leaders who had enhanced their political reputations in the wartime Coalition government.

The Conservative Party, on the other hand, did not try to analyse British problems by reference to the interwar years. The party tended to de-emphasise policy and rest heavily on the personality of Churchill, the successful war leader. Churchill was undoubtedly an asset and probably saved the party from even worse defeat. Yet his campaign did not benefit his party. He fought as leader of a National government, not as a party leader. He did his cause a disservice by trying to frighten the voters into the Conservative camp with spectres of socialist totalitarianism. His famous broadcast catches the flavour of his approach:

> I declare to you from the bottom of my heart, that no socialist system can be established without a political police ... They [Labour] would have to fall back on some form of Gestapo, no doubt very humanely directed in the first instance.[18]

However, there is no doubt that whatever their campaign, whatever their policy proposals, and irrespective of the state of their organisation, the Conservatives would have lost. The 1945 election was decided long before 1945. The Labour victory was a product of the movement of British opinion and expectations arising from the war. The 1945 election was a retrospective judgement of Conservative attitudes and policies in the interwar years. As the authors of the first Nuffield election study put it: 'The Conservatives were held to account for so many evil years, be the evil regarded as the result of misdoing or ill fortune.'[19] Thus the election was a result of a combination of long-term factors, the impact of the war years, and the desire not to squander the social benefits and promises.[20]

Notes to Chapter 7

1. This chapter has drawn upon an unpublished research paper by Adrian Lee and Alan Ball, 'The Electoral Truces, 1914–18 and 1939–45' (1973).
2. See A. J. P. Taylor, '1932–45', in *Coalitions in British Politics*, ed. D. E. Butler (London: Macmillan, 1978) p. 87.
3. H. Dalton, *The Fateful Years 1931–45* (London: Muller, 1957) p. 332.
4. A. Bullock, *The Life and Times of Ernest Bevin*, vol. 2 (London: Heinemann, 1967) p. 185.
5. House of Commons Debates (387) 1003–10.
6. Labour Party, *Report of the 39th Annual Conference*, 1940, p. 19. The Conservative Whip's Office has no record of the truce.
7. W. I. Jennings, 'Parliament in Wartime', *Political Quarterly*, 1940, p. 239.
8. Randolph Churchill in September 1942 on the need for a centre party 'based around all the best political elements'. See A. Calder, *The People's War* (London: Jonathan Cape, 1969) p. 533.
9. Conservative Party, *The Onlooker*, April 1940, p. 8 (meeting of the Central Council of the National Union held on 4 April 1940).
10. Ibid, June 1940, p. 8.
11. Major Dugdale, in *The Onlooker*, December 1943, p. 3.
12. The Kings Norton, Birmingham, CLP was disciplined in May 1941 for not supporting the Conservative candidate, and in February 1943 Portsmouth North CLP showed great reluctance in supporting the Conservative candidate, Admiral Sir William James, the original 'Bubbles' of the soap advert, and unofficially the CLP gave a great deal of help to Tom Sargant, the Common Wealth candidate.
13. Labour Party, *Report of the 41st Annual Conference*, 1942, p. 46.
14. H. Pelling, *Britain and the Second World War* (London: Collins, 1970) p. 185, See Calder for a description of the party. Calder is also the most interesting source for accounts of by-elections in these years – see particularly his hilarious account of the West Derbyshire election (pp. 522–4).
15. See D. E. Butler and A. Sloman, *British Political Facts, 1900–1979*, 5th edn (London: Macmillan, 1980) p. 234.
16. J. Wheeler Bennett, *King George VI* (London: Reprint Society, 1959) p. 630.
17. R. A. Butler, *The Art of the Possible* (Harmondsworth: Penguin, 1973) pp. 129 and 131. Ramsden argues not that the Conservative Party organisation was weaker than Labour's but that it was not as strong as it usually was compared with Labour. See Lord Butler (ed.), *The Conservative Party* (London: Allen & Unwin, 1977) p.419.
18. Quoted in Calder, p. 577.
19. R. B. McCallum and A. Readman, *The British General Election of 1945* (Oxford University Press, 1947) p. 268.
20. See H. Pelling, *The Labour Governments 1945–51* (London: Macmillan, 1984) pp. 17–33.

8

The Conservative Party and Consensus Politics, 1945-64

The Conservative Party and the Party System

Between 1945 and 1964 the party system displayed two overwhelming characteristics which, taken together, make these
years unique in the party politics of modern Britain. One
feature was the almost complete dominance of electoral
and parliamentary politics by the two main parties; the other
was the high degree of bipartisan agreement over large areas
of policy-making. The election results from the six elections
provide ample evidence of the first characteristic (see Table
8.1 overleaf).

The combined percentage votes of the two parties never fell
below 87.5 per cent of the votes cast at a time when the
lowest turn-out was just under 77 per cent in the lack-lustre
election of 1955. The two main parties continued to garner
the vast majority of seats. In retrospect there was not a great
deal of electoral imbalance between the two parties. In terms
of seats won 1945, 1955 and 1959 were convincing victories,
but the other three elections were close in terms of votes and
seats. By-elections emphasised the remarkable electoral
stability of the period. The Labour Party did not lose one by-
election between 1945 and 1950 (there was one ILP loss to
the Conservatives). Only one seat changed hands between
1951 and 1955. Swings were higher against the incumbent

TABLE 8.1

	Total seats	Conservatives	Labour	Liberal	Others
1945	640	212 seats 39.8% of vote	394 48.3%	12 9.1%	22 2.8%
1950	625	298 43.5%	315 46.1%	9 9.1%	3 1.3%
1951	625	321 48.0%	295 48.8%	6 2.5%	3 0.7%
1955	630	344 49.7%	277 46.4%	6 2.7%	3 1.2%
1959	630	365 49.4%	258 43.7%	6 5.9%	1 0.9%
1964	630	304 43.4%	317 44.1%	9 11.2%	0 1.3%

Sources: Nuffield election studies, 1950–64.

party after 1955, and there was the Torrington success of the Liberals in 1958. Yet over all from 1945 to 1959, only nine seats were lost to the opposition.[1]

From 1945 to 1964, and particularly in the 1950s, there was a broad consensus between the two major parties which was quite different from that existing before 1940 and after 1964. The origin of this consensus is complex. On the Conservative side the 1945 defeat was important; the party found itself in Opposition and faced by a governing party with an absolute majority in the House of Commons, a state of affairs unknown to Conservatives since 1910. Yet the origins of the consensus, as we have seen in the last chapter, are to be found in the war years.

Within this two-party consensual framework of party politics, the Conservative Party was the more electorally successful of the two parties, forming a single-party government for thirteen of the nineteen years. To investigate the nature of this success, we must look at the organisation, the policies and the leadership of the party in this post-war period.

The Organisation of the Conservative Party after 1945

The Conservative Party reacted to the 1945 defeat according to tradition; blaming the inadequacies of the organisation of the party, it proceeded to investigate and change certain aspects of its organisation. The post-1945 period is different from other such periods in that the organisational changes were accompanied by important re-emphasis of policy. In July 1946 Lord Woolton, a former member of Churchill's Cabinet, became chairman of the party organisation in succession to Ralph Assheton. Woolton had the authority and enthusiasm to win the party over to his ideas and to improve the grass-roots morale after the shattering election defeat. Lord Woolton was so depressed by the state of the party machine and so pessimistic of electoral improvement that he at first thought of changing the name of the Conservative Party to a more vote-catching one, believing that the Labour Party had a more advantageous title (in fact, he always referred to the Labour Party as the Socialist Party). Ironically, when the Labour Party was experiencing a similar period of electoral self-doubt after the 1959 election, there were similar suggestions.[2]

The organisational reforms, carried out between 1945 and 1951, may be generally classified under the following headings:

(1) *Policy and research.* In November 1945 the Central Council of the National Union established the Advisory Committee on Policy and Political Education under the chairmanship of R. A. Butler. This was to be a very important body in the new policy-making machinery. It came under the control of the Executive Committee of the National Union, but after the Maxwell Fife Report it was reconstituted as the Policy Advisory Committee, with the addition of an Advisory Committee on Political Education. These changes aimed at making the new committees more directly controlled by the party leadership; the influential Advisory Committee on Policy and Political Education had been far too remote from direct influence of the leader.[3] Another important step was to revive the Research Department of the Central Office which had withered during the war years. Here again Butler

was influential. He also established the Political Centre, which had a large degree of independence, though it was financed by Central Office. The CPC was quite important in educating the party rank and file and winning a large degree of acceptance for the new party policies. A final new development in this field was the establishment of Swinton College in 1948, the Conservative College of the North, for the training of party agents and providing weekend schools for party members. All these reforms provided the institutional framework for the debate on and the production of the party policies that were to underline the electoral successes of the party in the 1950s.

(2) *The Young Conservatives.* During the period 1945–6 the party took steps to revitalise its youth wing and as a result established the Young Conservatives, an organisation for party members under the age of 30. By December 1949 there were 2,375 Young Conservative branches with a membership of 160,433.[4] The organisation proved important in that it increased the supply of party workers in the constituencies, while the influx of young people was thought to improve general party morale. It was certainly never to give the party leadership the trouble that youth movements caused the Labour Party. The Young Conservatives were docile, loyal instruments of the Conservative Party.

(3) *Membership, candidates and constituencies.* In 1948 the famous Committee on Conservative Party Organisation under the chairmanship of David Maxwell Fife reported. The Committee's recommendations dealt with various aspects of the party's affairs; those dealing with the candidate– constituency party financial relationship led to certain significant changes. The Report recommended that constituency parties should bear the cost of the election expenses of Conservative candidates and the candidates should not contribute more than £25 p.a. (the limit was £50 in the case of MPs). Previously it was argued that constituency parties sought rich candidates who would make substantial donations to the local party. This was a move to democratise the party and to encourage candidates, even working-class candidates, of limited means. The reform was certainly not the revolutionary change that Lord Woolton claimed, and Maxwell Fife

had doubts later as to the beneficial aspect of the reform.[5] The reform came too late to affect the selection processes for the next two general elections and had only a limited impact on the social base of the party. Using the 1951 election, before the effect of the Maxwell Fife reforms, and comparing it with the evidence from the 1964 election, one is impressed by the similarities not the differences (see Table 8.2).[6]

TABLE 8.2

	1951 (321 Conservative MPs)	1964 (304 Conservative MPs)
Average age	47 yrs	45 yrs
Jews and RCs	7	22
Women	6	11
Education		
Chiefly elementary	4	3
Chiefly secondary	44	36
Secondary and university	33	36
Public school only	73	73
Public school and university	167	156
Oxbridge	168	159
Occupation		
Professions	132	146
Business	117	80
Miscellaneous	71	75
Workers	1	2

Sources: D. E. Butler, *The British General Election of 1951* (London: Macmillan, 1952) pp. 35–43; and D. E. Butler and A. King, *The British General Election of 1964* (London: Macmillan, 1965) pp. 230–40.

One might argue that the social background of MPs is irrelevant to their political views and holds no clue to progressive–conservative divisions in the party.[7] Yet the failure of the Maxwell Fife reforms to change the social basis of the Conservative Party could still have had significant electoral consequences. Certainly, the contrast between the social backgrounds of the two party leaders in the 1964 election and the aristocratic backgrounds of Macmillan's Cabinet members was used by the Labour Party, and even if it did not influence the voters, it could have benefited the Labour Party morale in the election campaign. However, the reform did have an important impact on party membership and party activity. The constituency parties could no longer rely on candidate subsidies and the only important alternative source of local finance was individual subscriptions. In 1953 the party claimed a membership of 2,805,832, compared with a figure of 1,200,000 in 1947 and 2,249,031 in 1948.[8] The constituency parties had benefited from Lord Woolton's reforms and from money spent on the training of agents. By 1950 the number of Conservative agents was double that of 1945; in England and Wales 527 out of 542 constituencies had full-time party officials.[9] Only a small minority of these agents had received no training. During this period in opposition, then, the training, pay and professional standing of agents improved substantially.

(4) *Finance.* One of Lord Woolton's greatest achievements, besides increasing party membership substantially, was in the field of party finance. His fund-raising appeals were highly successful, even his Fighting Fund appeal far exceeded its £1 million target. Fund-raising appeals also stimulated local party activity and recruitment. The Maxwell Fife Report did recommend changes in the financing of the central party organisation based on a system of variable quotas which the local party paid to the centre on a voluntary basis related to the size of the Conservative vote in the constituency. The changes had the advantage of guaranteeing money from the local parties to the hard-pressed central bodies on a permanent basis.

(5) *The National Union.* Changes in the structure of the National Union were few and insignificant. Small changes tended to increase the power of the smaller Executive Committee at the expense of the Central Council and to transfer more important functions to the sub-committee of the Executive Committee, the General Purposes Sub-Committee. Hoffman argues that the chief purpose of these changes was 'to bring the major functions of the party more closely under the Leader's control',[10] as was the case with the reconstitution of the Advisory Committee on Policy and Political Education. In 1950 the Conservative conference determined to maintain

its role as a mass political rally by defeating a proposal to reduce the number of constituency representatives who could attend the conference from seven to two and so create a working body.

All these organisational changes were very important for the party, but their impact and significance should not be overstated. Evidence from election studies shows that successes and failures cannot be directly related to the state of constituency organisation.[11] Certainly organisational improvements contributed to electoral successes in the 1950s but they did not win the elections.

More importantly, the reorganisation of the party after 1945 did not affect the distribution of power in the party: the influence of the rank and file over the leadership remained negligible; the party organisation was mainly devoted to winning elections. The policy-making bodies of the party were firmly in the hands of the parliamentary leadership. When the party conference 'rebelled' in 1950 to insist on the building of 300,000 houses a year by the next Conservative government, the platform felt it was wiser to give way to the conference demands. However, the leadership was not bound by the decision, no matter how embarrassing it would have been if they had ignored it. In the event the target was achieved, and the incident is the more important because it is so rare in the Conservative Party. Organisational change, then, increased the party centralisation and efficiency, but it did not generate an extension of intra-party democracy.

Conservatives and Policy, 1945—64

There is a persuasive myth in the Conservative Party that, as a result of the 1945 election defeat, the party looked hard at its policies and its public image. It found both wanting and with much hard thinking and internal debate, the party rethought its policies within the mantle of the Conservative tradition. The voters embraced these new policies and rejected socialism, and there followed years of unparalleled prosperity under Conservative auspices.

The myth has some truth. Many new approaches to policy

were adopted in the five years after the war and certainly electoral defeat was a most powerful spur to re-evaluation. But there are three serious qualifications. First, much of the new thinking that contributed to the new Conservatism had its roots in the war years. The party went to the electorate in 1945 with a programme not too dissimilar to that of the Labour Party; the main difference was one of priorities. Second, the Conservative Party was responding to the same social and economic pressures as the Labour Party; a political party often exaggerates its freedom of manoeuvre. Butler, the main architect of the new policy directives, put it in perspective when he observed: 'As in the days of Peel, the Conservatives must be seen to have accommodated themselves to a social revolution.'[12] Third, the 1951 election victory was not a direct result of the programmatic uplift of the Conservative Party, just as it was not a consequence of the structural reforms in the party. Yet even with these qualifications, the changes in the Conservative Party do mark important shifts of emphasis in modern Conservatism. The policy consensus to which the party contributed in these years has been aptly christened 'Butskellism'.

The policy rethinking after 1945 was neither the work of the rank and file of the party nor the product of the efforts of the party leader. In fact, Churchill was rather hostile to specific policy commitments, for fear they would provide 'hostages to fortune' or that the party could be dishonourably accused of trying to outbid the Labour Party for electoral support.[13] The new thinking was the product of a small group of influential figures in the party and the organisations that they controlled – the Research Department, the Advisory Committee on Policy and Political Education, and the Conservative Political Centre. Butler undoubtedly played the key role, supported by a new generation of Conservative leaders such as Macleod, Maudling, Powell and Heath.

The essence of the party policy facelift was not in the details of policy but in the new ordering of priorities. By 1951 the party was prepared to emphasise, not merely pay lip-service to, the concept of social welfare, the needs of the unemployed, the aged and the sick. The party now accepted Beveridge explicitly as well as implicitly. After laying down some of the foundations of the National Health Service before 1945, it was willing to accept Labour reforms almost completely. Equally vital, the party now accepted the goal of full employment and higher government spending.[14] There were to be differences between the Conservatives and the Labour Party over the extent of individual economic freedom, but the Conservatives, like Labour, had accepted Keynesian economics and the managed economy. Electorally the party was to place a great deal of emphasis on the evils of Labour's nationalisation programme, but in reality the Conservatives did not disagree fundamentally with much of that programme. The Conservative Party has never been averse to using the power of the state: 'Like Socialist Democracy, Tory Democracy legitimises a massive concentration of political power.'[15] The difference after 1945 was that the party was prepared to play down the *laissez-faire* aspects of Conservatism and promote its long-established corporatism.

The actual details of the new post-war party policies are less important in themselves than as serving as an indication of what the Conservatives would do if they returned to power. The most important in this respect is the *Industrial Charter* of 1947. The content was 'indeed "broad" rather than detailed, vague where it might have been specific'.[16] Other charters followed on agriculture, Wales, Scotland, the Empire and women. Although the actual election manifesto of June 1949, *The Right Road for Britain,* did have a greater stress on free enterprise than the *Industrial Charter,*[17] the essential differences were minimal.

The Conservative Party in government from 1951 to 1964 continued to subscribe to the political consensus formed between 1940 and 1950. In 1951 the Bow Group was formed to urge these new consensual policies; it became one of the most influential elements within the party. The Group stressed the need to appeal to the new affluent working classes, the need for a strong state sector in the mixed economy and the maintenance of the Welfare State. Conservative governments produced few controversial measures, particularly in the early period of their thirteen years of power. They maintained full employment, reached the housing targets promised, appeased the trade unions, increased the number of doctors, teachers and students and did not seek to erode the Welfare State in any serious way. The Conservative Party presided over one of the most affluent periods in British history. Generally the terms of trade altered in Britain's favour after the end of the Korean war, so the Conservatives were fortunate that they were returned to office to oversee these economic changes; they did not create them.

The consensus was not restricted to domestic matters; besides the continuing agreement on the outlines of British foreign policy (the 1956 Suez aberration excepted), there were no essential differences between the parties on matters of colonial policy. The Conservatives, particularly under Macmillan, proved as eager as the Labour Party to cast off formal control of large parts of the Empire. It is true that Conservative administrations had problems in Kenya, in Cyprus and in Central Africa, but these problems, though seized upon by Conservative critics as examples of the party's nostalgic longing for the old imperialism, did not, in the long run, disturb the main area of agreement between the two parties.

The Conservatives did denationalise iron and steel and attempted to denationalise road transport. However, the denationalisation proposals were surprisingly few, given the scale of Labour's programme between 1945 and 1951. In 1958 the much-criticised Rent Act and later in 1962 the Commonwealth Immigration Act did widen the gulf between the parties, but it was the Conservative government's apparent inability to handle the economy after 1960 that was to give the Labour Party its main ammunition.

The Conservative electoral successes throughout the period were based on the ability of the party to deliver the economic goods; the party began to falter electorally and internally when, for reasons partly beyond its control, it could no longer do so. Conservative policies were essentially pragmatic. The 1959 election slogan, 'Conservatives give you a better standard of living — don't let Labour ruin it', underlines this pragmatism. Compared with the period 1945–51, there was little theoretical speculation or conflict after 1951 in the party; the supporters of consensus dominated its upper ranks.

Leadership and Power in the Conservative Party, 1945–64

Between 1945 and 1964 the Conservatives had four leaders. One, Churchill, resigned at a time of his own choosing, but two, Eden and Macmillan, resigned because of ill-health at a time when there was strong, open opposition to their leadership. The fourth, Lord Home, losing a difficult election immediately after becoming leader, resigned after two years. Of the three leaders who followed Churchill, only Eden faced no challenge in the party for the leadership.

Yet the resignations of Eden and Macmillan, and the succession contests of 1957 and 1963, may give the impression of weak leadership constantly under attack. This is far from true. Churchill and Macmillan for the most part had few important critics in the party, and those that did challenge were easily disposed of.

Churchill was not a good leader of the Opposition. After his painful rejection by the electorate in 1945, he tended to withdraw from the routine work of party leadership, and to reserve himself for statements of international significance. He disliked his changed position and tended to be out of sympathy with much of the detail of policy rethinking and organisational reform. There were some rumblings of criticism that he did not attack the Labour government in a more partisan manner,[18] but there was no serious challenge to his leadership at any time after 1945. His national reputation and his stature in foreign affairs, plus the electoral success of 1951, were sufficient protection.

This political inviolability is slightly surprising given the state of his health and his age. In 1951 he was 77 and had suffered two strokes and was to suffer two more before his retirement. Also, Churchill was not essentially a Conservative; it has been said of the government he formed in 1951:

> There has rarely been a government that has contained so many members who held office merely by the will of the Prime Minister and who had no conventional political backing to support them in office. Perhaps there was never a one-party government that seemed to owe so little to the party that put it in office and kept it there.[19]

Anthony Eden had been heir apparent for so long that there was no opposition to his succession in April 1955. In fact, so smooth was the succession and so rapturous was his reception that it appeared ominously like the successions of Balfour and Neville Chamberlain. But Eden was in trouble politically long before the Suez debacle of the summer and autumn of 1956; in January 1956 he was forced to deny rumours that he was about to resign. He was indecisive and unwilling to delegate, generally failing to provide the type of leadership that had been expected of him, given his long experience of government. It is ironic that it was foreign affairs, long regarded as his particular forte, that was to bring his greatest failure. He resigned for genuine reasons of ill-health in January 1957, but his Suez failure had ensured that his tenure of the highest office would be short. Nutting, one of his Ministers, says of Eden in 1956: 'He had lost his grip on events, it was said. His inexperience of financial problems was beginning to show. The deft diplomat was no leader; he had no control over his Ministers.'[20]

In view of the political controversy that surrounded the Suez crisis and the fact that the Anglo–French intervention resulted in failure, little damage was done to the party. The strongest supporters of intervention, the Suez group, continued their opposition after Macmillan succeeded Eden, but there was no real threat to Macmillan's leadership. When Lord Salisbury left the government over colonial disagreements, the right-wing rebels were left without a powerful voice within the Cabinet. There were a few rebels on the left over Suez, but there was no concerted opposition from that quarter. Of the eight that abstained from supporting the government in November 1956, Boyle survived to gain high office, and some (like Nicolson) were denied renomination by their constituency parties.[21]

Eden's resignation was in the event surprisingly sudden, and his unavailability to give advice regarding the succession further complicated a difficult situation. There had been two other occasions in the twentieth century, 1923 and 1940, when the Conservative Party had no obvious successor to the retiring prime minister. Neither provided much guidance. In the event two senior party members, Lord Salisbury and

Lord Kilmuir (formerly Maxwell Fife), sounded out the views of the Cabinet members one by one, and the Chief Whip sounded the opinions of the MPs. This was 'so subtly conducted that many MPs . . . may be entirely unaware that they are taking place'.[22] Salisbury and Kilmuir also asked the opinions of the chairman of the party and the chairman of the 1922 Committee. Salisbury then reported to the Queen, who had consulted with Winston Churchill. On 10 January Macmillan was appointed prime minister and twelve days later unanimously elected leader of the Conservative Party.

Macmillan defeated Butler in this leadership contest mainly because of the suspicion that Butler would be the weaker of the two men in a political crisis. Butler had mutely opposed the Suez venture in contrast to Macmillan's strong support and was unfairly regarded in some quarters as 'a man of Munich', while Macmillan had gained much prestige from his successful period at the Ministry of Housing after 1951. If the post-1965 procedure for choosing the leader had been in operation, Macmillan would not have won more votes than Butler, but Macmillan divided the party least. As Butler himself was to remark: 'It was clear from the representations that had been made to the Chief Whip's office that there were many on the back-benches who would oppose my succession; there was no similar anti-Macmillan faction.'[23]

Macmillan was very successful in uniting the post-Suez party. His strength, style and confidence restored the morale of the party and he was to lead it to the impressive 1959 election victory: 1959—60 was the height of his popularity; large set-backs were to follow. Economic difficulties, particularly the 1961 balance-of-payments crisis, undermined the confidence of the government. Unemployment began to rise, there was a pay pause, a credit squeeze and higher taxes. Foreign policy failures, the collapse of the attempt to enter the EEC, and the appearance of race as a political issue in Britain, all added to Macmillan's difficulties. The disastrous loss of the Orpington by-election to the Liberals in March 1962 showed how far the popularity of the government had slumped. Macmillan tried to remedy the situation in July 1962 by sacking a third of his Cabinet, promoting younger progressives. However, fate was not kind to Macmillan. Two scandals, the Vassall scandal of October 1962 and the more damaging Profumo affair of June 1963, seemed to show that he had lost his ability to lead the government.[24] Although still determined to lead the party into the next election, Macmillan was admitted into hospital in October 1963 and he decided to resign.

The customary processes of selecting a successor would probably have followed the same pattern as 1957 since there was no clear heir-apparent; but there were two important differences. First, the party was on the eve of a general election that it looked likely to lose. Second, the announcement of Macmillan's resignation was made to a Conservative Party conference meeting at Blackpool. The conference was disastrous for Lord Hailsham, Macmillan's favourite for the succession. For on the unwise advice of Randolph Churchill, Hailsham attempted to turn the conference into an American-style political convention. With badges and enthusiastic speeches, Hailsham wooed the rank and file. At a meeting of the Conservative Political Centre on 10 October he announced that he was going to relinquish his peerage. His behaviour did him incalculable harm; the party was not accustomed to allowing the extra-parliamentary party to decide such matters. The conference was not an unmitigated success for the other two front-runners, Butler and Maudling, because their speeches too clearly reflected their relative dullness as potential party leaders.

Away from the heady air of Blackpool, Macmillan was determined to influence events from his hospital bed. He saw all the main actors and on 14 October he issued a memorandum suggesting methods for sounding out opinion in the party: the Lord Chancellor should ascertain the views of the Cabinet; the Chief Whip those of other ministers and MPs; the Chief Whip in the Lords those of Conservative peers; and Lord Poole, Joint Party Chairman, was to sound out the views of the National Union and of Conservative candidates.[25] By this time, Macmillan, realising that his favourite had ruined his chances, was now backing Lord Home, his foreign secretary. He was determined not to have Butler, whom he regarded as an electoral liability as leader; and certainly Butler suspected bias in the consultative process which hurt his chances.[26] Yet even as late as 16 October, Butler was still regarded as the favourite.

However, the MPs, the Lords and the constituency associations were prepared to accept Home; only members of the Cabinet appeared reluctant. There was still an attempt by Hailsham, Maudling and Powell to rally support behind Butler, but it came too late. Macmillan, in advising the Queen to send for Home, urged all speed. Home, in seeking to form his administration, first saw Butler; and Butler's sense of loyalty to the party ensured the collapse of any serious opposition to Home's succession.

The complex tangle of the succession crisis had a number of consequences. First, there was the claim that the whole affair had been managed by a 'magic circle' who controlled the party and prevented democratic practices in the party;[27] Macleod and Powell refused to serve in Home's administration. Second, the bad publicity for the 'customary processes' of leadership selection resulted in important changes in the selection procedures in 1965. Finally, the undignified and seemingly undemocratic choice of Lord Home had important consequences for Conservative Party fortunes in the 1964 election.

Notes to Chapter 8

1. See C. Cook, 'Note: 1945—1960', in *By-elections in British Politics*, ed. C. Cook and J. Ramsden (London: Macmillan, 1973) pp. 191—7.
2. Douglas Jay suggested 'Labour and Radical' or 'Labour and Reform'; see S. Haseler, *The Gaitskellites* (London: Macmillan, 1969) p. 163.
3. J. D. Hoffman, *The Conservative Party in Opposition, 1945—51* (London: MacGibbon & Kee, 1964) p. 109.
4. Ibid, pp. 74—6 and 118—19.
5. See Lord Kilmuir, *Political Adventure* (London: Weidenfeld & Nicolson, 1964) pp. 157—60.
6. See also C. Mellors, *The British MP* (Farnborough: Saxon House, 1978) pp. 30, 41—4, 62—70.
7. See D. E. Butler and M. Pinto-Duschinsky, 'The Conservative Elite, 1918—78: Does Unrepresentativeness Matter?', in *Conservative Party Politics*, ed. Z. Layton-Henry (London: Macmillan, 1980) pp. 198—204.
8. R. T. McKenzie, *British Political Parties*, 2nd edn (London: Heine-

mann, 1963) p. 187. Note comments on the vagaries of party membership figures.

9. H. G. Nicholas, *The British General Election of 1950* (London: Cass, 1951) p. 24.
10. Hoffman, p. 124.
11. Nicholas, pp. 40–1.
12. R. A. Butler, *The Art of the Possible* (Harmondsworth: Penguin, 1973) p. 135.
13. See H. Pelling, *Winston Churchill* (London: Pan Books, 1977) pp. 574–5. As Butler (p. 137) states: 'he [Churchill] would not have tolerated the binding of the Leader before the party was back in power'.
14. See A. Gamble, *The Conservative Nation* (London: Routledge & Kegan Paul, 1974) pp. 47–8.
15. S. Beer, *Modern British Politics*, 2nd edn (London: Faber, 1969) p. 91.
16. Butler, pp. 137 and 148–9. See also Gamble's comments on the *Charter*, pp. 42–3.
17. Hoffman claims this was the result of the party's disappointment at losing the Hammersmith South by-election in February 1949, but other historians of the party claim greater intra-party democracy, stress that the change was a product of the two-way movement of ideas in the party initiated by the CPC; the grass roots wanted more *laissez-faire*. Hoffman's electoral interpretation has history on its side. See Hoffman, pp. 185–6; and T. F. Lindsay and M. Harrington, *The Conservative Party, 1918–1970* (London: Macmillan, 1974) p. 158.
18. See criticism by the 1922 Committee in March 1949 after the Hammersmith South by-election failure, in P. Goodhart, *The 1922: The Story of the Conservative Backbenchers' Parliamentary Committee* (London: Macmillan, 1973) pp. 146–8.
19. Ramsden, in Lord Butler (ed.), *The Conservative Party* (London: Allen & Unwin, 1977) p. 427. Churchill, no doubt with fond memories of his wartime coalition, even offered the Ministry of Education to Clement Davies, the Liberal leader. See R. Douglass, *A History of the Liberal Party 1895–1970* (London: Sidgwick & Jackson, 1971) p. 265.
20. A. Nutting, *No End of a Lesson* (London: Constable, 1967) p. 24.
21. For an account of Nicolson's problems in Bournemouth East, see N. Nicolson, *People and Parliament* (London: Weidenfeld & Nicolson, 1958). Nutting resigned his seat after local criticism and Sir Frank Medlicott did not contest his Norfolk Central seat for the same reason. For details on the eight Suez rebels and their relations with their constituency parties see R. J. Jackson, *Rebels and Whips* (London: Macmillan, 1968) pp. 280–9.
22. McKenzie, p. 589. Macmillan gives a humorous account of the pattern of questioning of ministers in H. Macmillan, *Riding the Storm 1956–9* (London: Macmillan, 1971) p. 182.

23. Butler, p. 197.
24. The Vassall affair involved an Admiralty clerk who was a Russian spy being blackmailed for homosexual activities. Its political importance stemmed from rumours implicating two government ministers, Lord Carrington and Thomas Galbraith, and alleging that Vassall had been protected. The Radcliffe Tribunal cleared the two ministers in April 1963. John Profumo was the Minister for War, who shared a prostitute, Christine Keeler, with a Russian diplomat. Profumo compounded his sins by denying the relationship with Keeler in the Commons. He was finally forced to resign in great disgrace. Ironically, while politically damaging to Macmillan, the Profumo affair lessened the pressures on him to resign the party leadership. Lord Hailsham's emotional television outburst underlined why this was so: 'A great party is not to be brought down because of a scandal by a woman of easy virtue and a proved liar.' See W. Young, *The Profumo Affair: Aspects of Conservatism* (Harmondsworth: Penguin, 1963).
25. H. Macmillan, *At the End of the Day* (London: Macmillan, 1973) pp. 509—10.
26. Ibid, p. 496; and Butler, pp. 246—7.
27. In a review of Randolph Churchill's *The Fight for the Tory Leadership* (London: Heinemann, 1964) Macleod wrote a savage attack on the succession process (*Spectator*, 17 January 1965). The article was certainly a mistake for an ambitious politician: 'politically reckless', Macleod's biographer called it — see N. Fisher, *Iain Macleod* (London: André Deutsch, 1973) p. 254. See also Reginald Bevins, *The Greasy Pole* (London: Hodder, 1965). Bevins was a minister at the time and his badly written book is a fierce attack on the 'Tory Establishment'.

9

The Labour Party, 1945-64

Labour in Office, 1945–51

In 1945 the Labour Party, partly to its own surprise, achieved an over-all majority for the first time in its history. The new government had none of the limitations said to have shackled previous Labour governments, but it did not interpret the election results as a victory for 'socialism'; the reforms of the Labour government were essentially uncontroversial and fully in keeping with the consensus that had emerged from the Second World War. The Bank of England, civil aviation, coal, gas, electricity, inland transport and iron and steel were nationalised, but only the nationalisation of iron and steel was controversial and only the last two were to be denationalised. Even the government was lukewarm over iron and steel, leaving it to the last; moreover, compensation was extremely generous for the previous owners of all these industries. The form of public ownership was quite comforting for those suspicious of Labour's nationalisation programme; public boards or corporations, as favoured by the main architect, Herbert Morrison, ensured a degree of management continuity.

Labour implemented Beveridge, extended national insurance and social security, raised the school-leaving age and set up the government's most impressive achievement, the National Health Service. It repealed the hated Trade Disputes Act of 1927, but this repeal, or the reform of the House of Lords, or the changes in the franchise, could not be seen as politically divisive. Labour's planning controls have always been rather exaggerated. Rogow has shown that there was no

162

integrated system of planning, and what machinery there was was dismantled during the period of the retreat from planning after 1948.[1] On foreign and colonial policy the differences with the Conservative Opposition were almost imperceptible, and Ernest Bevin, Labour foreign secretary for most of the period, won high praise both from the Foreign Office itself and from Anthony Eden, the Shadow foreign secretary. Both parties were determined to maintain the Anglo–American alliance and rigidly oppose any Soviet-led Communist aggression.

It was this strong anti-Soviet line that provoked most opposition within the Labour Party, and most backbench rebellions tended to be concerned with defence and foreign policy. A 'Keep Left' group was formed within the PLP in 1947 and it occasionally criticised the government. Its membership, although small, was to form the basis of the 'Bevanite' group of the 1950s. There was a successful, albeit temporary, rebellion in 1947 to limit conscription for military service to one year, and other rebellions over Palestine and Ireland in 1948–9. But generally, in spite of the large Labour majority, these rebellions were fairly easily contained by the leadership without much recourse to sanctions. The most serious rift in the party was partly the result of the Cold War rigidity of the leadership. In 1948 thirty-seven members of the PLP sent a telegram to Nenni, leader of the more Marxist of the two non-communist socialist parties in Italy, congratulating him on electoral success. The PLP leadership reacted strongly, forced a retraction from some of the signatories and publicly warned others. The leadership was able to use the incident to expel 'fellow-travellers', and before the end of 1949, four Labour MPs (John Platt-Mills, Leslie Solley, Lester Hutchinson and Konni Zilliacus) had been ousted from the PLP. Another MP, Alfred Edwards, was expelled in 1948 and joined the Conservative Party.[1a]

However, the rebellions were relatively few and received little support from the extra-parliamentary party. There were several reasons for the strength of the parliamentary leadership in these years.

First, there was a firm sense of loyalty to the leadership in all sections of the party. The government was by and large implementing the NEC-inspired manifesto of 1945, and was seen as struggling to achieve these goals in very difficult economic and international circumstances. The leadership certainly used this goodwill wisely. The Standing Orders of the PLP were suspended for the duration of the government, theoretically giving MPs more freedom; the PLP strengthened certain institutional devices which improved communication within the PLP and possibly gave under-used backbenchers a feeling of utility. Thus the Liaison Committee was revived consisting of two members elected by the PLP, the Leader of the Commons, and a Labour peer. Backbench standing committees were set up to monitor or provide liaison with the relevant minister, depending on the minister's attitude, and the PLP continued to meet as usual. The narrow majority of 1950–1 further increased the pressure on backbenchers to conform.

Second, the circumstances of the international situation made persistent rebellion difficult in the one policy area where there was most disagreement. To take the stance that Britain should adopt a more neutralist, less hard-line policy at the height of the Cold War in the face of apparent Soviet aggression, particularly in Czechoslovakia in 1948 and Korea in 1950, took courage and some subtlety so as not to appear pro-communist. Without the restraints of office, foreign policy questions were to form the main basis of inter-party disagreement in the early 1950s. Notwithstanding these pressures, the most serious rift in the party exploded over defence spending. In 1950 economies in the NHS, imposed because of the outbreak of the Korean war, ultimately provoked the resignations of Bevan, Wilson, and Freeman from the government. The political insensitivity of Gaitskell, Chancellor of the Exchequer, was the main reason that prescription charges exploded into such a serious rift. Hugh Dalton believed Bevan was resentful because Gaitskell got the promotion that Bevan thought should be rightfully his own, but Leslie Hunter has argued that Bevan was just seeking an excuse to resign 'to gain freedom of action in mobilising the party against what he considered a disastrous and accelerating drift to the right'.[2]

A third and most important reason for the relative unity of

the Labour Party when in office was the leadership of Attlee. Underrated and regarded as a stop-gap leader after his appointment in 1935, he certainly went on to belie Churchill's gibe that he was 'a modest man with plenty to be modest about'. He was both a strong and conciliatory leader, both necessary ingredients after the trauma of 1931, especially given the prestige of the team he led after 1945. His cryptic terseness has probably added to the problem of appreciating his ability to lead the party.[3]

Attlee led a very powerful team of ministers, including Bevin, Cripps, Morrison and Dalton, yet he survived all attempts to curb his power or to replace him. During the summer of 1945 when Churchill invited Attlee to accompany him to the Potsdam Conference, Harold Laski, the chairman of the NEC, stated that Attlee could attend only as an observer. Churchill used this in the election campaign to claim that a Labour prime minister would be answerable to the party caucus. Attlee replied that the NEC had the right to be consulted but not to give orders.[4] Attlee showed a similar determination to protect himself when there was an attempt to replace him after the results of the 1945 election had been declared. Herbert Morrison suggested that Attlee should wait until he had been confirmed as leader by the PLP before going to the palace to be asked to form a government. Morrison rested his case on the Labour party conference decision of 1933. Attlee certainly ignored some of the safeguards introduced in 1933 in the wake of the MacDonald 'betrayal', but the conference did not say that the leader should be elected before forming a government, rather that consultation should take place. With the encouragement of Bevin, Attlee ignored Morrison's rather clumsy attempt to become leader and formed his government in exactly the same manner as his predecessor, MacDonald, had done in 1929.[4a]

There was one important attempt to undermine Attlee's leadership during the economic crisis of June 1947. This took the form of a conspiracy led by Cripps and Dalton for Attlee to be replaced by Bevin. The plot failed because of Bevin's steadfast loyalty to Attlee and because Morrison, who still had hopes of the leadership, could not possibly gain from a conspiracy which would instal his main enemy, Bevin, in power. The whole affair collapsed when Attlee wisely promoted Cripps, whose hostility to his leader then subsided.[4b]

However, although there was good reason for the survival of Attlee and the unity of the Labour Party and its governments, there remains the problem of why, given the huge majority in 1945, the party was out of office by 1951. The government's economic difficulties and the resulting austerities did provoke some disillusionment with the Labour government, as did Morrison's failure as foreign minister during the Abadan crisis of 1951. The state of the leadership was another factor: Cripps and Bevin died before the government's tenure of office came to an end, and Attlee was ill during the crisis over Bevan's resignation. Yet the argument that Labour had completed its reform programme and was intellectually exhausted lacks conviction. The programme endorsed by the Labour Party conference in June 1949, *Labour Believes in Britain,* provided a number of nationalisation proposals to implement. The tiny Labour majority in the House of Commons after the 1950 general election was not the only reason for the failure to act on this programme; the Labour government of 1950–1 deliberately chose not to attempt any implementation.

In one sense the Labour Party did not lose the 1951 election: it was not rejected by the electorate; it increased its share of the vote and gained more votes than the Conservative Party. It was the collapse of the Liberal Party vote (fewer Liberal candidates) working to the advantage of the improving Conservative Party and the vagaries of the electoral system that worked to the disadvantage of the outgoing government.

Labour in Opposition, 1951–64

The 1951–64 period proved to be a very stormy one for the Labour Party. Against the backcloth of three successive Conservative victories, the party was shaken by conflicts within the PLP and in the extra-parliamentary party. There are three strands in the Labour Party at this time which are often difficult to separate. First, there were divisions within the party over specific issues such as defence, public owner-ship and membership of the EEC. Second, there was the issue of power relationships within the party, questions of leader-ship, internal discipline, the relationship of the PLP to the extra-parliamentary party, and the role of the trade unions within the party. Third, there were the personalities of the leading figures within the party, notably Attlee, Bevan, Morrison, Gaitskell and Wilson.

All three strands are interwoven. The battles for particular policies are fought at every level within the party: the PLP, the trade unions and the CLPs. Generally, the Revisionists, supported by Gaitskell, tended to be for a stronger defence policy and to be suspicious of demands for more national-isation, while the left, led by Bevan until 1955, tended to the reverse. The centre was very important in all these struggles. The party that emerged in the mid-1960s was a party led by the centre–right with the rhetoric of the left, a party which for the most part saw the ascendancy of Revisionist policies, a party which was dominated by the parliamentary leadership which had the power and the willingness to ignore the extra-parliamentary party in matters of policy-making. To simplify the configuration of policy, power and personality, they will be treated separately, but their essential interrelationship must always be borne in mind.

Policy Conflicts

Defence proved a highly contentious area of conflict for the party. It was an area of disagreement when Labour was in power, and it continued to be a source of strife after 1951. There were differences of emphasis in relation to the American alliance and support of NATO; those who criticised both were often wrongly branded as sympathisers of the Soviet Union. There were disagreements over the scale of British rearmament during and after the Korean war, as well as over the question of German rearmament. The disputes over nuclear weapons reflected positions ranging from complete pacificism and unilateral disarmament through multilateralism to full-throated support for the British retention and develop-ment of the independent nuclear deterrent.

In March 1952 fifty-seven MPs defied the Whips' instructions to abstain and opposed the government motion asking for approval of its rearmament programme. Standing Orders were reimposed by the parliamentary leadership and the party leaders were successful in their demand for the end of 'parties within parties', a move against the Bevanite group in the Commons. The issue of German rearmament divided the party even more and the leadership only narrowly gained a majority at the 1954 party conference. In the same year Bevan resigned from the Shadow Cabinet on this issue, and in a Commons debate on the German question six MPs who defied the PLP leadership were temporarily expelled from the PLP. In 1955 Bevan himself attacked Attlee on the floor of the House of Commons on the use of nuclear weapons after sixty-two MPs had abstained under the Conscience Clause. His punishment was expulsion by the PLP, and he only narrowly missed expulsion from the party.[5]

However, 1955 marked the end of Bevan's rebellions, and his former supporters in the PLP were left without a leader. In 1956 he became Party Treasurer, rejoined the Shadow Cabinet as Shadow foreign secretary, and at the 1957 conference emphasised his complete unity with the leadership and Gaitskell on defence matters by making his 'naked into the conference chamber' speech in which he advocated British retention of nuclear weapons.

The period 1955 to 1959 saw relative peace within the party over defence matters. However, several factors came together to lead to further clashes which culminated in the 1960 conference disavowing the leadership position on defence and passing a confused motion favouring unilateral disarmament. There was a change of leadership in one of the largest unions, the TGWU, in 1956; in 1958 the Campaign for Nuclear Disarmament was formed and grew rapidly; the cancellation of 'Blue Streak' in 1960 effectively marked the end of an independent deterrent for Britain. Gaitskell's obstinate handling of the intra-party conflict served to inflame the situation. Gaitskell would not accept the verdict of the 1960 conference and campaigned vigorously to have the policy reversed at the following party conference. His success in 1961 virtually ended the struggle over defence policy for the time being.

A second source of policy conflict was provided by the issue of public ownership. Basically there were three groups: the left, which wanted more nationalisation; the centre, led by Morrison, which wanted 'consolidation' of the gains already made; and the Revisionists, led by Gaitskell, who believed that nationalisation was irrelevant. It was the views of the Revisionists which were ultimately to triumph. The 1953 policy document, *Challenge to Britain,* was a victory for the 'consolidators' with its 'shopping-list' of firms to be nationalised in the future but no general commitment to increasing state ownership. Miliband has stressed the good fortune of the leadership provided by the Conservative government's denationalisation of iron and steel: 'This soon became the well-gnawed bone which the leadership regularly threw back to the hungry activists, as a token of the leadership's belief in public ownership.'[6]

The election manifesto of 1955, *Forward with Labour,* marked another victory over the left, but the greatest triumph for the Revisionists was the conference acceptance of the policy document, *Industry and Society,* in 1957. The document contained proposals for only two industries to be nationalised, steel and road haulage. There was, of course, the obligatory reference to taking into public ownership those industries that were seriously failing the nation. The 1959 election manifesto was simply a diluted version of *Industry and Society.*

The effective elimination of nationalisation from the Labour Party programme was mainly the work of the Revisionists in the 1950s. The Revisionists were closely associated with Gaitskell and may be regarded as the 'radical right' of the Labour Party. They were very influential in the PLP, seeking to turn the party into new ideological paths. The essence of the Revisionist challenge to Labour Party orthodoxy can be found in such works as the *New Fabian Essays* of 1952, in the very influential *Future of Socialism* written by Crosland in 1956, and the numerous publications of the Revisionist pressure groups, *Socialist Commentary* and *Socialist Union.*[7]

The basic tenets of this 'rethinking' of Labour ideology can be stated as follows. The 'managerial revolution' meant a transfer of power from the hands of the capitalist owners to the professional managerial class; nationalisation of industry would not alter the new position. In addition, nationalisation should and can only be viewed as a means to certain goals, not as an end in itself; it does not, for various reasons, achieve socialist goals such as equality and a wider distribution of power. Therefore, fiscal means such as progressive taxation and control of the economy are much more efficient weapons, while state purchase of shares is a much more efficient means of state control. Finally, the goals of equality, political freedom and an improvement in the quality of life can best be achieved in a mixed economy.

Revisionist thinking was certainly vague in its goals and was partly, as Crosland later admitted, a product of the economic optimism of the 1950s. However, the essential characteristics of Revisionism was its concern with winning elections. The Revisionists believed that the Labour Party was continually losing elections because of its policies, especially nationalisation, and that the party's 'cloth-cap' image was electorally unpopular. In the Nuffield study of the 1959 general election, the authors claimed:

the old pattern of thinking about British politics is becoming progressively less meaningful. With the disappearance of many of the overt distinctions between middle and working class, the sense of class conflict has been reduced.[8]

Ruth Hinden, editor of *Socialist Commentary*, argued in a similar vein in *Must Labour Lose?* and concluded: 'The manual workers have not only vastly improved their position as manual workers, they have also "changed" their position: some are no longer manual workers at all.'[9] Besides its identification as a class party, she concluded that the Labour Party also suffered from its association with nationalisation.[10] In the *Socialist Commentary* survey section, Abrams underlines the class point forcibly:

The image of the Labour Party, held by both its supporters and its non-supporters, is one which is completely obsolete in terms of contemporary Britain. Both groups see Labour identified with the working class . . . and at the same time, many workers, irrespective of their politics, no longer regard themselves as working class.[11]

It was against this background of dubious 'embourgeoisement' theories, and in the context of the third successive election defeat, that Gaitskell launched his campaign to change Clause IV of the Labour Party Constitution in November 1959. Gaitskell claimed that he was not changing Labour Party goals (in truth they had already been varied by the successful attack on public ownership by the Revisionists in the early 1950s) but was solely concerned with the party image.[12] His failure to ensure support for his initiative and the strength of the emotion the 1918 Constitution aroused ensured Gaitskell's retreat by the middle of 1960.

Yet Gaitskell won in practice if not in theory. The issue of public ownership continued to be played down in policy documents and election manifestos. After Gaitskell's death in 1963, the election of 1964 saw the party fight on the classless basis of an emphasis on the scientific revolution. Harold Wilson had not opposed Gaitskell on either defence or nationalisation when he challenged him for the leadership of the party; the issue for Wilson was poor leadership. So on the issues of defence and public ownership there was to be much continuity.

The third aspect of policy that divided the party in the years of opposition was that of membership of the EEC. In July 1961 Macmillan's government formally opened negotiations to enter the EEC. The issue was to split the Labour Party as it also divided the Conservatives. There were various strands in the Labour Party thinking that prevented agreement. The idealistic internationalism of the party was countered both by the strength of Commonwealth ties and the tradition of 'little Englandism'. It was to the latter tradition that Gaitskell spoke when he emphasised 'the end of a thousand years of history' in his famous anti-EEC speech to the 1962 conference. The economic advantages of entry were offset by the disadvantages, though some members of the party were prepared to join if the terms of entry or certain institutions were changed. A very strong argument in the party was the political argument that joining the Europe of

Adenauer and De Gaulle, a conservative, capitalist, Catholic Europe, would inhibit socialist advance in Britain. Generally the left in the party was anti and the right pro. However, Gaitskell confused an already ideologically confused situation by at first sitting on the fence pondering on the electoral disadvantages and fearing that a trap had been set for him yet again by the wily Macmillan. When he finally came down against entry in very emotional terms at the 1962 conference, his former opponents on defence greeted him enthusiastically while his Revisionist friends were mortified. Gaitskell's wife summed up the position when she observed: 'All the wrong people are cheering.'[13]

Power in the Party
Throughout this period, given Conservative dominance and the policy conflicts within the Labour Party, power blocs and power struggles became more visible than usual. The PLP wing of the party was dominated throughout these thirteen years by the centre–right and it was this group that provided all three leaders. Thus there were only fifty-seven MPs involved in the 1952 revolt on rearmament and the leadership was easily able to reimpose discipline through Standing Orders and the demand for the breaking up of the Bevanite group in the PLP. Morrison from the centre easily defeated Bevan in the deputy leadership contests of 1953–4, and even when Bevan resigned his Shadow Cabinet place in 1954 he was powerless to prevent Wilson, his erstwhile supporter, from filling the vacancy. Bevan was expelled from the PLP by 141 votes to 112 in 1955, and when the leadership contest took place later in the same year Gaitskell, representing the Revisionist right, won easily by 157 votes to Bevan's 70 and Morrison's 40.

The task of the leader was eased after 1955 with the return of Bevan to the front bench. At the lowest point of his fortunes in 1960 (after his conference defeat) Gaitskell could still muster 166 votes to Wilson's 81 in the leadership contest, the first such contest since the title of leader was adopted in 1922. Gaitskell was aided inside and outside Parliament by the activities of the Campaign for Democratic Socialism, a Revisionist group successfully working for the reimposition of the authority of the leader and the acceptance of his policies throughout the party. The victory of Wilson over Brown and Callaghan in December 1963 should not be greeted as a shift to the left in the party. Rather, it represented the triumph of the Attlee type of leadership that masked centre– right politics with compromises and an emphasis on the need for party unity at the expense of principle.

Outside Parliament, the leadership was protected in the NEC and in the party conference by the 'praetorian guard' of trade-union leaders. In terms of NEC seats and conference votes, power lay with six large unions which controlled half the six million conference votes, the other seventy-odd unions[14] having two million and the CLPs having one million. Neither the trade unions nor the CLPs ever voted as a single bloc but three unions, the transport workers (TGWU), the general and municipal workers (NUGMW) and the miners (NUM), did tend to consistently support the parliamentary leadership for most of the 1950s, and, in the case of the last two unions, for most of the period. The General Secretary of the TGWU, Deakin, was a bitter anti-communist with a great dislike of Bevan and the left in the PLP. Williamson, the conservative General Secretary of the NUGMW, was more diplomatic, but fully embodied his union's long tradition of political conservatism. Lawther of the NUM had more diffi- culties with a more democratic union, but he shared the conservatism and equally stressed the need for party unity.

These three unions, with over three and a third million votes, sometimes with support from the other three large unions, the inconsistent engineers, more rarely the shop- workers' union (USDAW) and the railwaymen (NUR), consis- tently voted together. Until the more leftward stance of the TGWU after Cousins had become General Secretary in 1956, they had only been on opposite sides of the political fence on one major issue since 1945. Even in the 1960 defeat Gaitskell still received the support of the NUGMW and the NUM. For most of the period they ensured the leadership's conference victories in regards to policy; they also kept the left out of the women's section of the NEC and the office of Party Treasurer, both categories voted for by the whole conference.

The CLPs wielded less power and were generally regarded with some exaggeration as being left-wing. At the height of the Bevanite troubles from 1952 to 1954, the seven-seat constituency section of the NEC returned six Bevanites. However, the CLPs should not be regarded as being a monolithic left bloc. Harrison estimates that in Bevan's bid for the Treasurership at the 1954 conference the CLPs were only two to one in his favour; and at the 1960 and 1961 conferences it has been estimated that two-thirds of the constituency delegates' votes were cast in favour of Gaitskell.[15]

The Revisionists tended to dismiss constituency activists as less important in the winning of elections than the general image of the party. There is also a trace of the oligarchic suspicion that too much democracy and participation leads to populist instability.[16] In any case, because of the support of the stronger unions for the leadership, there was no basic problem with the doctrine of 'conference sovereignty' in the 1950s. With defeat, first over Clause IV and then at the conference over defence, the right in the PLP began to stress the constitutional independence of MPs and the duty to the constituents who elected them. Gaitskell rejected any compromise before the 1960 conference and, when defeated, he did not accept conference authority but worked to reverse the decision.[17] Gaitskell's defiance in 1960 destroyed the myth of conference sovereignty and paved the way for the ignoring of conference under Wilson.[18]

There is one great difference between the Conservative and Labour parties; when the Conservatives lose one election, never mind three successive ones, the party involves itself in some degree of organisational and ideological change. The Labour Party, perhaps because it is more democratic and there are more points of resistance, never indulges to the same degree. It is true that a sub-committee of the NEC was set up after the 1955 defeat. But even when the committee reported that it 'was deeply shocked at the state of the Party organisation' and that 'compared to our opponents, we are still at the penny-farthing stage in a jet-propelled era',[19] there was to be no change in party organisation. Gaitskell's tactless attempt to change Clause IV in 1959 also showed the conservatism of the party, in the sense that those who accepted the irrelevance of public ownership still held the clause with emotional reverence.

Personalities and Labour Politics, 1951—64
Party conflicts and power struggles within the Labour Party were interlaced with personality conflicts, as we have already seen to some extent. One basic problem for the party in the early 1950s was that Attlee stayed too long as leader. As usual he tried to maintain a balance within the party between the warring factions, but as he got older he became more and more unsuited to pacifying them. This inability was clearly evidenced by Attlee's failure to give a clear lead during the struggle to expel Bevan from the party in 1955, and he compounded his silence by blaming Gaitskell for the attempted expulsion.

Perhaps the main reason for Attlee's retention of power 'was to retain the leadership until Morrison was disqualified from succession by age'.[20] Certainly, when Dalton launched his crusade in 1955 to make the older men in the leadership make way for the younger ones, Morrison, then in his late sixties, was particularly damaged. But Morrison had more disadvantages than age and Attlee's hostility. He was remembered as a poor foreign secretary in the last Labour government, and he compared badly with Gaitskell in economic debates. Moreover, he had incurred the wrath of the powerful Deakin by not opposing the dying Greenwood for the party treasurership; instead, Morrison regained his place on the NEC, having been ousted by the Bevanites the previous year by means of having the deputy leader of the party made an *ex officio* member of the NEC. Deakin was furious and thereafter regarded Gaitskell as the best possible saviour of the party from the threat from the left. In addition, Morrison had a reputation as a political boss and an intriguer. The last-minute manoeuvre in the leadership contest of 1955, in which he and Bevan, long enemies, conspired to attempt to force Gaitskell to step down to give Morrison a clear run, did not enhance his reputation.

Bevan was the most effective orator and the most temperamental of Labour Party leaders in the 1950s. His emotional outbursts did him much damage in the party; but although he had a low opinion of Gaitskell and was identified with the left in the PLP, Bevan was not in fact ideologically distant from Gaitskell, as his acceptance of *Industry and Society* and the Clause IV initiative indicate. Bevan is the hardest to interpret of all the contemporary leaders. He was certainly ambitious, and perhaps that is a reason for the reconciliation with his old foes in 1955. Yet it is difficult to understand why he gave up his safe NEC seat in 1954 when he knew he would lose the fight for the post of treasurer against Gaitskell; the intense hostility of Deakin would see to that.[21] Probably the view that Bevan could have had the leadership if he had behaved differently is correct. Attlee was reported to have said: 'Nye had the leadership on a plate. I have always wanted him to have it. But, you know, he wants to be two things simultaneously, a rebel and an official leader, and you can't be both.'[22]

Gaitskell was not a 'desiccated calculating machine';[23] he would not have led the party into so many crises if the description was apt. He had a strictly middle-class background and was regarded as one of the more successful ministers in Attlee's governments. He was a firm Revisionist and was regarded by his supporters as the strongest bastion against the left wing of the party. His rigidity and political insensitivity led him into many mistakes. He regretted his attempts in 1955 to expel Bevan from the party, and his promise of no increase in income tax, alongside proposals for large increases in public spending, made during the 1959 election campaign, was regarded as a blunder. Perhaps his greatest error as party leader would not have reached a position in which he risked warning, no discussion and no promises of support; it was a fundamental misunderstanding of Labour Party politics. Certainly, he did not lack courage in 1960, but an abler party leader would have not reached a position in which he risked defiance by his own conference on such an important issue.

Gaitskell's problem, for all his personal, human qualities, was that he tended to be intolerant of opposition. He had a weakness for imputing dishonourable motives to his opponents. His famous 'fight, fight, and fight again' speech of 1960 after his defeat on the defence issue had a strong sense of this arrogance. He tended to see intra-party opposition as motivated by scurrilous political reasons. His infamous speech at Stalybridge in 1952 shows all these elements:

> I was told by some well-informed correspondents that about one-sixth of the Constituency Party delegates appeared to be Communist or Communist inspired . . . It is time to end the attempt at mob rule by a group of frustrated journalists and restore the authority and leadership of the solid sound sensible majority of the Movement.[24]

The similarities between this speech and the one of 1960 are very strong. It was ironic that a party-manager type such as Harold Wilson whom Gaitskell disliked should continue most of Gaitskell's policies with far less party conflict.

Notes to Chapter 9

1. A. A. Rogow, *The Labour Government and British Industry, 1945–51* (Oxford: Blackwell, 1955).
1a. For an account of internal Labour politics between 1945 and 1951, see K. D. Morgan, *Labour in Power* (OUP, 1984) pp. 45–81. Also H. Pelling, *The Labour Governments 1945–51* (London: Macmillan, 1984).
2. L. Hunter, *The Road to Brighton Pier* (London: Arthur Barker, 1959) p. 32. The book is a fascinating mixture of gossip and political history. See Hugh Dalton, *High Tide and After, 1945–60* (London: Muller, 1962) p. 359. See also M. Foot, *Aneurin Bevan, 1945–60*, vol. 2 (London: Davis Poynton, 1973) pp. 294–5, for the claim that health charges became 'an obsession' with Gaitskell. Compare Foot's account, very hostile to Gaitskell, with that of P. Williams, *Hugh Gaitskell* (London: Jonathan Cape, 1979), which is equally ungenerous to Bevan (see particularly pp. 238 and 267).
3. Certainly the Conservatives had difficulties in understanding Attlee: 'for Mr Attlee remains an enigma to the Tories'. See Lord Moran, *Churchill: The Struggle for Survival 1940–65* (London: Constable, 1966) p. 335.
4. See F. Williams, *A Prime Minister Remembers* (London: Heinemann, 1961) p. 91. Also K. Harris, *Attlee* (London: Weidenfeld & Nicolson, 1982) pp. 258–61.
4a. Ibid, pp. 262–3.
4b. For an account of the plot, see B. Pimlott, *Hugh Dalton* (London: Jonathan Caope, 1985) pp. 505–8. Also 'his [Morrison's] interpretation of the 1933 rules was open to question, while his personal

interest in provoking a leadership contents was embarrassingly obvious to all', B. Donoughue and G. W. Jones, *Herbert Morrison* (London: Weidenfeld & Nicolson, 1973) p. 343.

5. For a discussion of the Bevanites, see M. Jenkins, *Bevanism: Labour's High Tide* (Nottingham: Spokesman, 1979). The book has a particular concern with Eastern Europe but chs 5—6 are relevant here.
6. R. Miliband, *Parliamentary Socialism*, 2nd edn (London: Merlin Press, 1972) p. 322.
7. R. H. S. Crossman (ed.), *New Fabian Essays* (London: Turnstile, 1952); and C. A. R. Crosland, *The Future of Socialism* (London: Jonathan Cape, 1956). For details on *Socialist Commentary* and *Socialist Union* see S. Haseler, *The Gaitskellites* (London: Macmillan, 1969) pp. 66—80.
8. D. E Butler and R. Rose, *The British General Election of 1959* (London: Cass, 1970) p. 15.
9. In M. Abrams and R. Rose, *Must Labour Lose?* (Harmondsworth: Penguin, 1960) p. 105.
10. Ibid, p.100.
11. Ibid, p. 23.
12. Williams, pp. 245—6.
13. Ibid, p. 736.
14. Various amalgamations reduced the number of affiliated unions in the 1950s and 1960s and there were many more changes. See L. Minkin, *The Labour Party Conference*, rev. edn (Manchester University Press, 1980) pp. 369—73. It is difficult, therefore, to give exact figures.
15. M. Harrison, *The Trade Unions and the Labour Party Since 1945* (London: Allen & Unwin, 1960) p. 316. Also K. Hindell and P. Williams, 'Scarborough and Blackpool: An Analysis of Some Votes and the Labour Party Conferences of 1960 and 1961', *Political Quarterly*, vol. XXXIII, no. 3, July—September 1962, pp. 306—20.
16. Compare Crosland, p. 341, with the views of an American conservative-pluralist, S. M. Lipset, *Political Man* (New York: Anchor, 1963) pp. 227—9.
17. It could be argued that in seeking a reversal at the 1961 conference Gaitskell was in fact recognising conference authority and if defeated again would have resigned. There is, however, no evidence to support this view.
18. See Minkin, pp. 287—9.
19. See R. T. McKenzie, 'The Wilson Report and the Future of the Labour Party Organisation', *Political Studies*, vol. 4, no. 1, February 1956, pp. 93—7.
20. Williams, p. 535.
21. Willaims claims it was to split the union vote and so weaken Deakin (ibid, p. 327).
22. Quoted in Foot, p. 484.

23. Bevan's words were said to refer to Gaitskell, but Bevan's biographer denies it (ibid, p. 452).
24. Quoted in Williams, pp. 304–5. Williams comments: 'It was a familiar if not endearing characteristic of Gaitskell to spy Communists among his opponents' (p. 711).

PART FOUR

The Challenges to the Two-Party System After 1964

10

The Conservative Party After 1964

Introduction

One of the most persistent and striking themes of this book
has been the adaptability and electoral success of the Conservative Party since the late nineteenth century. The history
of the party since 1964 re-emphasises both these characteristics. There have been three significant aspects of the modern
party. Firstly, the continuing electoral success of the party;
the election of 1964 was narrowly lost after thirteen years of
uninterrupted power and although the party lost the 1966
election more convincingly, it surprisingly won in 1970. It
lost the February 1974 election in terms of seats and was
defeated in the October election of the same year, but it was
to be faced by a Labour government with an absolute majority
in the Commons for only a brief period. The 1979 and 1983
elections were complete success stories for the Conservatives.
Secondly, power in the party remained firmly in the hands of
the party in Parliament, although there were to be important
innovations in the method of selecting the party leader.
Thirdly, the ideological changes in modern Conservatism enabled the party to succeed electorally and to set and indeed
dominate the political agenda of British politics in the later
part of this period. Since the electoral successes of the modern

170.

183

Conservative Party are examined elsewhere, the remainder of this chapter will look at the other two themes of firstly, leadership power and organisation, and secondly, the changing ideological currents and ideological conflicts within the party since 1964.

Parliamentary Leadership

Home and Heath

Ostrogorski's fears at the turn of the century of parliamentary democracy being threatened by local, self-appointed political caucuses have not been realised by the modern Conservative Party. Policy making and leadership selection have remained firmly in the hands of the party in the House of Commons and the extra-parliamentary party has not seriously challenged this power relationship. Furthermore, power within the parliamentary party has continued to lie with the leader but only as long as the leader maintained the confidence and support of MPs. The successful Conservative leader has won general elections and has maintained a power balance within the party in the Commons.

Since the retirement of Macmillan in 1963 and the succession of Home, new procedures for the selection of the leader were adopted and have changed the relationship between leaders and followers in some respects. Following the unfavourable publicity and dissatisfaction within the party with the procedure that led to the appointment of Home in 1963, a radical new system was adopted. The essentials of this new system were the selection of the leader by MPs, with provision for up to three ballots to ensure both that the choice of the leader was the clear choice of all Conservative MPs and that compromise candidates could be put forward in the event of a deadlock. In the first ballot a successful candidate had to win an absolute majority of the votes cast plus 15 per cent more votes than his or her nearest rival. On the second ballot other candidates could stand and the winner had to gain an absolute majority. On the third ballot the three leading candidates from the second ballot competed and a preferential voting system was used to eliminate the weakest candidate and allow the eventual winner to emerge with an absolute majority of the votes.

The new procedures were soon put to use. Home was seen as an inadequate adversary for Wilson in the 1964 election and he hastened his own departure by his constant reiteration that he would resign when the party wished. To add to the parliamentary criticism, constituency party feeling turned against Home and he resigned in July 1965. In the ensuing election, Heath won by 150 votes, Maudling gaining 133 and Powell 15. There was no need for a second ballot as both Maudling and Powell withdrew.

Edward Heath's leadership was full of difficulties. He was socially aloof and found communication difficult except among his close friends.[1] Throughout the 1965-70 period in opposition, he lagged behind his party in popularity. He became more immersed in the detail of policy formulation than in the task of boldly attacking the Wilson government as his critics within his party wished. He did win the 1970 election, but the difficulties of the 1970-74 period increased his unpopularity within the party. His infamous 1972 U-turn in economic policy was not helped by soaring oil prices, which harmed most industrial countries; the failure to implement the 1971 Industrial Relations Act effectively and his bruising encounters with the miners further weakened his authority and the party lost five by-elections in this period.[2] More importantly, Heath lost the two elections in 1974; Heath lost altogether three out of the four general elections he fought as party leader – shades of Arthur Balfour.

Immediately after the October 1974 election, the 1922 Committee, whose chairman, Edward du Cann, had been dismissed by Heath as party chairman in 1967, made public backbench criticisms of the leader. In the face of growing hostility in all sections of the party, Heath agreed to the establishment of a committee under Lord Home to draw up new rules for the selection of the party leader. The Home committee proposed the following system:

(1) Annual elections would be held for leader.
(2) The successful candidate could only be elected on the first ballot if there were an absolute majority plus 15 per cent of those eligible to vote, not merely of those voting.

(3) There were to be consultations with the National Union and these views would be conveyed to MPs during the voting process.

(4) The second and third ballots would follow the 1965 practice.

The first election under this new system took place in February 1975. Sir Keith Joseph, one of Heath's chief critics and the architect of much that was to become known as 'Thatcherism', could not stand because of certain indiscreet public statements on the subject of population control. Heath's friends refused to challenge him. Margaret Thatcher emerged to take up the cudgels on behalf of Heath's opponents and surprisingly won the first ballot with 130 votes to Heath's 119; Hugh Fraser won 16 and there were 11 abstentions or non-voters. Thatcher's votes were undoubtedly anti-Heath but not necessarily pro-Thatcher votes. However, as a recognition of her bravery she easily won the second ballot with 146 votes to Whitelaw's 79, Prior's 19, Howe's 19 and Peyton's 11.

Thatcher
Margaret Thatcher achieved the leadership of the Conservative Party almost by accident. She, unlike Heath, would never have emerged under the pre-1965 method of selection. She was different from other Conservative Party leaders in many ways. With only the experience of being Minister for Education and Science, she had had the least experience of ministerial office of any leader since Bonar Law; she was the most abrasive and strident Conservative leader since possibly Neville Chamberlain. The 'grocer's daughter' taunt was less important than the fact that she represented a lower middle class upwardly mobile section of the party which was wresting power from the older patrician gentlemen. Yet she possessed two traditional qualities held by nearly all successful Conservative Party leaders since Balfour; firstly, she maintained her communications with the Conservative backbenchers and the grass-roots of the party; secondly, she won general elections. To maintain her supremacy she needed an element of luck; the state of the Labour Party before 1983, the split in the

anti-Conservative vote since 1981 and the Argentinian invasion of the Falkland Islands in 1982 were examples of her
good fortune. Yet she adroitly exploited situations. In 1981
she had the worst popularity rating in the opinion polls of any
other modern prime minister and there was even talk of a
leadership challenge being mounted within the party in the
autumn of that year. After the 1983 general election, the by-
election defeats at Brecon, Fulham and Ryedale dented her
popularity within the party and the resignation of Cecil
Parkinson over his personal life and the departures of
Heseltine and Brittan over the Westland helicopters affair in
1985–6 raised doubts concerning her competence and ministerial selection.

Yet she survived with little real challenge. She routed the
'wet' element in her governments; the departures of St John
Stevas, Gilmour, Carlisle, Soames and Pym plus the resignation of Carrington and the demotion and final resignation of
Prior provided ample evidence of the necessary ruthlessness.

However, in spite of the supremacy of her own supporters,
especially in the economic field, her Cabinets were not solely
reflections of her own ideological preferences. Her appointment of ministers, especially after 1984 of ministers who were
more critical, underlined her awareness of the need to avoid
isolation within her own party. The attempted difficult
balancing act over South African sanctions in 1986 further
underlined her concern with party cohesion. All organised
opposition within the party failed to weaken her position;
the dramatic failure of Francis Pym's 'Centre Forward' initiative in the Spring of 1985 was but one example. Thatcher
successfully performed the most basic task of any Conservative leader: she won the two elections of 1979 and 1983,
thus ensuring her safe tenure of office.   457

The Extra-Parliamentary Party After 1964

The National Union
There were few changes in the extra-parliamentary party
after 1964. The National Union continued to be chiefly a

vote winning and fund raising machine. By the 1960s the leader attended the annual conference throughout its sessions instead of just the last day and since 1967 there has been the opportunity to record conference votes; but the conference never became the forum for decision-making and it continued to have little say in the direction of party policy.

There were attempts to democratise the party by making the leadership more accountable to the rank and file and increasing the political emphasis of the National Union. In July 1970 the Chelmer Review Committee on Party Organisation was set up by the Executive Committee of the National Union. It produced two reports, an interim one on candidate selection in 1972 and the final report of 1975. It was a radical report but generally ignored by the party, although some of its recommendations were implemented. By the 1980s the Tory Charter Movement which campaigned for greater internal democracy and the lifting of the veil of secrecy concerning party finances found that successive party chairmen successfully resisted calls for party reform.

Probably the main reason for the failure to democratise the Party as a whole and increase the power of the extra-parliamentary party was the lack of demand from below. When changes in the procedures for the election of the leader were implemented in 1975, the provisions for consultation with the party outside Parliament were not regarded as particularly successful and there was little protest.[3] While other British political parties became more internally democratic and made the leadership more accountable to their extra-parliamentary supporters, even if only formally in some cases, the internal distribution of power within the Conservative Party was largely untouched.

However, the National Union itself continued to have a fairly democratic structure. The Central Council, the governing body of the NU with 3,600 members represented MPs, Central Office, prospective candidates, the NU Executive Committee and area councils and constituency parties. It was too big to govern effectively and only met twice a year, delegating the day-to-day business to the Executive Committee. This committee of 150 met once a month and was fully representative of all sections of the party. Most of the detailed work of the Executive Committee was performed by the powerful General Purposes Committee, including the compilation of the agenda for the annual conference, an agenda always designed to encourage unity rather than criticism.[4]

Central Office

Central Office continued in its subordinate role to the party leader, although like all bureaucracies it developed varying degrees of independence. However, with its lack of patronage, its lack of an independent financial base and an inability to control candidate selection significantly, its political power remained weak. After 1964 its dependence on the leader increased. Heath made it more of a personal tool of the leader and used it to control other organisations such as the Research Department and the Conservative Political Centre. Heath was accused of using Central Office to attack his political opponents within the party and when he lost the leadership in 1975 retribution was swift.[5] Severe economies cut the staff of Central Office and reduced staff morale, control of the party election agents was returned to the constituency parties and there was a purge of the staff judged to be too sympathetic to Heath; Wolf, the Director General, was one of the victims. The appointment of Peter Thorneycroft in 1979 as party chairman ensured loyal Thatcherite support from a man not in the Cabinet and without further political ambitions and the subsequent selections of Cecil Parkinson, John Gummer and Norman Tebbit maintained the leader's control.

Party Membership and Finance after 1964

It has always been difficult to discover the exact membership of the Conservative Party, but it is clear that membership declined from the peak of 2,805,032 in the early 1950s. The Houghton Committee estimated that the average membership in 1974 for the constituency parties was approximately 2,400 which would have given the Party a total membership of 1½ million dropping to possibly 1.2 million in 1982.[6]

It is equally difficult to come to any firm conclusion about the financial state of the Conservative Party in the 1980s, although some accounts have been published since 1967. The

Houghton Committee estimated that for the year 1975-6, the Party had a total income of £6,290,000: £1,790,000 for the centre and £4,500,000 for the constituencies.[7] It was the financial health of the constituency parties that chiefly distinguished the Conservative Party from the Labour Party and gave the Conservatives such a marked advantage. The constituency parties raised money from various sources – individual subscriptions, small business donations, lotteries and social functions – and they spent the money on election expenses, agents and local administrative costs. They also contributed to Conservative Party headquarters under a system of quotas determined by the all-round strength of the local party.

This locally derived money constituted about one-third of the income of the central organisation. There were small investments and some money from state aid to the party in the House of Commons, but the other two-thirds of central funds came mainly from company donations. Only about one-fifth of the 1,000 largest companies made political donations, but of the estimated £2.83 m in political donations from 313 British companies in 1984, £2.22 m went to the Conservative Party.[8] Part of the problem of estimating Conservative income from companies lies in the fact that part of the total money went directly to the party and part indirectly through the British United Industrialists (BUI), an organisaexisting solely to raise money for the Party.[9] There were other organisations such as the Economic League and Aims (formerly Aims of Industry) which assisted the party and received money from private companies.

The Conservatives opposed more state aid to political parties recommended by the Houghton Committee, unsurprisingly given the party's relative advantage over the other political parties. Its income and expenditure varied according to the timing of general elections, but generally the financial health of the party remained relatively good; in the 1983 election it was able to employ nearly 320 agents.[10] However, when the Conservative government passed the Trade Union Act of 1984 which forced trade unions to hold ballots every ten years for the establishment of political funds, there was criticism of the lack of similar legislation to enforce the balloting of shareholders in companies donating money to the Conservative Party.[11]

Candidate Selection and Social Composition
Besides electoral organisation, fund raising and intra-party communication, the extra-parliamentary party continued to exercise one other important function: the selection of parliamentary candidates. The period after 1964 showed little friction between the sitting MP and his or her constituency association nor between the central party organisations and constituency parties over candidate selection. The methods of selection remained fairly uniform with the local chairman and agent (if there was one) as the influential actors and the constituency executive committee appointing a smaller selection committee to draw up a short-list from the hopefuls that applied; the executive committee acted as the selection committee. The choice of the committee was nearly always acceptable to the wider membership and only Southport in 1952 and Nelson and Colne in 1969 provided rare exceptions of the members' rejecting the executive's advice in the wider party meeting. In 1973 in the Langstone constituency near Portsmouth, the executive committee dropped the sitting MP, Ian Lloyd, choosing Janet Fookes instead, but Lloyd forced a meeting of all members and the executive choice was overruled in his favour.

Re-adoption conflicts have been in fact relatively rare.[12] Conflicts tended to arise from personal rather than political disagreements although some members on the left of the party, such as Nigel Fisher in 1970 or Nicholas Scott in 1977, had to fight hard for renomination. Commander Courtney had a difficult struggle in Harrow in 1966 as a consequence of compromising pictures taken during a visit to Moscow, and Christopher Brocklebank-Fowler's decision to move to the SDP in 1981 was encouraged by his uncomfortable relations with his local constituency party. The boundary changes before the 1983 general election threw up a few disputes as a result of dispossessed MPs looking for new seats and others looking for safer ones. The most bitter and public conflict occurred in Clwyd North-West where two dispossessed MPs from previously neighbouring seats were defeated in the original selection process by a Euro-MP, Beata Brookes. After bitter public wrangling, the High Court forced the local general meeting of the constituency association to reconsider and one of the former contenders, Sir Anthony Meyer, was nominated.

Just as local disputes were rare in the period after 1964, so conflict between the centre and the local party was an exception. The Interim Report of the Chelmer Committee caused some indignation in 1972, when it appeared to recommend increases in central control, suggesting revised model rules and formal re-adoption for each MP, but the controversial aspects were ignored. The Standing Advisory Committee on Candidates (SACC) maintained a short-list of candidates for constituencies to choose from, but the pressure on local parties is very light and informal. Central Office had great difficulty in finding an amenable local party to select Reg Prentice, the Labour defector from Newham NE before obtaining his selection in Daventry for the 1979 election. In 1974 the SACC refused to endorse Conservative candidates in Wigan, South East Leeds, Manchester Blackley, and in Liverpool's Scotland and Exchange division because of their Powellite leanings. The threat of withdrawal of financial help, prominent speakers and party literature with the ultimate sanction of disaffiliation was sufficient.

Given this continuity in the selection procedures, it was not surprising to find little change in the social composition of the Party, especially in regards to MPs. Conservative MPs remained totally unrepresentative in social background of the electors who vote Conservative. Between the two elections of October 1974 and 1983, the percentage of university graduates varied only between 69 and 71 per cent; public school products declined slightly from 75 to 70 per cent and those with a professional background declined from 46 to 35 per cent, while businessmen rose slightly from 32 to 36 per cent.[13]

The background of the extra-parliamentary élites such as constituency chairmen was more difficult to ascertain, but all the available evidence underlined the consistent pyramidal nature of the Conservative Party: the higher the position in the party, the higher the social class.[14] However, the composition of Cabinets under Macmillan was far more aristocratic than those of Thatcher; the identification of some of the more patrician landowners with the 'wet' element inside the Conservative Party was a factor in the predominance of ministers from professional and business backgrounds in the 1980s.

The Ideology of the Conservative Party after 1964

After 1964 there were marked changes in the direction and style of the political ideas of the Conservative Party. Ideological conflict was not new to the party, and Conservative history has amply illustrated the conflict of ideas and tendencies within the party. Yet it is important to remember while discussing ideological differences that more has united warring Conservatives than has divided them and that often rhetorical flourish may be mistaken for substance. The essential basis of Conservatism was untouched in this period; it continued to be a party of pragmatic adjustment to electoral pressures. Conservatives still saw history as a unity; there was a continuing relationship with the past and a duty to the future. Thus the legacy of the past should not be subject to sudden widespread change but slowly improved and handed to future generations. Conservatives continued to have a pessimistic view of man's nature. Man and society cannot be improved by societal blueprints; man is evil unless curbed by authority and there is the need for a strong state; the enforcement of order is one of the prime duties of the state. There continued to be no room for equality, neither political nor social, in Conservative thinking; leadership had to be provided by those best fitted to rule and in the British context this meant the upper and middle classes. Of course, this political élite would govern with the interests of the governed in mind; a form of social paternalism has always been an aspect of Conservatism.[15] The party steadfastly supported all British political institutions and succeeded in maintaining their identification with the party. Private property naturally figured importantly in Conservative thinking and membership of the EEC was an important necessity to protect the national interest.[16]

Yet there are three difficulties in analysing Conservative ideology after 1964. First is the long-standing Conservative belief that Conservatism is not an ideology and the long established anti-intellectual bias of the party.[17] Secondly, the cruder style of Conservative leaders since 1964, especially that of Thatcher, emphasised, often misleadingly, changes of ideological direction. Thirdly, the period did witness genuine ideological differences and amid this conflict it was understandable that the older themes of Conservatism were temporarily eclipsed in emphasis to provide ideological space for the newer ones. It should not be forgotten in discussing the ideological approaches of political parties that these parties are heavily influenced by external constraints which the party cannot control.

The election of Heath in 1965 and subsequently that of Thatcher in 1975 did emphasise ideological changes of direction for the Conservative Party to such an extent that from the 1970s one could identify two broad schools of thought within the party that were given the identification tags of 'wets' and 'dries'. They were crude generalisations but useful in tracing ideological developments after the 1960s.

The 'wets' were the inheritors of the Keynesian interventions of the post-1945 period; they represented the post-war consensus. The 'wets' believed in more state intervention to alleviate the social consequences of harsh market forces. They had a more humanitarian view of social policies: they were for conciliation especially in industry; and they wished to incorporate 'sensible' trade unionists into the decision-making structure, at least to some extent. They frowned on the abrasive rhetoric of the right of the party and had little sympathy with racist attitudes. After 1980, they were largely excluded from key posts in the Thatcher Cabinets, but some like Peter Walker did maintain their positions inside government. They organised themselves in such groups as the Tory Reform Group (TRG), established in 1975 as a successor to PEST (Pressure for Economic and Social Toryism). The TRG disapproved generally of the Conservative governments' monetarism, its lack of a clear pay policy, needless attacks on trade unionists and it supported, significantly, the adoption of proportional representation as a means of avoiding political extremism of either right or left.[18]

The 'dries' or the New or Radical Right of the Party were more difficult to classify. There was disagreement both about whether this new right was different from the older consensual Tory Party of the 1950s and also about the exact nature of this new ideological tendency within the party. Some commentators denied a clear ideological flavour to Thatcherism and its supporters on the new right; Peter Riddell claimed that there was a mistaken wish to confer on Thatcherism 'greater coherence and consistency than it has in practice'. Thatcherism, he argued was 'essentially an instinct, a series of moral values and an approach to leadership rather than an ideology.'[19]

Certainly the leadership played an important part in setting the agenda for the modern Conservative Party, but the New Right was based on more than the accidents of leadership selection. The Selsdon Park Conference of 1970 was one organised appearance of these new views and the Centre for Policy Studies, initiated by Keith Joseph in 1974, became one of the mechanisms for their dissemination throughout the party. The ideas of the New Right espoused economic policies that appeared to owe more to nineteenth-century liberalism than Tory collectivism. The new gurus were the American economist Milton Friedman and the Austrian, Friedrich von Hayek. The New Right followed the policy of monetarism: if one reduces the supply of money in circulation and gives priority to reducing the rate of inflation, many economic ills will disappear. The economic role of the state should be reduced; market mechanisms should replace state intervention to regulate the economy, direct taxes reduced to encourage private initiative, public spending reduced, and people should be encouraged to rely less on state welfare benefits. Naturally, the power of trade unions should be reduced.

However, there were significant divisions within the New Right.[20] On one hand there were the neo-liberals and on the other, the authoritarian populists. The neo-liberals consisted of various ideological groups, but generally they pushed the liberal economic arguments further and advocated more freedom in social and moral areas such as the absence of censorship and freedom to use drugs. To further complicate matters, part of the neo-liberal New Right became identified with a number of causes not clearly identified with economic or social *laissez-faire* doctrines. Thus within the New Right one could find strong support for white South Africa and for the 'repatriation' of black British citizens. Although organisationally many of the supporters of these discriminatory views within the party were identified with such organisations as the Federation of Conservative Students, these views had much wider support as a confidential report in September 1983 was to show.[21]

Yet there was a stronger case for identifying the Conservative leadership of the 1980s with the authoritarian populist wing of the party. The liberalism of this section only extended to some aspects of the economy and certainly did not imply the absence of a strong centralised state. This variety of the New Right was more accurately to be identified with Thatcherism; it was for hierarchy, authority, and nationalism; it was opposed to welfare spending and was strongly anti-trade union. Above it was closely identified with governmental centralisation of decision-making and it had a strong concern with questions of morality and public order through stronger police powers. It received support from a wide array of pressure groups such as the Festival of Light, anti-abortionists, Right-to-Life associations, supporters of the re-introduction of capital punishment and moral bodies such as the Listeners' and Viewers' Association. This brand of Conservatism was strongly nationalistic. Its popular appeal was partly witnessed by the 1979 and 1983 general elections; it had the ability to touch popular chords and lacked the distant élitism of the older patrician face of Conservatism.[22]

There is no doubt that Thatcherism had captured the Conservative Party by the middle of the 1980s and determined the agenda for British politics as a whole. Yet the question of the permanence of this authoritarian populism had still to be determined. Thatcherism certainly owed a great deal to style and rhetoric and naturally was linked closely to the type of leadership of Thatcher herself; new leadership of different circumstances such as a 'hung' Parliament and the necessity of coalition building could lead to different approaches and emphases; even a Conservative election defeat would strengthen the position of the dormant 'wets'. Above all it is important to re-emphasise two key aspects of modern Conservatism: it represents a coalition of views and it is pragmatic and flexible in its search for electoral success.[23]

Notes to Chapter 10

1. Norton firmly puts the blame on Heath for backbench rebellions between 1970 and 1974, in particular for 'his failure to communicate effectively with backbenchers'. See P. Norton, *Conservative Dissidents: Dissent Within the Conservative Party, 1970—77* (London: Macmillan) p. 284.
2. For an account of Heath's social and economic problems in the 1970—74 period, see P. Whitehead, *The Writing on the Wall* (London: Michael Joseph, 1985) pp. 70—115.
3. See P. Seyd, 'Democracy within the Conservative Party', *Government and Opposition*, vol. 10, no. 2, Spring 1975, pp. 219—37.
4. For a more detailed account of the contemporary Conservative Party organisation, see P. Norton and A. Aughey, *Conservatives and Conservatism* (London: Temple Smith, 1981) pp. 190—239.
5. For example, see P. Cosgrove, *Margaret Thatcher: A Tory and Her Party* (London: Hutchinson, 1978) pp. 51—5. For a more detailed view of the power of Central Office in the early 1970s, see M. Pinto-Duschinsky, 'Central Office and 'Power' in the Conservative Party', *Political Studies*, vol. 20, no. 1, March 1972, pp. 1—16.
6. *The Report of the Houghton Committee on Financial Aid to Political Parties*, Cmnd. 6601 (London: HMSO, 1976) p. 31. Also, see D. Butler and G. Butler, *British Political Facts, 1900—1985* (London: Macmillan, 1986) p. 139.
7. *Houghton Committee*, ibid. p. 41. Also see M. Pinto-Duschinsky, *British Political Finance 1830—1980* (Washington: American Enterprise Institute, 1981) pp. 126—54.
8. See *Labour Research*, August 1985, vol. 74, no. 8, pp. 202—5. Also 'Who Owns the Tories', *Trades Union Co-ordination Committee* (London: Co-operative, 1985).
9. In 1984, for example, £400,000 out of £500,000 of company donations that went to sources other than the Conservative Party went to the BUI. See *Labour Research*, ibid.
10. D. Butler and D. Kavanagh, *The British General Election of 1983* (London: Macmillan, 1984) p. 32.
11. See *Company Donations to Political Parties: a Suggested Code of Practice*, Constitutional Reform Centre and the Hansard Society for Parliamentary Government, June 1985, which recommended

shareholder ballots. This would probably be no threat to Conservative income from this source, and indeed may encourage donations from more companies. The Rank Organisation was probably the first large company to ballot its shareholders and the result was a foregone conclusion given the dominance of institutional shareholders. See *The Financial Times*, 14 March 1986.

12. See A. D. R. Dickson, 'M.P.'s Re-adoption Conflicts, Causes and Consequences', *Political Studies*, vol. 23, no. 1, March 1975, pp. 71–99.

13. See D. Butler and D. Kavanagh, *The British General Election of October 1974* (London: Macmillan, 1975) p. 215 and Butler and Kavanagh, *The British General Election of 1983*, pp. 235–7.

14. It is estimated that 85 per cent of constituency chairmen come from the A/B social categories, i.e. upper middle and middle class. See Z. Layton-Henry (ed.), *Conservative Party Politics* (London: Macmillan, 1980) pp. 193–8. See also J. Blondel, *Voters, Parties and Leaders*, rev. edn (Harmondsworth: Penguin, 1974) pp. 97–103.

15. See R. F. Leach, 'Thatcherism, Liberalism and Tory Collectivism', in *Politics*, vol. 3, no. 1, 1983 (The Political Studies Association) pp. 9–14 for a qualification of this view of Tory paternalism. For a more sympathetic view of collectivism in the Party, see A. Beattie, 'Macmillan's Mantle: The Conservative Party in the 1970s', *Political Quarterly*, vol. 50, no. 3, July–Sept 1979, pp. 273–85.

16. Membership of the EEC did produce divisions in the party in the 1960s and 1970s; British entry enraged the more romantically inclined Conservatives, but the champions of membership saw it as consistent with British national interest.

17. I. Gilmour wrote: 'Ideology seems inseparable from class; hence the Tories can only remain a national party if they remain free from ideological infection'. I. Gilmour, *Inside Right: A Study of Conservatism* (London: Hutchinson, 1977) p. 132.

18. For examples of the political ideas of the 'wets', see P. Walker *The Ascent of Britain* (London: Sidgwick & Jackson, 1977); T. Russel, *The Tory Party* (Harmondsworth: Penguin, 1978; Gilmour, *Inside Right: A Study of Conservatism*; F. Pym, *The Politics of Consent* (London: Hamish Hamilton, 1984).

19. P. Riddell, *The Thatcher Government* (Oxford: Martin Robertson, 1983) p. 7.

20. For an analysis of these divisions see R. Levitas (ed.), *The Ideology of the New Right* (Cambridge: Polity Press, 1986).

21. 'The Report of the Committee of Inquiry on Infiltration by the Extreme Right into the Conservative Party and the Level of Collaboration within the Right-Wing of the Conservative Party', written by the Young Conservatives was never made public and caused an outcry when it was leaked in 1984. It named several Conservative MPs and groups espousing right-wing and fascist causes and identified some National Front supporters who had joined the Conservative Party.

22. This view of the modern Conservative Party is persuasively set out in S. Hall and M. Jacques (eds), *The Politics of Thatcherism* (London: Lawrence & Wishart, 1983), although the book does not represent a uniform view of modern Conservative ideology.
23. See A. Gamble, 'Thatcherism and Conservative Politics', in Hall and Jacques, *The Politics of Thatcherism*, pp. 109–31.

11

The Labour Party After 1964

Leadership and Crisis: 1964-80

After winning the narrow electoral victory of 1964, the Labour Party held power for eleven of the next fifteen years before its heavy defeat in May 1979. They were troublesome years for the party and culminated in a series of the most damaging internal crises that the party has had to face in its history. The causes of these internal conflicts were many and complex, but the events of the 1960s and 1970s, together with the party's policies and power relationship of leaders and led, were to play significant roles.

Harold Wilson was a pragmatic leader of the party with the rhetoric of the left and the policy inclination of the right; he skilfully led the PLP through the 1964–6 period of a small parliamentary majority but he was beset with difficulties on all sides, not all of his own making, and the periods of his prime ministerial office, 1964–70 and 1974–6, were trying ones for the party. Economic problems were to the forefront, particularly the damaging devaluation crisis of 1967. However, Rhodesian UDI, support for America's Vietnam entanglement, EEC membership application, legislation to limit Kenyan Asian entry into Britain and the proposed trade union legislation contained in the White Paper, *In Place of Strife* of 1969 all added to the government's difficulties.

However, Wilson was secure as party leader in spite of the many problems he faced. There were murmurs of a plot against him in 1966, but they had little substance. Wilson's skill as party leader ensured the absence of real challenge; he did lose the 1970 election, but it was his only defeat in the five into which he led the party. His resignation in March 1976 came as a surprise although he had been planning it for several years.[1] Yet his period as party leader left two legacies of significance for the future of the party; his proposals for trade union reform in 1969 and his consistent ignoring of Labour Party Conference resolutions[2] helped both to radicalise the trade unionists in the party and to strengthen those party members on the left who sought constitutional change.

James Callaghan, Wilson's successor as party leader, was to pursue similar policies in similar adverse circumstances. He needed three ballots to become leader:

1st ballot		*2nd ballot*		*3rd ballot*	
Foot	90	Callaghan	141	Callaghan	176
Callaghan	84	Foot	133	Foot	137
Jenkins	56	Healey	38		
Benn	37				
Healey	30				
Crosland	17				

Callaghan was an avuncular figure who had carefully built up allies within the trade union movement and who in Crossman's words of ten years before realised 'his monomaniac belief that some day he would replace Harold'.[3] He had occupied all the main offices of government in his political apprenticeship, although many did not regard his periods of Chancellor of the Exchequer or Home Secretary as the most successful periods of his political life. He was centre-right in ideological inclination and was determined to maintain the prerogatives of the leader and the PLP. Callaghan certainly had difficulties with rebellious MPs, devolution being the outstanding example, but he could always count on the loyalty of the PLP on matters which were central to the survival of his minority government. The 1976—9 period was atypical because of this numerical weakness in the Commons and the PLP was managed rather than disciplined, with the emphasis on co-operation not sanctions. Yet the left, furious at Callaghan's approach to the IMF crisis of 1976 with its monetarist solutions, was angered further by Callaghan's ignoring of the vast amount of preparatory work that had gone into the party programmes of 1973 and 1976 when he rushed the drawing up of the 1979 election manifesto without proper discussion even in the PLP.[4]

Economic difficulties gave Callaghan some excuse for policies that found disfavour among large sections of his party, but ironically, given his past reliance on union support within the party, it was his insensitivity to union reaction to his 5 per cent wage policy late in 1978 that was to contribute so much to his party's electoral defeat in 1979 after he had decided, unwisely in retrospect, against an autumn 1978 election.

The Roots of the Constitutional Crisis

It was against this background that serious conflict broke out within the party in the late 1970s. There were intra-party arguments about defence and EEC membership but the critics of the leadership were mainly determined to democratise the party and widen the distribution of power. The left had won ideological arguments before and had produced the radical programmes of 1973 and 1976 only to see their victories reversed because of the lack of control over the leadership. Callaghan could not hold back the pressure for more internal party democracy that grew in the late 1970s and this pressure was skilfully orchestrated by the Campaign for Labour Party Democracy (CLPD), an organisation with strong roots in the CLPs.

An important factor in the pressure for reform was the attitude of the trade unions. The trade unions exerted much power in the party when they possessed the unity and the will to exert that power. After the 1979 election, 134 of the 269 Labour MPs were union sponsored; unions directly elected 12 of the 29 members of the NEC and controlled the election of the 5 women members and the Treasurer, they wielded 6 million of the 6½ million votes at the annual conference and contributed 80 per cent of the total party income. However, some unions were more powerful than others; in 1983 the six strongest of the 47 affiliated unions held four-fifths of the total union vote, and if united these unions could out-vote every other section of the party.[5] In the 1950s Attlee and Gaitskell could rely on the three largest unions most of the time for the support of the centre—right but selected by the CLPs formed the PLP and these MPs internal power structure changes in the unions themselves, led the affiliated unions to view more sympathetically attempts to introduce constitutional changes.[6]

Constitutional Reform

The formal constitutional structure of the Labour Party had changed little in the post-1945 period. MPs elected by voters but selected by the PLPs formed the PLP and these MPs enjoyed the sole right to elect the party leader. The CLPs, the affiliated TUs and the socialist societies such as the Fabian Society, together with the affiliated Co-ops, sent delegates to the annual conference which in theory was the sovereign body of the party. Between conferences the party was managed by the NEC, elected annually by the conference. The party leader and deputy leader sat ex-officio on the NEC, and besides the 12 trade unionists, five from the women's section and the Treasurer, the last two elected by the whole conference, there were seven from the CLPs, one from the affiliated socialist societies and one Young Socialist. By convention the block voting system was used at the conference so that all the votes of a single union, CLP or group were cast together.

There were three constitutional changes proposed in the late 1970s: the proposal to widen the franchise for the selection of the party leader; the proposal to give more power to the NEC in the drafting of election manifestos; and the proposal to introduce mandatory reselection of MPs, whereby every CLP must set in motion reselection procedures between general elections whether or not they wish to change their sitting MP. The disputes over the three proposals polarised the party into right and left factions and the arguments were bitter. The leadership selection proposal was discussed at the 1979 Conference with a motion to establish an electoral college consisting of MPs, trade unionists and CLPs. The proposal was defeated but in the following year a motion in favour of widening the franchise was surprisingly passed by a small majority. A special conference was convened at Wembley in January 1981 to agree on the details and there it was finally decided that the electoral college should be held at each annual conference and the votes in the college should be divided according to the formula of 40 per cent to the trade unions, 30 per cent to the PLP and 30 per cent to the CLPs. Mandatory reselection was accepted by the 1980 Conference but the proposal to give the NEC greater power in drawing up the manifesto was defeated.

The Consequences of Reform

The two reforms had important consequences for the Labour Party. They increased the degree of participatory democracy but served to bring attention to certain undemocratic aspects of the trade union block vote in leadership elections. Moreover, the electoral college did not satisfy all and there continued to be demands in the party for the adoption of the principle of one member/one vote. More immediately the reforms provided the final straw for many on the right of the party who broke away to form the SDP in the Spring of 1981. A large number of MPs were opposed to the widening of the franchise and when Callaghan announced his intention to retire, the PLP had no hesitation in deciding to go ahead with the selection of a new leader in the November of 1980, although the Wembley Conference of January 1981 had already been arranged. The result of this election was a victory for Michael Foot on the second ballot.

1st ballot		2nd ballot	
Healey	112	Foot	139
Foot	83	Healey	129
Silkin	38		
Shore	32		

Foot was an old-style radical, very common on the left of the British Labour Party. Throughout most of his parliamentary career he had been a rebel, closely identified with the Bevanites in the 1950s and a prominent member of the Tribune Group. When he finally entered government in the 1970s he worked particularly amicably with Callaghan in the post of Leader of the House and was invaluable in the government's early successful co-operation with the trade unions. Unlike Healey, he was not identified as much with the failures of the 1974–9 governments. He was certainly on the left of the PLP, a supporter of CND and an opponent of British membership of the EEC, but he also possessed a certain underlying conservative streak best illustrated by his reverence for the floor of the House of Commons and his opposition to such innovations as stronger Select Committees. Foot was elected to unify the party in a period of acute crisis, but his poor leadership during the 1983 election campaign — in which he was more concerned with party unity than in projecting the party's image to the electorate — proved a disaster for the party.

The extremely poor image of the Labour Party in the eyes of the electorate was made worse by the most damaging contest for the post of deputy leader in the middle of 1981. Tony Benn, ignoring the advice of many in the party, decided to challenge the incumbent, Denis Healey, at the 1981 Conference under the new electoral college rules. The fierce battle for a relatively unimportant post (invented to console Herbert Morrison in 1953) further polarised the party and inflicted serious electoral damage. Healey narrowly won the contest, but the party entered the 1983 campaign in disarray; it was deserted by its supporters on a larger scale than 1979 and grave doubts were raised concerning its electoral future.[7]

However, even before the election of 1983, there were signs of change within the intra-party power relationships. The centre–right began making gains in terms of elections to the NEC and the trauma of the massive election defeat began to concentrate minds on the electoral difficulties of the party and away from the internal power struggle. With the resignation of Foot, Neil Kinnock was elected leader in October 1983 with Roy Hattersley elected as his deputy:

	TU	CLP	MP	Total
Kinnock	29,042	27,452	14,778	71,272
Hattersley	10,878	577	7,883	19,288
Heffer	46	1,971	4,286	6,303
Shore	33	—	3,103	3,137

The election had a dramatic unifying effect on the party and in spite of the potentially harmful effects of the miners' dispute of 1984—5, the party began to recover in the opinion polls, capturing Fulham from the Conservatives in 1986. The left split into what was termed the soft and hard left, with Kinnock from his left-of-centre position having the increasing support of the former as well as the centre and right of the party inside and outside the Commons, allowing the party to recover to some extent from the ravages of the 1979—83 period.

The CLPs and Candidate Selection

The continuing crises of the late 1970s and early 1980s inevitably affected the membership of the party and there were great fears after 1980 that the CLPs would abuse the new powers of mandatory reselection. There was further concern about infiltration from the left, particularly from the Militant Tendency. The CLPs have been traditionally weak compared with the trade unions and their respective voting strengths within the party has been reflected in the financing of the party: the trade unions have long provided nearly 80 per cent of the income of the Party.[8] The most significant and autonomous power of the CLPs has always been that of selecting parliamentary candidates.

The official statistics indicated a decline in the individual membership of the party from a high of over one million in 1952—3 to 295,000 in 1983. Figures before 1980 tended to be unreliable, but there is some evidence that membership rose after a steep fall in the late 1960s and early 1970s. Besides the problem of numbers, there was the problem of distribution; parties in the safe Labour seats of the inner cities tended, from the 1960s, to be the smallest. The fall in membership was mirrored by a decline in the number of full-time agents from nearly 300 in the 1950s to 52 full-time agents in the 1983 general election. The reasons for the fall in membership were complex, but of crucial importance was the decline of working-class involvement in politics, and that given a more instrumental approach to political activity, an approach which stressed specific gains and losses to the participant rather than a generalised loyalty based on abstract principles. Consequently, the middle class began to play a disproportionately active role in the CLPs.[9] This development had important consequences for the ideological direction of the Party.

The CLPs generally welcomed the 1980 changes in the procedures for the selection of parliamentary candidates. Before 1980 the method had largely been unchanged since 1945; the local executive committee drew up a short-list from those nominated by different sections of the CLP; the candidates had to have their names on one of the two approved lists maintained by the NEC (the A list for those nominated by an affiliated body and therefore promising financial support). The general committee then acted as a selection body with the final nomination being approved by the NEC. Usually the whole procedure ran smoothly and if the candidate became an MP, there was generally a lack of drama in the MP–CLP relationship. Conflict, when it did arise, often stemmed from personal factors such as the age of the MP as in the case of S. O. Davies in 1970.

However, in the 1970s greater attention was focused on reselection battles where right-wing MPs were being opposed by CLPs for ideological reasons. In 1970, Margaret McKay was ousted for her pro-Arab views, but this case did not fit into the pattern of the four conflicts concerning Griffiths, Tomney, Taverne and Prentice. Griffiths was replaced in Sheffield Brightside and fought the October 1974 election unsuccessfully as an independent; Tomney was replaced in Hammersmith North before the 1979 election; Taverne resigned his seat in Lincoln and successfully fought the ensuing by-election as an independent (he survived one further election).[10] The long-running saga of the Prentice affair in Newham NE received most publicity and underlined the fact that even in those cases where ideological factors were to the fore, personal factors were still crucial. Prentice had personal views that were to the right of many of his supporters and the problem of personality clashes became more acute after he entered the Cabinet in 1974. The media presented the complex case as one of an heroic MP opposed by Marxist infiltrators, in spite of evidence of infiltration from the right financially aided by the right-wing pressure group, the National Association for Freedom. Prentice was subsequently elected as a Conservative MP in Daventry in 1979.[11] The Maureen Colquhoun reselection battle at Northampton North underlines this combination of ideological and personal factors; Colquhoun was a left-of-centre MP, criticised for her views on immigration but rejected for reasons of personal conduct.

In 1974 the NEC adopted the Mikardo doctrine that the NEC would intervene in the process of candidate selection only when the rules were broken, not when the NEC disapproved of candidates on ideological grounds. The left wanted further changes and fought for the ending of automatic reselection, which made opposition to the sitting MP difficult and cumbersome. The 1978 Party Conference left the choice of mandatory reselection with each CLP, and in 1979, the Conference approved of it for all CLPs in principle. The new procedure of mandatory reselection for all Labour MPs was finally approved in 1980.

The consequences of the adoption of the new procedure have been to further politicise the process. The CLPD which fought hard for the change, published a booklet in 1981, *How to Select and Re-Select Your MP*.[12] The casualty list before the 1983 election was certainly higher than usual, but less than many feared or hoped. Altogether eight MPs were refused reselection and they were nearly all on the right of the Party;[13] of course this list does not include those who had defected to the SDP or who had been dispossessed by boundary changes. Likewise, there were fewer ideological battles after 1983 than had been predicted. By the beginning of 1986 only four of the 150 Labour MPs seeking reselection had been dropped by their CLPs: Atkinson in Tottenham, Roberts in Hackney North, Forrester in Stoke North and McGuire in Makerfield; these do not include the MPs who decided not to seek renomination on the grounds of sure non-reselection, such as Freeson in Brent East where Ken Livingstone was selected. Thus the post-1980 period has not seen the widespread ideological purges anticipated, but the new processes helped to highlight a further problem for the party in the 1980s, the difficulties with Militant Tendency.

Militant Tendency and the Labour Party

The problems with the Militant Tendency first surfaced in the early 1970s. Militant Tendency was founded in 1964 by a group of Trotskyites centred around the newspaper, *Militant*. It grew from the Revolutionary Socialist League, and the two organisations remained secretly synonymous. A shadowy organisation, Militant claimed no membership, only readers and sellers of the newspaper; but its actual membership probably reached 4,500 by the early 1980s and at one of its annual conferences (rallies of newspaper readers), it claimed an attendance of 4,000. Everything was shrouded in secrecy, but it probably had over 140 full-time organisers by the mid-1980s and financially it was very healthy.[14]

Militant, unlike other Trotskyite groups, prospered with its entryist tactics and its influence grew within the Labour Party. By 1970 it had seized control of the Young Socialists, more important after 1972 when the YS organisation was granted a seat on the NEC.[15] In 1983 two Militant MPs were elected under Labour Party colours, Nellist in Coventry SE and Fields in Liverpool Broadgreen besides having a number of unsuccessful candidates in seats such as the Isle of Wight and Bradford. The organisation captured control of several parties, the most noticeable being the Liverpool District Party; and many non-Militant MPs, such as Frank Field in Birkenhead, had to fight hard to avoid being de-selected in favour of Militant candidates.

There were two basic arguments advanced in favour of the expulsion of Militant Tendency from the Labour Party: Firstly that the group was a separate organisation with its own distinct structure contrary to Clause 2(3) of the Labour Constitution. Secondly, the ideology of Militant was deemed contrary to the social democratic principles of the Labour

Party. The Tendency stressed for public consumption that its ideological goals were identical with Labour Party socialism, but like all Trotskyite groups, its public policies are but 'transitional demands', a means to heighten working-class consciousness. In Militant's view the working class will be betrayed by their leaders and with the inevitable collapse of capitalism, the Tendency will seize power in the ensuing revolutionary crisis.[16]

Labour Party concern with activities of the group was first reflected in the commissioning of the unpublished Underhill Report in 1975, with its 1977 supplement. In 1981 the Hayward–Hughes Report led to the proscription of the group in 1982 and the expulsion from the Party of five prominent Militant members, the editorial board of the *Militant* newspaper. In June 1982 a Register of groups within the party was established as a means of dealing with such entryist groups.

Many on the left were afraid that expulsions would not stop at Militant and would be used as ideological witch-hunts against the left-wing of the party if precedents were created. However, the severe 1983 election defeat led to more calls for action against Militant; the group was seen as a heavy electoral handicap and with the unfavourable publicity given to the Militant-controlled Liverpool Party, demands for tougher disciplinary action grew. The NEC instituted an inquiry into the Liverpool Party in 1985 and the District Party was suspended; expulsions of several prominent members followed in 1986. By the beginning of 1986 42 members of Militant had been expelled from CLPs.

Yet there were problems not foreseen by Militant opponents in the Party. As Militant became more unpopular and isolated in the party, Militant began to employ the effective weapon of recourse to the law to maintain its position in the Labour Party. In December 1985, the Courts stopped the expulsion of ten members from the Stevenage CLP and there were similar successful actions elsewhere based on the arguments of natural justice. Early in 1986, expulsions other than those of Liverpool ceased and the opponents of Militant looked to the 1986 Party Conference for a change in the party rules to facilitate more expulsions.

The Ideology of the Labour Party After 1964

The Labour Party has always been an ideological coalition. The party was established in 1900 by trade unionists who saw it as an extension of their industrial struggles, as well as liberals, social democrats of various hues and even a few Marxists. Therefore, not surprisingly, ideological conflict has never been absent from the party and the period after 1964 witnessed one of the periodic intensifications of intra-party argument. Yet before discussing the nature, causes and consequences of the post-1964 ideological crises two important aspects of the conflict should be stressed. First, the issues that produced party strife, particularly in the 1970s, were difficult to classify in simple left—right terms. There is no doubt that the party as a whole moved to the left, but the issues themselves often produced support from various sections of the party. It has always been too simplistic to categorically place, for example, the CLPs on the left and the PLP uniformly on the right. Alliances were fluid depending on the issue. Secondly, the disputes in the party broke out among the party élite and left the less active members of the party largely untouched.[17]

The nature of the ideological ferment and the signs of the move to the left can be illustrated in various ways. The 1973 Labour Programme was the most radical since 1945. It put renewed emphasis on public ownership and democratic control of British industry it forcibly argued the case for industrial restructuring on the premise that private enterprise had failed the nation, especially in terms of investment, and it laid great stress on central planning. The EEC controversy, only partially settled by the 1975 referendum, and the adoption of unilateral nuclear disarmament as official party policy together with the rows over candidate selection provided further examples. Conference resolutions, motions in Parliament and surveys of party opinions all to differing extents illustrate the ideological conflict.[18] Also in the 1980s the party chose two clear left-of-centre leaders in Foot and Kinnock.

As we have seen, the left responded to the Wilson and Callaghan ignoring of Conference resolutions and the emasculation of the party programmes of 1973 and 1976 with a campaign to reform the Party Constitution and to redistribute power within the party. In this it was partly successful with the establishment of the electoral college and mandatory reselection. Moreover, unlike the 1950s, this time it was the left that had coherent policies and strategies whilst the right was intellectually bankrupt; Crosland had been able to arm the Revisionists in the 1950s, but there was no equivalent in the 1970s. The collapse of consensus politics and the apparent inability of Keynesian economics to tackle the economic crises effectively intellectually enfeebled the right. The response was the establishment of the SDP; the continued absence of a coherent intellectual framework for the new party illustrated the ideological problems of the right at the time of the defections.[19]

The reasons for this turn to the left in the 1970s are many and controversial. The failure of the economic policies of successive Labour governments culminating in the IMF crisis of 1976 and the abandonment of full employment and the adoption of monetarism was one. The trade unions were pushed further to the left by internal changes and by Labour government policies of wage restraint and trade union 'reform'. The growth of single issue pressure groups such as CND, women's groups, black organisations, environmentalists, a whole host of organisations concerned with economic and social deprivation such as Shelter, Age Concern, and civil liberty groups, all helped to radicalise Labour Party members and bring in new recruits. There was some validity in the claim that this increasing middle class membership of the party coincided with a working-class withdrawal and so further radicalised the party.[20] Also the left organised itself more effectively than at any time in the past with such organisations as CLPD; the Campaign for Labour Victory of 1977 was but a pale shadow of the right's Campaign for Democratic Socialism that succeeded in turning back the unilateralist tide of the 1960s.

The results of this process of moving to the left were traumatic for the party; the rows over entryism continued, some of the right defected to the SDP and the electoral harvests of 1979 and 1983 were bitter.[21] Yet political parties are not immune from external pressure and the magnitude of the 1983 defeat affected both the policy options and the rhetoric of the party. After 1983 there was a greater yearning for unity and a distrust of people and organisations that exacerbated party disagreements. There was a greater willingness to change some of the policies that had been deemed to be electoral liabilities and the left split into what were termed the soft and hard left, with the former tending to rally around the greater pragmatism of the Kinnock leadership.

Yet the Labour Party remained an ideological coalition and in spite of the formation of the SDP, the party had a right, centre and various hues of the left. The Labour Party of the 1980s remained a recognisably social democratic party. There is little doubt that events after 1964 moved the party leftwards, but as with all political parties, the real test is the experience of government and the restraints of office.[22]

Notes to Chapter 11

1. See Joe Haines, *The Politics of Power* (London: Jonathan Cape, rev. edn, 1977) pp. 220—21.
2. 'Rarely in modern times can a parliamentary leadership have appeared as impervious to the policy preferences of its extra-parliamentary supporters as the Wilson Government did in the late 1960s.' L. Minkin, *The Labour Party Conference*, rev. end (Manchester University Press, 1980) p. 316.
3. R. Crossman, *The Diaries of a Cabinet Minister, 1964—66*, vol. 1 (London: Hamilton/Jonathan Cape, 1975) p. 596.
4. This control exercised by the leader drew angry comments from Tony Benn at the 1980 Labour Party Conference who claimed that Callaghan's veto had blocked important policies approved by past conferences. See *The Report of the Annual Conference of the Labour Party, 1980*, pp. 146—7.
5. The six unions were as follows: TGWU (Transport and General Workers' Union), AUEW (Amalgamated Union of Engineering Workers — changed in 1986 to AEW), NUGMW (National Union of General and Municipal Workers), NUPE (National Union of Public Employees), USDAW (Union of Shop, Distributors and Allied Workers) and EETPU (Electrical, Electronic, Telecommunication and Plumbing Union).
6. See Minkin, *The Labour Party Conference*, p. 326. Also A. Fenley, 'Labour and Trade Unions', in *The Labour Party*, C. Cook and I. Taylor (eds) (London: Longman, 1980) pp. 50—83. Also C.

Crouch, 'The Peculiar Relationship: the Party and the Unions', in *The Politics of the Labour Party*, D. Kavanagh (ed) (London: Allen & Unwin, 1982) pp. 171–90. The history of the period should not be seen as a continual clash of Labour governments and unions. The 1974–6 period was marked by a great deal of co-operation; the Social Contract, the abolition of the defunct 1971 Industrial Relations Act, the granting of certain legal privileges under the 1975 Industry Act, the absence of an imposed incomes policy, the Advisory Conciliation and Arbitration Service and the personalities of union leaders such as Scanlon and Jones all assisted this relative harmony.

7. See D. Butler and D. Kavanagh, *The British General Election of 1983* (London: Macmillan, 1984) pp. 295–7; p. Whiteley, *The Labour Party in Crisis* (London: Methun, 1983) pp. 208–219; A. Heath *et al.*, *How Britain Votes* (Oxford: Pergamon Press, 1985); P. Dunleavy and C. T. Husbands, *British Democracy at the Cross-roads* (London: Allen & Unwin, 1985).

8. See M. Pinto-Duschinsky, *British Political Finance 1830–1980* (Washington: American Enterprise Institute, 1980) pp. 155–78; D. Butler and G. Butler, *British Political Facts 1900–1985* (London: Macmillan, 1986) p. 157. In 1984 the Conservative Government, in an attempt to weaken the links between the trade union movement and the Labour Party and as part of a campaign to increase democratic participation inside the trade unions, passed the Trade Union Act. It stipulated that all trade unions had to ballot their members every ten years and a majority vote would be needed to establish a political fund. As most trade unions with important political funds were affiliated to the Labour Party this was a graver threat to the financial health of the Party than the Conservative legislation of 1927 which replaced 'contracting out' by 'contracting in'. Fortunately for the party, the campaign organised by the unions to counter the threat succeeded impress-ively. By 1986 every union balloted found a majority of over 80 per cent in favour of maintaining a political fund. See *The Financial Times*, 6 January 1986.

9. There is a detailed analysis of the problem in Whiteley, *The Labour Party in Crisis*, pp. 53–80; see also B. Hindess, 'The Decline of Working Class Politics: A Re-Appraisal', in *Trade Unions in British Politics*, B. Pimlott and C. Cook (eds) (London: Longman, 1982) pp. 237–57.

10. See D. Taverne, *The Future of the Left* (London: Cape, 1974).

11. See P. McCormack, *Enemies of Democracy* (London: Temple Smith, 1978) for an account by one of the anti-left Oxford infiltra-tors.

12. See also A. Young, *The Re-selection of MPs* (London: Heinemann, 1983).

13. See Butler and Kavanagh, *The British General Election of 1983*, pp. 219–25. The selection of Peter Tatchell in Bermondsey and

the opposition of the former MP Mellish, also received a great deal of unsavoury publicity in February 1983, see P. Tatchell, *The Battle for Bermondsey* (London: Heretic Books, 1983).

14. See M. Crick, *Militant* (London: Faber & Faber, 1984); T. Forrester, 'The Labour Party's Militant Moles' *New Society*, 10 January 1980, pp. 52—4; P. Wintour, 'Militant's Resolutionary Socialism', *New Statesman*, 18 January 1980, pp. 77—8.

15. The NEC decided in 1986 to make changes in the structure and financing of the Young Socialists in order to lessen Militant influence.

16. See Crick, *Militant*, pp. 63—77. Militant did differ from other Marxist groups in that. it reduced all to an economic interpretation of the class struggle and therefore tended to be more hostile to the demands of groups such as CND, the Anti-Nazi League, women's rights, blacks and homosexuals. It tended to have a far more puritan, humourless image than other Trotskyite groups.

17. See Whiteley, *The Labour Party in Crisis*, pp. 24—30.

18. See ibid., pp. 30—39; H. Berrington and J. Leece, 'Measurement of Backbench Attitudes by Guttman, Scaling of Early Day Motions: a Pilot Study, Labour, 1968—9', *British Journal of Political Science*, vol. 7, pp. 529—40.

19. See M. Hatfield, *The House the Left Built* (London: Gollancz, 1978); S. Holland, *The Socialist Challenge* (London: Quartet Books, 1975); Tony Benn, *Arguments for Socialism* (London: Jonathan Cape, 1979).

20. See D. Kavanagh, 'Still the Workers' Party? Changing Social Trends in Elite Recruitment and Electoral Support', in *The Politics of the Labour Party*, pp. 95—134.

21. Labour was the more popular of the parties in 1981 in spite of the formation of the SDP, but the Benn—Healey contest proved disastrous for Labour's standing in the opinion polls, see D. Butler and G. Butler, *British Political Facts, 1900—1985*, p. 263.

22. See R. Rose, *Do Parties Make a Difference?* 2nd edn (London: Macmillan, 1984).

12

The British Party System Since 1964

The Challenge to the Two-Party System

By the mid-1980s, the British party system could still be characterised as a two-party system in that the majority of seats in the House of Commons were won by the two largest parties, one of them having won an absolute majority of seats at the previous election and willing to govern alone.[1] However, developments in the 1970s and 1980s led many observers to question the future existence of this party system and argue that Britain was entering a period of multi-partyism.

Certainly the party system that had existed from 1945 to the 1960s was under threat; the dominance of the two major parties was under strain and in 1974 neither of the major parties was able to secure an absolute majority of seats in the House of Commons for the first time since the 1929 election. Two possibilities were predicted; firstly, that one of the major parties would ultimately be replaced by a challenger in the way that Labour replaced the Liberal Party as a major party in the early part of the twentieth century; secondly, that multi-partyism would become a permanent feature of British politics, especially if hung parliaments were to lead to a change in the electoral system. We have already examined

the contributions and reactions of the Conservative and
Labour parties to these uncertainties. We now turn to the
other agents of change: elections, voting behaviour, the electoral system and the challenging parties themselves.

Elections, Voting Behaviour and the Electoral System

In terms of election results and the degree of electoral support, there is little doubt that the period after 1964 saw a
weakening of the British two-party system. The number of
MPs owing no loyalty to the two major parties increased
and the total share of the vote won by the Conservative and
Labour parties dropped dramatically. In 1951, the two major
parties won 96.8 per cent of all the votes cast and 98.6
per cent of the seats in the Commons. In 1974 (Feb.) the
figures were 74.9 per cent of votes and 94.0 per cent of seats;
in 1983 the figures were 70 per cent of votes and 93.0 per
cent of the seats. The vagaries of the electoral system were
protecting the parties in the House of Commons more than
they were protected in terms of votes. The general election
results since 1964 underline the nature of the changes that
were taking place (see Table 12.1).

TABLE 12.1

	Conservatives (seats)	Conservatives (% votes)	Labour (seats)	Labour (% votes)	Others (seats)	Others (% votes)
1964	304	43.4	317	44.1	9	12.5
1966	253	41.4	363	47.9	14	10.2
1970	330	46.4	288	43.0	12	10.6
1974 (Feb.)	297	37.8	301	37.1	37	25.1
1974 (Oct.)	277	35.8	319	39.2	39	25.0
1979	339	43.9	269	37.0	27	19.1
1983	397	42.4	209	27.6	43	30.0

Sources: Nuffield election studies, 1964—83.

The numbers voting in general elections did not decline
noticeably after 1964 but there were fluctuations between a
high of 78.1 per cent in February 1974 and a low of 71.2 per

cent in October of the same year. However, the number of seats won on minority votes increased to over 50 per cent in 1983 compared with under 13 per cent in 1959,[2] an indication both of more candidates and the greater willingness of the voters to choose candidates from other than the two major parties, opinion polls began to measure the increasing volatility of the electorate's voting intentions.[3] One of the more striking changes in electoral behaviour was to be seen in the outcome of by-elections. From 1945 to 1955 no government lost a by-election, and the Conservatives only lost two between 1955 and 1959; only nine seats changed hands in the whole 1945–59 period. In the 1960s and afterwards there were dramatic changes. Labour lost 16 by-elections between 1964 and 1970, the Conservatives lost five in the 1970–74 government, there were seven losses for the 1974–9 Labour government, and eight for the Conservatives between 1979 and 1986. The sizes of some of the swings against the government party were often very high. The percentage changing hands in the respective periods make an interesting comparison:

1951–55	2%
1955–59	12%
1959–64	14%
1964–66	15%
1966–70	42%
1970–74	30%
1974–79	23%
1979–83	35%

Source: *British Political Facts, 1980–85.*

There are many explanations and not a few disagreements on the reasons for the changes in voting behaviour in the last two decades, but despite the differences of opinion two basic interpretations have been advanced.[4] Firstly, there is the sociological model which particularly stresses the relationship between social class and voting behaviour and secondly, there is the economic or rational model which emphasises rational behaviour on the part of the individual voter and the absence of long-term loyalties to a particular political party. Neither model is presented as a total explanation of the behaviour of the British voter and most explanations seek to interpret recent electoral results with varying degrees of synthesis. However, the following arguments have been advanced:

(1) *Social class*. There is agreement that social class continued to be an important factor in British voting behaviour[5] but disagreement over its definition[6] and uncertainty whether voters ceased to vote along class lines (class de-alignment) or whether the British class structure was in the process of a transformation with the decline of the traditional manual working class and the growth of the white collar sector. If the latter, it would then be more sensible in explaining voting behaviour to distinguish between public and private sector workers, not middle and working class. Nevertheless, it is clear that either interpretation in regards to social class would help to explain the poor performances of the Labour Party in 1979 and 1983 and the rise in the number of Alliance supporters.

(2) *The political parties*. Partly as a result of the class changes, there was less long-term loyalty to particular political parties (partisan dealignment). Voters became more inclined to pass electoral judgement on a party's ideological position and the perceived competence of its leadership. Parties were punished for being moderate/extreme, too left/right, etc.

(3) *Government performance*. Elections had become a retrospective judgement on the government in office. Thus Heath was punished for the economic and industrial troubles of 1973–4, Callaghan for his failures during the 'winter of discontent', 1978–9, and Thatcher rewarded in 1983 for her courage during the Falklands war.

(4) *Issues*. If the electorate had become more instrumental in terms of individual interests, then the importance of particular issues was enhanced. Thus the continuing unpopularity of nationalisation continued to damage the electoral prospects of the Labour Party, and the sale of council houses to their tenants boosted the Conservative Party's support.

(5) *The mass media*. Of varying importance to all these interpretations was the role of newspapers and television in

carrying political messages and political images of the political parties. There is little doubt that the media played an important part in raising interest in the SDP and the Alliance in the early 1980s, but the role of the media in particular elections and its influence over long-term behaviour is a matter of some dispute.[7]

However, amid all these various explanations of the changes in electoral behaviour, the British electoral system was of utmost importance in the structuring of the party system particularly in not translating accurately votes for a party into seats in the House of Commons. There is little doubt that if a system of proportional representation had been in use instead of the 'first past the post' or simple plurality system, then the shape of the party system in the House of Commons would have been radically changed. Thus in 1979 the Conservatives won 53.4 per cent of seats with only 43.9 per cent of votes, Labour 42.4 per cent of seats with 36.9 per cent of votes and the unfortunate Liberals won only 1.7 per cent of seats with 13.8 per cent of the vote. The discrepancies were even greater in 1983 with the Conservatives winning 61 per cent of seats with 42.4 per cent of votes, Labour benefited also, gaining 32.2 per cent of seats with 27.6 per cent of votes, while the Alliance won only 3.5 per cent of seats with 25.4 per cent of the vote. In 1983 the Conservatives managed to lose votes yet gain seats.

As a result of these and other distortions, the campaign for adopting another electoral system, preferably a form of proportional representation, gathered pace in the 1970s and 1980s especially in the ranks of the Liberals, Social Democrats and their academic supporters. The electoral system, it was argued, produced an 'adversarial' form of party politics,[8] produced undemocratic, minority governments and failed to produce efficient, strong, or stable governments. Of course, there were strong arguments produced in defence of the status quo and controversy hinged crucially on the desirability or otherwise of coalition government.[9] It was essential to recognise the ideological basis of both sides; the reforms were proposed or opposed because basically they were likely to result in a type of government that was or was not desired.[10]

Yet the consequences of the electoral system, although of prime importance, was not the only factor determining the nature of the party system. The same electoral system did not prevent the Labour Party overhauling the Liberal Party or the multi-partyism of the 1920s or indeed the minority governments of the 1970s. In times of electoral volatility, change and 'hung parliaments', the likelihood of the introduction of a different electoral system is enhanced, as was the case during the minority Labour Government of 1929– 31. A change in the electoral system would revolutionise the British party system. The political parties themselves, however, are not passive onlookers of these political changes; we have seen the responses of the two major parties and we must now look at the significance of the Liberals, the SDP and the smaller parties during this period of change.

The Liberal and Social Democratic Parties

In the post-1964 period the main threat to the supremacy of the two major parties came firstly from the Liberal Party and after 1981 from the Alliance, the combination of the Liberals and the Social Democratic Party (SDP). The creation of the SDP in 1981 and its alliance with the Liberals was an important landmark in the history of the British party system; the Liberals were making gains, but these were inconsistent and did not seriously threaten the existence of the two-party system. However with the creation of the SDP, the new combination of Liberals and Social Democrats was able to secure a degree of electoral progress that had largely been denied to the Liberal Party before 1981. Yet the creation of the SDP, while important, should not disguise the fact that the progress of the Alliance after 1981 was still based on the same foundations that gave the Liberals encouragement before its formation nor that the problems that beset the Liberals during their revival in the 1960s and 1970s still presented difficulties to the Alliance. Therefore to examine the nature of this threat to the dominance of the Conservative and Labour parties, it would be more rewarding to look first at the Liberal Party and its electoral fortunes before 1981, then proceed to examine the nature of the SDP, finally investigating the alliance of the Liberals and the SDP.

The Post-1945 Liberal Party

The Electoral Fortunes of the Liberal Party
The Liberal Party had been in continual decline since the 1920s and reached the lowest point in its fortunes in the 1950s; the 1951 general election, in terms of candidates and votes, was the most disastrous election the Liberals have experienced. In the late 1950s and early 1960s there were some signs of a Liberal revival; the party pushed the Conservatives into third place in Rochdale in 1958, won a by-election, its first in nearly thirty years, at Torrington in the same year and turned a 14 000 Conservative majority into a 9000 Liberal majority at Orpington in 1962 (the Liberal vote rose from 21 per cent in 1959 to 53.9 per cent in 1962). The general election results from 1950 to 1979 indicate the extent of the revival (see Table 12.2).

TABLE 12.2

Election	Liberal seats won	% vote	No. of Liberal candidates	No. of lost deposits
1950	9	9.1	475	319
1951	6	2.5	109	66
1955	6	2.7	110	60
1959	6	5.9	216	55
1964	9	11.2	365	52
1966	12	8.5	311	104
1970	6	7.5	332	184
1974 (Feb.)	14	19.3	517	23
1974 (Oct.)	13	18.5	619	125
1979	11	13.8	577	303

Source: D. Butler and G. Butler, *British Political Facts 1900–1985* (London: Macmillan, 1986) (6th ed) pp. 226–8, 249.

In 1951, five out of the six successful Liberals faced no Conservative opposition; after 1964, the party won its seats mainly in three-cornered contests. The party began to run strongly in Conservative seats, the Labour vote suffering from tactical voting; thus, in February 1974, the Liberal candidate finished either first or second in 51 of the 76 south coast constituencies.

Just as general elections after 1964 represented rises and falls in Liberal support, so by-elections before 1981 presented an uneven picture. The Liberal Party tended to perform well during periods of Conservative government; the anti-Labour vote during Labour administrations mainly went to the Conservative Party. From 1964 to 1970, Birmingham Ladywood in 1969 was the sole Liberal success. Similarly, between 1974 and 1979, there was only the late victory in 1979 at Edge Hill Liverpool to record. Yet during the Conservative government of 1970—4, the Liberals won five English seats — Rochdale, Sutton and Cheam, the Isle of Ely, Ripon and Berwick-upon-Tweed, besides gaining Rochdale from the Labour Party. The paucity of Liberal gains during Labour governments since 1964 should be set against 16 Labour by-election losses before 1970 and a total of seven between 1974 and 1979.

The unevenness of electoral successes supported the findings of opinion polls in that the chief attraction of the Liberal Party in this period lay in the unpopularity of the two main parties. When the Liberals did attract voters on the basis of the protest vote, they were unable to translate this negative support into a clear positive appreciation of Liberal policies. One-half of the party's support in the February 1974 election had disappeared by the October election, although the party was compensated by winning voters who had not voted Liberal in February. A survey of Liberal electoral support in 1974 showed that the party lacked a large stable core of persistent Liberal voters, thus the volatility of Liberal support. The survey indicated that the party's occasional supporters were less interested in general politics than the small, stable core of middle class, middle aged voters. Only the small core had clear attitudes to Liberal policies; generally, the Liberal Party lacked a clear image.[11] When the party did not field a candidate, the Communists or National Front were likely to increase their votes.[12] In 1974, opinion polls indicated that a majority of Liberal voters were opposed to a major plank in the Liberal programme — continued membership of the EEC.

Organisation and Power in the Liberal Party

Power in the Liberal Party has proved difficult to locate with the same accuracy one could use with the Conservative and Labour Parties for several reasons. Membership was small and the turnover in members was marked, and the party had no experience of government since 1945. It will be recalled that the growth of the Labour Party to second party status and government responsibility in 1922 and 1924 had a significant effect on the strengthening of the power of the PLP and the leader of the party. Also, the Liberal Party organisation and formal decision-making process were extremely complex; indeed, this complexity encouraged the Liberal leader to ignore the party machinery and make decisions without consultation. Fortunately for the unity of the party, Thorpe's discussions with Heath after the February 1974 election on the possibility of a Conservative–Liberal coalition produced nothing; Thorpe had not consulted the party organisation and there was strong opposition to the proposal inside all sections of the party. Likewise, Steel did not fully consult the party over the Lib–Lab Pact of 1977 and the arrangement produced unease in the party.[13] Certain conditions were subsequently imposed on any similar future arrangements.

However, the party leadership was fortunate after 1964 in that few issues led either to clashes between the parliamentary wing of the party and the members outside or between the leader and his followers. There were rumbles over the leadership's imposition of an arrangement to share seats with the SDP after 1981 but as the division generally benefited the Liberals, the opposition was not serious. The most important clash was over defence policy. In 1981, the Liberal Assembly opposed the siting of Cruise missiles in Britain and Steel immediately made it clear that he would not agree with such a decision. The issue was not debated in the 1982 and 1983 Assemblies, but in 1984, the Liberal Council, which formally decided party policy between assemblies, voted for the immediate withdrawal of the missiles and the leadership was again defeated on the same issue at the 1984 Liberal Assembly. However, the unresolved clash did not lead to any serious crisis within the party though the issue did underline the ambiguity of the leader's powers.

The leadership was strengthened by the party's adoption of a more democratic method of electing the party leader. The high political profile adopted by Jeremy Thorpe after he replaced Grimond as leader in 1967 certainly had political advantages, but it also gave rise to certain embarrassments for the party. The scandal of the mysterious donor of a large sum of money led to criticisms within the party as to the most advantageous use of the money. In the mid-1970s the Norman Scott affair, involving Thorpe in allegations of homosexuality and murder plots, hung over the party, and Thorpe's involvement in the collapse of a fringe bank while he was leader further damaged the party.

In 1976 the Liberals pioneered an important innovation in British politics; they established a new method for electing the party leader which involved the extra-parliamentary wing of the party. A candidate had to be nominated by at least three Liberal MPs and each member of the party could vote, each constituency vote being weighted according to the size of the constituency Liberal vote in the last election, the size of the local membership, and the payment of affiliation fees. In 1981 this was changed to one member/one vote with at least five MPs or one-fifth of the parliamentary party nominating the candidates, the candidates having themselves to be MPs; the existing leader could be challenged by at least 50 constituency associations. David Steel was elected leader by this new method in 1976 after Thorpe's resignation, defeating John Pardoe by 12,546 votes to 7,032 and subsequently was not seriously challenged. The reforms not only increased the democratic participation of the rank and file, but also increased the legitimacy and therefore the power of the leader *vis-à-vis* his parliamentary followers.

The extra-parliamentary organisation of the party was both complex and decentralised. At first glance the structure bore some resemblance to those of the two main parties; the National Executive Committee meeting eight times a year consisted of representatives of the regional and national parties (12 English regions and the Scottish, Welsh and Ulster Liberal Parties). The Executive Committee was responsible to the Liberal Council which met four times a year and was in turn responsible to the Liberal Annual Assembly. The Assembly consisted of representatives from regional, national and constituency parties but although it debated and decided party policy, these decisions were not binding on the parliamentary party. However, this is where the simplicity of party organisation ended. Besides a multitude of *ad hoc* bodies with overlapping responsibilities, there were four other distinct institutions: the Liberal Central Association which survived the 1936 reforms and became a means of channelling state aid to Liberal candidates; the Finance and Administration Board which had a great deal of autonomy being responsible neither to the NEC nor to the leader; Standing Committee consisting of MPs and candidates meeting 14 times a year; the Liberal Party organisation which replaced the NLF in 1936 and became the bureaucratic machine of the party.

A factor which added to the organisational difficulties of the Liberals and impaired their electoral strategy was the shortage of money. The party optimistically expanded too rapidly after the pre-1964 by-election results and after the electoral disappointments of 1964 and 1966, its efforts at fund raising were failures. For example, its one million pound target of 1967 produced little more than a few thousand pounds and the party had to reduce its permanent staff by half before the 1970 election. By the 1979 election, the party was cut to only seventeen full-time agents and there had been a further trimming of the permanent staff. The grant of government money to political parties in 1975 helped, but the party was forced into its familiar electoral expedient of concentrating its efforts and financial resources on special constituencies irrespective of the total number of Liberal candidates. A 'special seats' programme was launched in 1973, concentrating mainly on sixteen constituencies, and this strategy was more or less followed in 1979. It has always been difficult to estimate accurately the sources and size of Liberal Party funds, but there is no doubt that the party has always been at a relative disadvantage to the major parties.[14] The main source of Liberal money remained membership subscriptions and personal donations,[15] but with the formation of the Alliance, company donations although small became less erratic. The largest single donation from a company to a political party was, in fact, £188,000 from the British School of Motoring in 1983 to the Liberal Party. This was to prove of some embarrassment in 1985 when Steel admitted that Liberal MPs had tried to secure changes in a Private Member's Bill affecting the operations of driving instructors.

The Ideology of the Modern Liberal Party
There are many difficulties in the discussion of the political ideas of the modern Liberals. The party had long been out of office; it was a small party and furthermore, as noted earlier, the voters tended to have confused negative images of what exactly the party stood for. Certainly, as with the two major parties, the Liberal Party could not be clearly identified with just one set of ideological positions. Indeed, the ideological divisions that were apparent on the eve of the First World War, the divisions between social and radical Liberals, were still evident in the post-1945 Liberal Party.[16] The same dichotomy can be seen in the career of Grimond, elected leader of the party in 1956, pursuing a radical programme of re-alignment of the left and by the late 1970s regretting the Conservative monopoly of the free market ideas of economists such as Hayek.[17]

Yet the modern Liberal Party was not opposed to state power in the manner in which Thatcherism espoused the Conservative version of nineteenth-century *laissez-faire* liberalism. The emphasis on individualism and freedom was still there, and modern Liberals still quoted John Stuart Mill; but the influence of the mid-twentieth-century liberals such as Beveridge and Keynes was apparent. Modern Liberals believed in the exercise of state power for the pursuit of social and economic reforms, but strongly qualified this partial collectivism with a stress on individual civil liberties, administrative and political decentralisation and a rejection of any class interpretation of political conflict. However, the ambivalence to social and economic redistributive policies could be seen in the party's largely negative attitude to organisations such as trade unions.

A central plank in the approach of the modern Liberal Party continued to be constitutional reform. The party pioneered British entry into the EEC and it continued to advocate full federal union for Western Europe, an echo of the old Gladstonian internationalism. The party stressed regional devolution, including a degree of self-government for Scotland and Wales and accompanying changes in parliamentary government, particularly reform of the House of Lords. However, all these constitutional proposals were secondary to the one overriding aim which the party has advocated since it dropped to third place in 1922: that of reform of the electoral system. The espousal of a form of proportional representation and the condemnation of the existence of the alleged 'adversarial system' of British politics was echoed again and again in all Liberal Party literature and by academic and journalistic supporters of the Party.[18]

The ideas of the Liberal Party were heavily influenced by the emergence of single issue pressure groups that sprang up in the 1960s and 1970s, groups concerned with deprived sections of the community, moral and environmental issues. The radicalism of the Young Liberals in espousing these causes often embarrassed the staider leaders of the party; an example was the campaign led by Peter Hain, a prominent Young Liberal before joining the Labour Party, to stop the South African cricket tour of Britain taking place in 1970. This essentially populist approach was reflected in the 'community politics' strategy by which the party concentrated on local issues and the problems of direct concern to the voters. This approach yielded certain electoral successes of which Liverpool was, perhaps, the best example.

The Social Democratic Party Since 1981

The Emergence of the SDP and the Formation of the Alliance
The SDP was officially born on the 26 March 1981 with the initial support of 14 defectors from the Parliamentary Labour

Party together with the active backing of several members of past Labour governments and approving noises from the leadership of the Liberal Party. Before the 1983 election, the new party was to win the support of 29 MPs including one who defected from the Conservative Party. However, the gestation period of the new party stretched over several years. Roy Jenkins, ex-Labour Home Secretary and Chancellor of the Exchequer and at one time deputy-leader of the Labour Party gave the annual BBC Dimbleby Lecture in November 1979 in which he issued a call for a new radical centre party; a defeated candidate in the 1976 leadership election, he had long come to the conclusion that he had no future with the existing Labour Party. The Labour Party Conference of 1980 disillusioned many right-wingers in the party over issues of party policy and internal party democracy to such an extent that by the autumn of 1980, prominent members of the PLP such as David Owen and Bill Rodgers with the wavering support of Shirley Williams who had lost her seat in 1979, were envisioning and discussing a break. The first public sign came with the Limehouse Declaration of 25 January 1981, the day after the Wembley Conference approved the new method of electing the Labour leader. It was signed by the 'Gang of Four', Jenkins, Owen, Rodgers and Williams, supported by nine other Labour MPs. The formation of the SDP was now only a matter of timing.

The causes of these defections and the reasons for the establishment of the new party were complex, the product of the interrelationship of many factors; there was no inevitability about the birth of the SDP. The principal factors were:

(1) The collapse of the post-1945 consensus and the problems of applying Keynesian solutions to current economic problems. The defectors came principally from the Labour right and had come to prominence in the 1950s and 1960s. They recognised the need for re-thinking but could not in the final analysis support the alternative economic strategy of the left which could be said to have been a logical extension of the revisionist analysis of Crosland.[19]

(2) The power of the trade unions in the Labour Party, further strengthened by their new role in the leadership

selection process in 1981. Rodgers presented this as one of the principal reasons for his defection.[20]

(3) Discontent with many aspects of Labour policies, particularly nuclear unilateral disarmament and the hostility to membership of the EEC.

(4) Infiltration from the left, particularly Militant Tendency.

(5) The constitutional changes in the Labour Party. The proposals for a new method of leadership selection and the mandatory reselection of MPs threatened the power base of the Labour right, the PLP. The defectors were opposed to greater accountability of MPs to their CLPs.

However, it is important to stress the lack of inevitability of the breakaway; even at the last moment many of the principal defectors were wavering. Nor did the whole Labour right secede; many right-wingers stayed on in the Labour Party. There was no unanimity among the defectors about what sort of party should emerge from the split. Roy Jenkins wanted a non-socialist party and was quite close to the Liberals but had been persuaded by Steel not to join the Liberal Party but to encourage a massive break within the Labour Party. Owen, Williams and Rodgers, with closer sympathies to the old social democratic consensus, worked for the establishment of an alternative Labour Party of the right.[21] The collective leadership that emerged after the birth of the new party was a testament both to the personal friction between the leaders and to their different concepts of what form the new party should take.[22]

Four main factors contributed to immediate successes for the new party: firstly, the national prominence of the leaders; secondly, the wide and sympathetic mass media coverage of both the birth of the new party and the staggered process of defections from the Labour Party; thirdly, the continuing conflict within the Labour Party and particularly the fight for the deputy leadership between Healey and Benn; fourthly, the economic problems of the Conservative government. In fact, the existence of a Conservative government which had aided Liberal by-election successes in the past[23] came to the aid of the new party. In July 1981, Jenkins nearly won Warrington from Labour and in November, Shirley Williams,

guilty of public uncertainty over a decision whether to contest Warrington, won the safe Conservative seat of Crosby. In
March 1982, Jenkins won Glasgow Hillhead and together
with the Liberals, the SDP stood high in the opinion polls. It
was the Falklands War that helped to halt the upward progress of the new party in late March 1982.

The Organisation and Ideology of the SDP

The organisation adopted for the SDP reflected the chief
motivations of the architects of the new party in defecting
from the Labour Party. At every level and in all the important
areas of decision-making, power resided heavily with the
party in Parliament. The SDP leader was elected by a ballot
of all members of the party but he/she had to be nominated
by at least 15 per cent of MPs. Jenkins defeated Owen by
26,300 votes to 20,900 votes in July 1982, but Owen was
elected unopposed in 1983. The parliament of the party, the
Council for Social Democracy, had a 400 strong membership
and met four times a year, but although it adopted policy,
its decisions were not binding on MPs. The National Committee was responsible for organisation and the Policy Committee
was responsible for both policy and the election programme,
but it was dominated by MPs and furthermore could not bind
the parliamentary party. A novel feature of the SDP was the
creation of Area Parties instead of the usual constituency
parties, a result of both the weakness of support in certain
constituencies and the fear that unrepresentative minorities
might seize control. However, these area parties were primarily
electoral machines, and it was stressed that although they
selected candidates, MPs were solely responsible to the electorate, not to their local parties.

The SDP introduced many novel features into British
politics; computerised lists of members, credit card payment
of fees[24] and direct mailing system soliciting for party funds,
a system common in the United States. These innovations
reflected the overwhelming middle class character of the SDP
at all levels, a party created from the top by a London-based
middle class élite.[25]

Creating a distinct policy image was a serious problem for
the SDP and indeed, the lack of distinct policies was seen by

some as a virtue. One journalist supporter said at the birth of the party: 'If they are wise, the Social Democrats will not be drawn into exaggerating the importance of policy. Most people do not know what the policies of their parties are and when they find out, they usually don't like them much'.[26] Owen warned very early about the dangers of the political disease of 'manifestoitis'. The blurring of the ideological image of the party was compounded by the nature of the break with the Labour Party; the SDP wished to denounce the Labour Party but wished to be seen as the inheritors of the post-1945 consensus; the Social Democrats wished to hold the middle ground in British politics and win votes and also had to keep from straying too far from the Liberal Party.[27] The ideological problems of the party were exacerbated by the dominance of the leader after 1983 and there was no doubt that on economic issues particularly he pushed the SDP further to the right of the Liberal Party. The SDP was the nearest British equivalent to the American party model of an electoral organisation with the minimum of ideological baggage. It was no surprise to find that electoral reform was the top of its priorities.[28]

The Alliance of the Liberal and Social Democratic Parties
The Liberal–SDP Alliance was cemented by the end of 1981. There were certainly critics of the close relations between the two parties; Liberal MPs Michael Meadowcroft and Cyril Smith were open in their fears of damage being done to Liberalism and the Liberal Party, and the Association of Liberal Councillors was a continual sceptic regarding the fruits of close co-operation. The friction between the two parties resulted from the belief of many Liberals, particularly at the grass-roots, that their party was a democratic party with roots in the local community and with a long history of struggling to 'break the mould' of British politics, while the SDP with fewer local organisations was dominated by London and the parliamentary wing of the party. Furthermore, Owen appeared to push the SDP further to the right, especially on economic and defence issues. Yet the chief source of irritation was the allocation of seats between the two parties; a complex formula was adopted for the 1983 election with the

Liberals having the most winnable seats, so although the arrangement caused friction in certain areas, the conflict was resolved remarkably smoothly.[29] The question of the leadership of the Alliance was settled in a less satisfactory manner with Jenkins assuming the position of 'prime minister designate' if the Alliance were to form a government after the 1983 election, a solution that was to be strenuously avoided in future elections.

In terms of co-operation and the winning of electoral support, the Alliance proved to be quite successful.[30] There were a series of by-election victories for both parties before the 1983 election at Croydon, Crosby, Glasgow Hillhead, Mitcham and Morden and Bermondsey. The general election result, while disappointing in terms of seats, was good in terms of votes:

	MPs	Candidates	% share of the vote
Alliance	23	633	25.4
Liberals	17	322	13.7
SDP	6	311	11.6

With the return of a Conservative government in 1983, the Alliance continued to perform well in by-elections and the two parties moved closer together, particularly at local level. At the parliamentary level there was sustained resistance mainly from the SDP and Owen against any form of merger between the two parties even though, *de facto*, this was happening with joint conferences and joint selection of parliamentary candidates. A serious rift between the two parties is highly unlikely in the near future, and although an absolute majority for the Alliance in the House of Commons remains a distant goal, the bargaining power derived from a hung Parliament remains a distinct possibility.

The Minor Parties

The Nationalist Parties
The period after 1964 saw the rise and fall in the fortunes of the political parties representing Scottish and Welsh nationalism. The Scottish National Party (SNP) made a significant

breakthrough with its by-election victory in Hamilton in 1967, increased its candidates and votes in 1970 and had dramatic successes in 1974. However, in spite of the party's increased importance resulting from Labour's lack of a parliamentary majority before 1979, there was a gradual ebbing away of support with reversals in the 1975 EEC Referendum, the disappointment of the devolution referendum in March 1979, and the setbacks in the 1979 and 1983 general elections. The Welsh Nationalist Party, Plaid Cymru, experienced a similar history. After a by-election breakthrough in 1966 in Carmarthen, the next three general elections saw an increase in electoral support, support that was to disappear in the two referendums of 1975 and 1979 and in the general elections of 1979 and 1983 (see Table 12.3).

TABLE 12.3

Election	SNP			Plaid Cymru		
	Seats	% vote in Scotland	Candidates	Seats	% vote in Wales	Candidates
1959	0	0.8	5	0	5.2	20
1964	0	2.4	15	0	4.8	23
1966	0	5.0	23	0	4.3	20
1970	1	11.4	65	0	11.5	36
1974 (Feb.)	7	21.9	70	2	10.7	36
1974 (Oct.)	11	30.4	71	3	10.0	36
1979	2	17.3	71	2	8.1	36
1983	2	11.8	72	2	7.8	38

Source: Nuffield election studies, 1959–83.

The SNP, founded in the 1930s and winning its first parliamentary seat in the Motherwell by-election of 1945, did not emerge as a major threat to the established parties in Scotland until the 1960s. Yet after the high hopes of the early 1970s, it was to suffer a major disappointment when only 33 per cent of the Scottish electorate voted for a separate Scottish Assembly in 1979. Plaid Cymru did not have so far to fall, but only 12 per cent of the Welsh electorate voted for a Welsh Assembly in 1979.

The reasons for the rise and relative decline of the nationalist parties are far from clear and it is difficult to draw close
parallels between the SNP and Plaid Cymru. Certainly they
were the recipients of the protest vote that principally went
to the Liberals in England, and both Wales and Scotland
shared a feeling of neglect by a London-based central government in a period of severe economic difficulties and decline
in traditional heavy industries; the expansion of the oil
industry in Scotland was an additional factor there. There is
no doubt that the Labour Party tended to neglect its organisations in the safe industrial seats of central Scotland and
South Wales. These factors must be put in the context of the
upsurge in nationalist feeling in other European states during
this period.[31]

However, the two parties were quite distinctive. The SNP
remained essentially a middle class party, pragmatic but with
a distinctive division between its right and left wings. The
leadership came from the right, but after the failures of 1979,
a '79 Group' was formed. This faction stressed a more radical,
socialist approach to Scotland's problems and favoured a
strategy of fighting more forcibly in Labour held seats. The
'79 Group' succeeded in pushing the policies of the SNP
more to the left, but in spite of bitter internal battles, the
control of the party remained in the hands of the right and
the SNP continued to be peripheral to the mainstream of
British politics.

Plaid Cymru had always been a more radical party and unlike the SNP has laid more stress on cultural and linguistic
roots as a basis for independence.[32] After 1979, the split
between the more rural, conservative, Welsh-speaking elements
from the West and the North and the more radical, urban,
English-speaking members from the South became more pronounced. However, the radicals triumphed; the party espoused
a nationalist version of decentralised socialism, it stood for
unilateral nuclear disarmament, and it strongly supported the
miners in the prolonged and bitter strike of 1984/5. The
election of Dafydd Elis Thomas as president of Plaid Cymru
in 1984 appeared to confirm this turn to the left.

Despite the ideological differences between the two
nationalist parties, in 1986 they finally achieved an agree-

ment to form an alliance to fight the next election. The agreement, modelled on the politically successful Liberal–SDP combination, was mainly aimed at increasing media attention during the next general election, and providing a basis for political co-operation between the two in the event of a future 'hung Parliament'. Neither party has quite regained the momentum and enthusiasm of the 1970s, but they still remain potential reservoirs for the protest vote and established channels for a further upsurge of nationalist feeling.

Political Parties in Northern Ireland
Political parties in Northern Ireland have always been different to those elsewhere in the United Kingdom. Before 1972, the Province of Northern Ireland enjoyed a large measure of self-government and therefore elections to the Stormont Parliament were more important than the politics of Westminster. Economic and class factors that played such an important role in the rest of the United Kingdom were absent from Northern Irish politics. The test of political allegiance and voting behaviour in Northern Ireland was religion. Protestants voted for the various Unionist parties and for the maintenance of links with Britain while the Roman Catholics, who formed one-third of the Province's population, voted for candidates and parties whose ultimate goal was Irish unification.

This self-contained political system emerged from the political and military conflicts of the period 1912–22. The six counties of Northern Ireland with overall Protestant majorities refused to countenance any form of Irish Home Rule which gave power to the Irish Catholic majority. The Protestant majority was successful and under the 1921 Act a self-governing Province of Northern Ireland emerged. The boundaries of the new Province conformed to the old local government boundaries and made little sense in terms of the all-important religious divisions, retaining the presence within the Northern Ireland boundaries of a large Catholic minority who generally looked to Dublin and Irish unification. The establishment of the Irish Free State based on the twenty-six counties of the South in 1922 added to Protestant unease in the North.

The religious divisions in Northern Ireland and the Irish Free State's declared goal of Irish unification established the type of party system in Northern Ireland that was to endure until the 1970s. The Protestant majority voted for the Unionist Party which dominated Stormont politics and always won eight or more of the twelve Westminster seats, while the Catholic minority voted for the Nationalist Party. Parties which attempted to cut across the sectarian divide, such as the Northern Ireland Labour Party, had little success. The Unionist Party in the House of Commons was indistinguishable from the British Conservative Party, and Northern Ireland politics intruded little into British politics. Thus in 1964 the Ulster Unionist Party won all twelve Northern Ireland seats, and it won eleven in 1966; these Unionist MPs were regarded as part of the Conservative Party total.

Events in the late 1960s shattered this party configuration and added to the multiplicity of parties in the House of Commons in the 1970s.[33] In 1963 O'Neill became prime minister of Northern Ireland and leader of the Unionist Party; his attempts to moderate the political attitudes of the Protestants and bring the Catholics into the Northern Ireland political system produced a great deal of unease among his Protestant supporters. The Catholics, long dissatisfied with their lowly place in the social, economic and political life of the Province, attempted to come out of the political ghetto and demand greater equality. The spark was lit by the Civil Rights Movement which began demonstrating for equal political rights in 1968. At first non-denominational, the campaign became increasingly identified with the Catholic minority; a Protestant backlash ensued and the violence finally led to the direct intervention of the British government and the use of the army in Northern Ireland. In 1972 the Stormont Parliament was suspended and direct British rule established. All subsequent attempts to restore some form of self-government, involving Protestants sharing power with the Catholics, failed.

The consequences of these events for the Northern Ireland political parties were far-reaching. New political parties appeared and these parties had attitudes and acted in ways very different from their predecessors. The changes can be summarised as follows:

(1) The Unionist Party was shattered. In the general election of 1970 an early indication of events to come was the election of Paisley as an independent Protestant Unionist, demanding a harder line against the demands of the Catholic minority. The Unionist Party of O'Neill, Chichester-Clark and Faulkner suffered a series of splits and a majority formed the Official Unionist Party under West; Faulkner formed a new Unionist Party of Northern Ireland. In the election of February 1974 the Protestant opponents of the former Unionist Party leadership came together in the Ulster United Council (UUC) and won eleven of the twelve Westminster seats; this Protestant coalition won ten seats in the October 1974 election. The continuing divisions in the Protestant ranks were again evident in the 1979 election; the UUC broke up and the Official Unionist Party won only five seats; the former, more moderate Unionists of the O'Neill–Faulkner lineage were entirely eliminated, and various Protestant groups, such as Paisley's Democratic Unionist Party won five seats.[34] In the general election of 1983, with the Northern Ireland seats increased to seventeen, the Official Unionists won eleven seats, the Democratic Unionists won three, and one seat went to an independent Unionist. The divisions within the Protestant camp were underlined by the fact that thirteen of the seventeen seats represented an inter-Protestant struggle.

(2) The old Nationalist Party disappeared and its place was taken in 1971 by the Social Democratic and Labour Party (SDLP). The new party saw unification as an ultimate solution to the Irish problem, but was far more flexible in seeking concessions within the existing political framework; it regarded social and economic demands as equally important as constitutional questions. The SDLP returned one MP to parliament in the three general elections of October 1974, 1979 and 1983, with a further by-election success in 1986 when the Protestant MPs challenging the Hillsborough agreement between the British and Irish Republican governments, forced a series of by-elections.[35] However, as in the Protestant camp, significant divisions between the Catholics remained. In 1970 there were three Catholic MPs elected to the House of Commons, each from a different group and after 1979,

Sinn Fein, the political wing of the Provisional IRA, began to fight local and parliamentary elections in a more determined manner. Profiting from the perceived timidity of the SDLP, Sinn Fein succeeded in electing Bobby Sands, a convicted IRA prisoner in April 1981, although he fought the election under non-party colours. In 1982, in the elections for the newly constituted Northern Ireland Assembly, Sinn Fein won 10 per cent of the vote to 19 per cent of the SDLP and in the 1983 election, Gerry Adams, of the Sinn Fein defeated independent Catholic, Gerry Fitt, who had represented West Belfast for 17 years. In this election, the SDLP fought all seventeen seats winning 17.9 per cent of the vote and Sinn Fein fought fourteen with 13 per cent of the vote. The mainly Catholic Workers Party fought fourteen also but only managed less than 2 per cent of the vote. The SDLP and Sinn Fein won one seat each.

(3) These new political groupings, both Protestant and Catholic, were far more independent of the major political parties and more volatile in terms of their voting behaviour in the House of Commons. After the 1972 abolition of the Stormont Parliament, the Unionists refused to take the Conservative whip in the House of Commons and could not be relied on to vote against the minority Labour government in the period leading up to the 1979 election. Even in the Labour government's defeat in the Commons in March 1979, Callaghan was able to secure two Irish Protestant votes by his promise of more parliamentary seats for Northern Ireland but at the same time managed to alienate the two Catholic MPs. Protestant MPs from the Province became even more hostile to the Conservative Party in the 1980s and temporarily shelving their boycott of the Commons, even helped to secure a major defeat for the Conservative government in 1986 over a Bill dealing with Sunday trading as revenge for the Hillsborough Agreement. The comfortable Conservative majorities of 1979 and 1983 reduced the political significance of the Northern Irish parties in the House of Commons, but in the event of a 'hung' Parliament, the complex pattern of the seventeen seats of Northern Ireland could again be politically significant.[36]

The Smaller Parties

Apart from the nationalist and Northern Ireland parties, the other small parties in Britain have played a most insignificant role in the British party system. The Communist Party of Great Britain has been the most conventional of these groups in terms of its search for parliamentary seats and it has always had the largest membership. After 1964 it fought between twenty-nine and fifty-seven seats at each general election but in all 317 contests it only succeeded once in saving a deposit — Jimmy Reid in Dumbartonshire in February 1974. In 1983 the 35 CPGB candidates had an average of 0.8 per cent of the votes per contested constituency; by 1985 the membership of the party had declined to less than 11,000. An intensely bitter intra-party dispute took place in the years following the 1983 election. The issues were complex but basically involved a struggle between the 'hardliners' or 'Stalinists' who kept control of the party newspaper, the *Morning Star*,[37] and the Eurocommunists who could be roughly identified with the influential and prestigous monthly journal, *Marxism Today*.[38] The Eurocommunist or liberal wing of the Party maintained control of the party institutions, including the important Executive Committee, and by 1985 had begun to expel some of the 'hardliners'. Previous splits within the CPGB have resulted in the formation of rival parties; in 1977 supporters of the Soviet Union and its policies in Eastern Europe broke away to form the New Communist Party. While the CPGB remained politically irrelevant, it remained the most important of all the Marxist parties in Britain and its industrial influence remained out of all proportion to its size; the intellectual influence on the rest of the British left, especially with the popularity of *Marxism Today*, was also significant.

Other Marxist groups were even less important to the British party system. The Socialist Workers' Party and the Workers' Revolutionary Party have contested elections, but mainly for propaganda reasons with no hope of success; all 60 candidates in 1979 and the 20 in 1983 standing under the WRP label lost their deposits. Membership of these parties, although difficult to estimate, remained small and declined from its relative peak in the 1960s to below 6,000 in the

1980s. They were prone to splits and defections; the WRP experienced the most newsworthy schism when in 1985 its veteran leader, Gerry Healey, was expelled for alleged sexual misdemeanours. The International Marxist Group disbanded itself in the early 1980s and its members sought entry into the Labour Party. The most politically successful of these groups, the Trotskyite Militant Tendency, was only able to advance under the protective umbrella of the Labour Party.[39]

During the 1970s the most important of the minor parties was the National Front. It was founded in 1967 with the amalgamation of various racist groups and although adopting a wider programme which included leaving the EEC and dismantling the trade unions, its only real platform was the abolition of all non-white immigration and a general hostility to non-whites. The Front fought every election since its formation, increasing its candidates from 10 in 1970 to 303 in 1979, all these candidates losing their deposits. It had some successes in local elections, for example in Leicester in 1977 and in the Greater London Council elections of the same year when it pushed the Liberal Party into fourth place, but the Front's strongest by-election performance was at West Bromwich in 1973 where it polled just over 16 per cent of the vote.

However, the immigration policies of various British governments since the 1960s tended to nullify the race issue as a potential vote winner and the continual ferocious intraparty battles reduced the importance of the independent racist right in British politics; all 60 National Front candidates lost their deposits in 1983. After 1979, the National Front suffered another damaging party leadership battle, with one of its well known leaders, Tyndale, forming the rival British National Party after his expulsion from the National Front; all 53 BNP candidates lost their deposits in the 1983 general election. The NF's membership dropped from approximately 20,000 in the mid-1970s to less than 6,000 by the early 1980s. Paralleling Trotskyite entryism into the Labour Party, many ex-National Front members joined the Conservative Party and in 1983 caused some embarrassment by standing as official Conservative candidates.[40]

One of the most interesting of the minor parties that have

appeared in the period since 1964 was the Ecology Party; it changed its name to the Green Party in 1985. It was formed in 1973 and was another manifestation of the growing concern with environmental issues which in the late 1960s and 1970s spawned numerous pressure groups.[41] By the mid-1980s the Green Party had a small membership of 5000 but its participation in general and local elections was growing and its share of the vote was increasing relative to the other small parties. From only five candidates in the October 1974 election and 53 in 1979, it fielded 108 in the 1983 election, the largest number for any minor party. It sought to emulate the success of the Greens in West Germany, but unlike that party, it was harshly penalised by the British electoral system.

All the minor parties in the British party system continued to be discriminated against by the nature of the British electoral system and there is no doubt that a change in the present electoral system to a type of proportional representation would constitute the major ingredient of change in the nature of all the political parties and the party system they constitute.

Notes to Chapter 12

1. For a definition of a two-party system, see G. Sartori, *Parties and Party Systems, Vol. 1* (Cambridge University Press, 1976) pp. 185–92.
2. R. Rose and I. McAllister, *Voters Begin to Choose* (London: Sage, 1986) p. 25.
3. See D. Butler and G. Butler, *British Political Facts 1900–1985* (London: Macmillan, 1986) pp. 258–64.
4. For recent interpretations of British voting behaviour, see D. Butler and D. Stokes, *Political Change in Britain*, 2nd ed. (London: Macmillan, 1974); P. Dunleavy and C. T. Husbands, *British Democracy at the Cross-roads* (London: Allen & Unwin, 1985); A. Heath, R. Jowell and J. Curtice, *How Britain Votes* (Oxford: Pergamon Press, 1985); Rose and McAllister, *Voters Begin to Choose*.
5. Heath, Jowell and Curtice, *How Britain Votes*, p. 44.
6. For example, see Rose and McAllister, *Voters Begin to Choose*, p. 162.
7. For the role of the mass media see the contrasting views of I. Crewe, 'Why the Conservatives Won', in *Britain at the Polls, 1979*, H. R. Pennimar (ed.) (Washington: American Enterprise Institute,

1981) pp. 270–1; Dunleavy and Husbands, *British Democracy at the Cross-roads*, pp. 110–17; Heath, Jowell and Curtice, *How Britain Votes*, pp. 148–9.

8. Defined as, 'a stand-up fight between two adversaries for the favour of the lookers-on', S. Finer, *Adversary Politics* (London: Anthony Wigram, 1975) p. 3. These views were echoed in *Report of the Hansard Society Commission on Electoral Reform* (London: HMSO, June 1976) p. 3. It was also argued that the two-party system resulted in huge discontinuities of government policy, see S. E. Finer, *The Changing British Party System 1945–1979* (Washington: American Enterprise Institute, 1980) p. 19. See also the criticisms of V. Bogdanor, *The People and the Party System* (Cambridge University Press, 1981) pp. 177–205.

9. For discussion of the problems of coalitions and 'hung' parliaments, see V. Bogdanor, *Multi-party Politics and the Constitution* (Cambridge University Press, 1983); D. Butler, *Governing Without a Majority* (London: Collins, 1983); D. Butler (ed.), *Coalitions in British Politics* (London: Macmillan, 1978). Besides the problems of coalition-making coalition stability and the undemocratic nature of horse-trading after the election, coalitions sometimes produce unrepresentative governments from representative assemblies; the exclusion of the Italian Communist Party with one-third of the vote from governments since 1947, and the power of the small West German Free Democratic Party to force changes of government without elections and without itself losing government office as it did in the autumn of 1982, are some examples of this disproportionality.

10. Two Conservative members of the Tory Reform Group have put the argument clearly: 'A "coalition" of moderates — Tories, Liberals and Social Democrats in the Labour Party — would ensure stable government and guarantee sensible, middle of the road policies excluding the extremes of both Left and Right'. T. Russel, *The Tory Party* (Harmondsworth: Penguin, 1978) p. 153, and 'Thus the main argument for electoral reform is that it would prevent control of Government by extremist minorities'. I. Gilmour, *Inside Right* (London: Hutchinson, 1977) p. 225. There was electoral reform of a minor nature in 1985 which extended the franchise to Britons living abroad, increased the deposit for standing in Parliamentary elections, and reduced the threshold for forfeiture of the deposit.

11. J. Alt, I. Crewe and B. Sarlik, 'Angels in plastic: The Liberal Surge in 1974', *Political Studies*, vol. 25, no. 3, Sept. 1977, pp. 343–68. See also P. H. Lemieux, 'Political Issues and Liberal Support in the February 1974 British General Election', *Political Studies*, vol. 25, no. 3, Sept. 1977, pp. 323–42. Also, J. Curtice, 'Liberal Votes and the Alliance: Re-alignment or Protest', in *Liberal Party Politics*, V. Bogdanor (ed.) (Oxford University Press, 1983) Ch. 5. Also H. Himmelweit *et al.*, *How Voters Decide* (London: Academic Press, 1981) pp. 157–75.

12. See D. E. Butler and D. Kavanagh, *The British General Election of February 1974* (London: Macmillan, 1974) pp. 336–7.
13. See A. Mitchie and S. Hoggart, *The Pact* (London: Quartet, 1978).
14. See M. Pinto-Duschinsky, *British Political Finance 1830–1980* (Washington: American Enterprise Institute, 1981) pp. 179–211. Also see *Houghton Committee Report on Financial Aid to Political Parties.*
15. The membership of the Liberal Party has fluctuated over this period. From 250,000 in 1964 there was a decline in the late 1960s Houghton estimating a membership of 190,000. The membership in 1986 was less than 100,000
16. See pp. 79–82.
17. See A. Gamble, 'Liberals and the Economy', in *Liberal Party Politics*, pp. 191–216.
18. See V. Bogdanor, *The People and the Party System* (Cambridge: CUP, 1981) and I. Bradley, *The Strange Rebirth of Liberal Britain* (London: Chatto & Windus, 1985) pp. 224–30.
19. This argument is developed quite persuasively in N. Tracy, *The Origins of the Social Democratic Party* (London: Croom Helm, 1983) pp. 33–6. Crosland's own unflattering opinion of Rodgers is in S. Crosland, *Tony Crosland* (London: Jonathan Cape, 1983) p. 227.
20. See W. Rodgers, *The Politics of Change* (London: Secker & Warburg, 1982) pp. 167–70. It was pointed out that Rodgers looked to the trade unions in the 1960s to reverse Labour policy on unilateralism and Shirley Williams had a seat on the NEC for ten years thanks to the block vote of the unions. See S. Williams, *Politics is for People* (Harmondsworth: Penguin, 1981) pp. 126–140.
21. See H. Stephenson, *Claret and Chips: The Rise of the SDP* (London: Michael Joseph, 1982) pp. 28–38.
22. For a discussion on the relations between the leaders, see I. Bradley, *Breaking the Mould? The Birth and Prospects of the Social Democratic Party* (Oxford: Martin Robertson, 1981) pp. 84–6. Bradley's account is useful but marred by excessive admiration for the key defectors.
23. See p. 223.
24. This initiated Roy Hattersley's remark that the SDP came into existence to make the world safe for Access card-holders.
25. See R. Samuel, 'The SDP and the New Political Class', *New Society*, 22 April 1982, pp. 124–7. Membership of the SDP increased dramatically at first, nearly 50,000 in the first few months: 65,000 ballot papers were sent to members in 1982. It dropped to 50,000 in 1984. In 1986 it stood at officially 58,000.
26. Peter Jenkins, *The Guardian*, 25 March 1981.
27. Stephenson, *Claret and Chips*, pp. 103–4.
28. Taverne, *The Future of the Left* and Williams, *Politics is for People*, for example, never mention PR. The books published by the SDP

leaders since 1981 reflected this ambivalence towards a distinct ideological stance. D. Owen in the revised edition of *Face the Future* published in 1981, removed all references to socialism.

29. For details, see D. Butler and D. Kavanagh, *The British General Election of 1983* (London: Macmillan, 1984) pp. 75–6.

30. There is some evidence that the Alliance vote was more coherent and less of a protest vote than the previous support for the Liberals before 1979. See Heath, Jowell and Curtice, *How Britain Votes*, pp. 142–6.

31. See T. Nairn, *The Break Up of Britain: Crisis and Neo-Nationalism* (London: New Left Books, 1977).

32. For a discussion of the cultural and political backgrounds of Scottish and Welsh nationalism, see A. H. Birch, *Political Integration and Disintegration in the British Isles* (London: Allen & Unwin, 1977) pp. 98–133.

33. For a more detailed discussion of the changes in the party system in the 1970s, see I. McAllister and S. Nelson, 'Modern developments in the Northern Ireland Party System', *Parliamentary Affairs*, vol. XXXII, no. 3, Summer 1979, pp. 279–316.

34. It should be noted that elections in Northern Ireland differed in many ways from those in the rest of the United Kingdom. A form of proportional representation (the single transferable vote) is used; there are more voters per constituency; turn-out is generally higher; there is a greater use of the postal vote. Before the 1970s electoral corruption of various forms was widely practised; a favourite slogan was 'vote early, vote often'.

35. The SDLP success was in Newry and Armagh where Seamus Mallon defeated the sitting OUP member. This divided the NI seats as follows: OUP 10; DUP 3; Popular Unionist 1; SDLP 2; Sinn Fein 1.

36. In discussing NI's political parties, I have ignored the Alliance Party. This party was avowedly non-sectarian and attempted to attract electoral support from both communities. In 1983 it contested eleven seats with its usual lack of success and won only 8 per cent of the vote.

37. The circulation of the *Morning Star* dropped to 28,250 by 1984 of which only 13,835 were sold in Britain.

38. For one account of the nature of the divisions within the CPGB, see D. Cook, 'No Private Drama', *Marxism Today*, vol. 29, no. 2, Feb. 1985.

39. See Chapter 11 for a discussion of the position of Militant Tendency within the Labour Party.

40. For discussions of the National Front in this period, see M. Walker, 'The National Front', in *Multi-Party Britain*, H. Drucker (ed.) (London: Macmillan, 1979) pp. 183–203. M. Harrop *et al.*, 'The Bases of National Front Support', *Political Studies*, vol. 28, no. 2, June 1980, pp. 271–83. S. Taylor, *The National Front in English Politics* (London: Macmillan, 1982).

41. For an analysis of environmental politics in Britain, see P. Lowe and J. Goyder, *Environmental Groups in Politics* (London: Allen & Unwin, 1983). For a discussion of environmental politics in a wider context, see A. R. Ball and F. Millard, *Pressure Politics in Industrial Societies* (London: Macmillan, 1986) Ch. 6.

Important Dates since 1867

1867   The Second Reform Bill
       The Formation of the Conservative National Union
1872   The Ballot Act
1877   Foundation of the National Liberal Federation
1881   Social Democratic Federation Founded
1883   The Corrupt Practices Act
1884   Third Reform Act
       Fabian Society established
1885   Redistribution of parliamentary seats
1886   Liberal Unionists secede
1891   The Newcastle Programme of the Liberal Party
1893   The Independent Labour Party established
1900   Formation of the Labour Representation Committee
1901   Taff Vale decision
1903   Liberal–Labour Electoral Pact
       Chamberlain's tariff campaign begins
1906   Liberal landslide electoral victory
1909   The Lloyd George Budget
       The Osborne judgement
1911   The Parliament Act
1915   Asquith forms his coalition government
1916   Lloyd George becomes prime minister
1918   Fourth Reform Act
       Labour Party Constitution
       Coupon election
1922   Fall of Lloyd George's coalition
       Labour becomes second largest party
1923   Liberals reunited
1924   First Labour government

1926	The General Strike
1928	Universal suffrage
1931	Political crisis and the formation of the National Government
1935	Baldwin replaces MacDonald as prime minister
1938	Chamberlain goes to Munich
1939	Outbreak of war; the electoral truce
1940	Churchill forms coalition
1942	The Beveridge Report
1945	Labour electoral victory
1949	Representation of the People Act
1955	Gaitskell defeats Bevan and Morrison for Labour leadership
1956	Suez
1957	Macmillan defeats Butler in leadership contest
1960	Gaitskell defeated at Labour conference on defence issue
1962	Liberal by-election victory at Orpington
1963	The Profumo affair Conservative leadership crisis
1965	Heath becomes first elected leader of the Conservatives
1969	Wilson defeated over *In Place of Strife*
1972	Heath's government's U-turn
1974	February election produces minority Labour government
1975	Thatcher becomes Conservative leader
1975	EEC referendum
1977	Lib—Lab Pact
1979	March devolution referendums May Conservative election victory June European elections
1980	Labour conference agrees to widen franchise for leadership selection
1981	January Labour conference on party constitution Formation of SDP
1982	Falklands War
1983	Conservative election victory Kinnock replaces Foot as Labour leader

Leaders of British Political Parties

The Liberal Party		The Conservative Party	
1868	W. Gladstone	1868	B. Disraeli
1874	Lord Hartington*	1881	S. Northcote*
1880	W. Gladstone	1885	Lord Salisbury
1894	Lord Rosebery	1902	A. Balfour
1899	H. Campbell-	1911	A. Bonar Law*
	Bannerman	1921	A. Chamberlain*
1908	H. Asquith	1922	A. Bonar Law
1926	D. Lloyd George	1923	S. Baldwin
1931	H. Samuel	1937	N. Chamberlain
1935	A. Sinclair	1940	W. Churchill
1945	C. Davies	1955	A. Eden
1956	J. Grimond	1957	H. Macmillan
1967	J. Thorpe	1963	A. Douglas-Home
1976	D. Steel	1965	E. Heath
		1975	M. Thatcher

* Leader of the party in the House of Commons

The Labour Party

Chairman of the PLP		*Party leader*	
1906	K. Hardie	1922	R. MacDonald
1908	A. Henderson	1931	A. Henderson

Chairman of the PLP		*Party leader*	
1910	G. Barnes	1932	G. Lansbury
1911	R. MacDonald	1935	C. Attlee
1914	A. Henderson	1955	H. Gaitskell
1917	W. Adamson	1963	H. Wilson
1921	J. Clynes	1976	J. Callaghan
		1980	M. Foot
		1983	N. Kinnock

The Social Democratic Party

1982	R. Jenkins
1983	D. Owen

Select Bibliography

Political Parties: General

Beyme, K. von (1985) *Political Parties in Western Democracies*, Aldershot, Gower.

Day, A. J. and Degenhardt, H. W. (1980) *Political Parties of the World*, London, Longman.

Duverger, M. (1954) *Political Parties,* London, Methuen.

Michels, R. (1954) *Political Parties,* New York, Collier-Macmillan (first English edn published 1915).

Ostrogorski, M. (1964) *Democracy and the Organisation of Political Parties,* 2 vols, Chicago, Quadrangle Books (first published 1902).

Sartori, G. (1976) *Parties and Party Systems,* vol. 1, Cambridge University Press.

British Political History

Addison, P. (1975) *The Road to 1945,* London, Jonathan Cape.

R. Bentley (1984) *Politics Without Democracy 1815–1914,* London, Fontana.

Butler, D. (ed.) (1978) *Coalitions in British Politics,* London, Macmillan.

Calder, A. (1969) *The People's War: Britain 1939–45,* London, Jonathan Cape.

Cook, C. and Ramsden, J. (1978) *Trends in British Politics since 1945,* London, Macmillan.

Cowling, M. (1971) *The Impact of Labour 1920–24,* Cambridge University Press.

Dangerfield, G. (1970) *The Strange Death of Liberal England,* London, Palladin (first published in 1935).

Morgan, K. O. (1979) *Consensus and Disunity: The Lloyd George Coalition Government 1918–22,* Oxford, Clarendon Press.

O'Day, A. (ed.) (1979) *The Edwardian Age: Conflict and Stability 1900–1914,* London, Macmillan.

Pelling, H. (1979) *Popular Politics and Society in Late Victorian Britain,* 2nd edn, London, Macmillan.

Pugh, H. (1982) *The Making of Modern British Politics, 1867–1939,* London, Blackwell.

Sked, A. and Cook, C. (1979) *Post-War Britain: A Political History,* Harmondsworth, Penguin.

Taylor, A. J. P. (1965) *English History 1914–1945,* Oxford, Clarendon Press.

Whitehead, P. (1985) *The Writing on the Wall. Britain in the Seventies,* London, Michael Joseph.

British Political Parties: General

Beattie, A. (ed.) (1970) *English Party Politics,* 2 vols, London, Weidenfeld & Nicolson.

Beer, S. (1969) *Modern British Politics,* 2nd edn, London, Faber.

V. Bogdanor (1983) *Multi-party Politics and the Constitution,* Cambridge, Cambridge University Press.

Brown, K. D. (ed.) (1974) *Essays in Anti-Labour History,* London, Macmillan.

Bulmer Thomas, I. (1967) *The Growth of the British Party System,* 2 vols, 2nd edn, London, Baker.

Butler, D. and Butler, G. (1986) *British Political Facts 1900–1985,* London, Macmillan.

Finer, S. E. (1980) *The Changing British Party System 1945–79,* Washington, American Enterprise Institute.

Guttsman, W. L. (1965) *The British Political Elite,* London, MacGibbon & Kee.

Hanham, H. J. (1959) *Elections and Party Management in the Time of Gladstone and Disraeli,* London, Longman.

Houghton Committee (1976) *Report on Financial Aid to Political Parties*, Cmnd 6601, London, HMSO.

Jennings, Sir Ivor (1960–2) *Party Politics,* 3 vols, Cambridge University Press.

McKenzie, R. T. (1963) *British Political Parties,* 2nd edn, London, Heinemann.

Pinto-Duschinsky, M. (1981) *British Political Finance, 1830–1980*, Washington, American Enterprise Institute.

Rose, R. (1984) *Do Parties Make a Difference?* 2nd edn, London, Macmillan.

Thompson, P. (1967) *Socialists, Liberals and Labour: The Struggle for London 1885–1914,* London, Routledge & Kegan Paul.

A. Young (1983) *The Re-selection of MPs*, London, Heinemann.

British Elections

Alderman, G. (1978) *British Elections: Myth and Reality,* London, Batsford.

Blewett, N. (1972) *The Peers, the Parties and the People: The General Elections of 1910,* London, Macmillan.

Butler, D. (1952) *The British General Election of 1951,* London, Macmillan.

Butler, D. (1955) *The British General Election of 1955,* London, Macmillan.

Butler, D. and Kavanagh, D. (1974) *The British General Election of February 1974,* London, Macmillan.

Butler, D. and Kavanagh, D. (1975) *The British General Election of October 1974,* London, Macmillan.

Butler, D. and Kavanagh, D. (1980) *The British General Election of 1979,* London, Macmillan.

Butler, D. and Kavanagh, D. (1984) *The British General Election of 1983*, London, Macmillan.

Butler, D. and King, A. (1965) *The British General Election of 1964,* London, Macmillan.

Butler, D. and King, A. (1966) *The British General Election of 1966,* London, Macmillan.

Butler, D. and Pinto-Duschinsky, M. (1971) *The British*

General Election of 1970, London, Macmillan.

Butler, D. and Rose, R. (1970) *The British General Election of 1959,* London, Cass.

Butler, D. and Stokes, D. (1974) *Political Change in Britain,* 2nd edn, London, Macmillan.

Cook, C. (1975) *The Age of Alignment: Electoral Politics in Britain 1922–29,* London, Macmillan.

Cook, C. and Ramsden, J. (1973) *By-Elections in British Politics,* London, Macmillan.

Craig, F. W. S. (ed.) (1981) *British Electoral Facts, 1832– 1980,* 4th edn, Chichester, Parliamentary Research Services.

Dunleavy, P. and Husbands, C. T. (1985) *British Democracy at the Crossroads,* London, Allen & Unwin.

Heath, A., Jowell, R. and Curtice, J. (1985) *How Britain Votes,* Oxford, Pergamon Press.

Helmore, L. (1967) *Corrupt and Illegal Practices,* London, Routledge & Kegan Paul.

Lloyd, T. (1968) *The General Election of 1880,* Oxford University Press.

McCallum, R. B. and Readman, A. (1947) *The British General Election of 1945,* Oxford University Press.

Nicholas, H. (1951) *The British General Election of 1950,* London, Macmillan.

O'Leary, C. (1962) *The Elimination of Corrupt Practices in British Elections 1868–1911,* Oxford University Press.

Pelling, H. (1967) *The Social Geography of British Elections 1885–1910,* London, Macmillan.

Rose, R. and McAllister, I. (1986) *Voters Begin to Choose,* London, Sage.

Russell, A. K. (1973) *Liberal Landslide: The General Election of 1906,* Newton Abbot, David & Charles.

Stannage, C. T. (1980) *Baldwin Thwarts the Opposition. The British General Election of 1935,* London, Croom Helm.

The British Electoral System

Blewett, N. (1965) 'The Franchise Factor in the United Kingdom 1885–1918', *Past and Present,* vol. 32, pp. 27– 56.

Bogdanor, V. (1981) *The People and the Party System. The Referendum and Electoral Reform in British Politics,* Cambridge University Press.

Finer, S. E. (ed.) (1975) *Adversary Politics and Electoral Reform,* London, Anthony Wigram.

Hansard Society (1976) *Report of the Commission on Electoral Reform,* London, Hansard Society.

Harrison, B. (1978) *Separate Spheres: The Opposition to Women's Suffrage in Britain,* London, Croom Helm.

Lakeman, E. (1982) *The Case for Proportional Representation,* London, Heinemann.

Liddington, J. and Norris, J. (1978) *One Hand Tied Behind Us. The Rise of the Women's Suffrage Movement,* London, Virago.

Maud, A. (1982) *Why Electoral Change? The Case for P.R. Examined,* London, Conservative Political Centre.

Morgan, D. (1975) *Suffragists and Liberals,* Oxford, Blackwell.

Pugh, M. (1978) *Electoral Reform in War and Peace 1906– 18,* London, Routledge & Kegan Paul.

Smith, F. (1966) *The Making of the Second Reform Bill,* Cambridge University Press.

The Conservative Party

History and Organisation

Behrens, R. (1980) *The Conservative Party from Heath to Thatcher,* Farnborough, Saxon House.

Blake, R. (1970) *The Conservative Party from Peel to Churchill,* London, Eyre & Spottiswoode.

Butler, Lord (ed.) (1977) *The Conservative Party: A History from its Origins to 1965,* London, Allen & Unwin.

Goodhart, P. (1973) *The 1922: The Story of the Conservative Party Backbenchers' Committee,* London, Macmillan.

Hoffman, J. (1964) *The Conservative Party in Opposition, 1945–51,* London, MacGibbon & Kee.

Holmes, M. (1985) *The First Thatcher Government 1979– 83,* Brighton, Wheatsheaf.

Layton-Henry, Z. (ed.) (1980) *Conservative Party Politics,* London, Macmillan.

Lindsay, T. and Harrington, M. (1980) *The Conservative Party 1918–1979*, London, Macmillan.

Norton, P. (1978) *Conservative Dissidents: Dissidents within the Parliamentary Conservative Party 1970–74*, London, Temple Smith.

Norton, P. and Aughey, A. (1981) *Conservatives and Conservatism*, London, Temple Smith.

Pugh, M. (1985) *The Tories and the People 1830–1935*, Oxford, Blackwell.

Ramsden, J. (1978) *A History of the Conservative Party: The Age of Balfour and Baldwin 1902–1940*, London, Longman.

Ideology

Gamble, A. (1974) *The Conservative Nation*, London, Routledge & Kegan Paul.

Gilmour, I. (1977) *Inside Right: A Study of Conservatism*, London, Hutchinson.

Hailsham, Viscount (1959) *The Conservative Case*, Harmondsworth, Penguin.

Hall, S. and Jacques, M. (eds) (1983) *The Politics of Thatcherism*, London, Lawrence & Wishart.

Levitas, R. (ed.) (1986) *The Ideology of the New Right*, Cambridge, Polity Press.

O'Sullivan, N. (1976) *Conservatism*, London, Dent.

Riddell, P. (1983) *The Thatcher Government*, Oxford, Martin Robertson.

Russel, T. (1978) *The Tory Party: Its Policies, Divisions and Future*, Harmondsworth, Penguin.

Smith, P. (1967) *Disraelian Conservatism and Social Reform*, London, Routledge & Kegan Paul.

Biography/Autobiography

Blake, R. (1955) *The Unknown Prime Minister: The Life and Times of Andrew Bonar Law 1858–1923*, London, Eyre & Spottiswoode.

Blake, R. (1969) *Disraeli*, London, Methuen.

Butler, R. A. (1973) *The Art of the Possible*, Harmondsworth, Penguin.

Eden, A. (1960) *Memoirs: Full Circle*, London, Cassell.

Feiling, K. (1946) *The Life of Neville Chamberlain*, London,

Macmillan.

Fisher, N. (1973) *Iain Macleod*, London, André Deutsch.

Macmillan, H. (1971) *Riding the Storm 1956–9*, London, Macmillan.

Macmillan, H. (1972) *Pointing the Way, 1959–61*, London, Macmillan.

Macmillan, H. (1973) *At the End of the Day, 1961–3*, London, Macmillan.

Middlemas, K. and Barnes, J. (1969) *Baldwin*, London, Weidenfeld & Nicolson.

Pelling, H. (1974) *Winston Churchill*, London, Macmillan.

Rhodes-James, R. (ed.) (1969) *Memoirs of a Conservative: J. C. C. Davidson's Memoirs and Papers*, London, Weidenfeld & Nicolson.

Salvidge, S. (1934) *Salvidge of Liverpool: Behind the Political Scenes 1890–1928*, London, Hodder & Stoughton.

Sampson, A. (1967) *Macmillan: A Study in Ambiguity*, London, Allen Lane.

Taylor, A.J.P. (1974) *Beaverbrook*, Harmondsworth, Penguin.

Woolton, Lord (1959) *Memoirs*, London, Cassell.

Zebel, S. H. (1973) *Balfour*, Cambridge University Press.

The Labour Party

History and Organisation

Bealey, F. and Pelling, H. (1958) *Labour and Politics 1900–1906*, London, Macmillan.

Briar, A. M. (1962) *Fabian Socialism and English Politics 1884–1918*, Cambridge University Press.

Coates, D. (1980) *Labour in Power? A Study of the Labour Government 1974–79*, London, Longman.

Cole, G. D. H. (1948) *A History of the Labour Party from 1914*, London, Routledge & Kegan Paul.

Cook, C. and Taylor, I. (eds) (1980) *The Labour Party*, London, Longman.

Crick, M. (1984) *Militant*, London, Faber & Faber.

Crick, M. (1986) *The March of Militant*, London, Faber & Faber.

Dowse, R. E. (1966) *Left in the Centre: The ILP 1893–1940*,

London, Longman.

Harrison, M. (1960) *The Trade Unions and the Labour Party since 1945*, London, Allen & Unwin.

Haseler, S. (1969) *The Gaitskellites*, London, Macmillan.

Howell, D. (1983) *British Workers and the Independent Labour Party, 1888–1906*, Manchester University Press.

Kavanagh, D. (ed.) (1982) *The Politics of the Labour Party*, London, Allen & Unwin.

Kogan, D. and Kogan, M. (1982) *The Battle for the Labour Party*, London, Fontana.

McKibbin, R. (1974) *The Evolution of the Labour Party 1910–1924*, Oxford University Press.

Minkin, L. (1980) *The Labour Party Conference*, rev. edn, Manchester University Press.

Moore, R. (1978) *The Emergence of the Labour Party, 1880–1924*, London, Hodder & Stoughton.

Pelling, H. (1964) *The Origins of the Labour Party*, 2nd edn, Oxford, Clarendon Press.

Pelling, H. (1972) *A Short History of the Labour Party*, 4th edn, London, Macmillan.

Pimlott, B. (1977) *Labour and the Left in the 1930s*, Cambridge University Press.

Whiteley, P. (1983) *The Labour Party in Crisis*, London, Methuen.

Ideology

Bealey, F. (1970) *The Social and Political Thought of the Labour Party*, London, Weidenfeld & Nicolson.

Benn, T. (1979) *Arguments for Socialism*, London, Jonathan Cape.

Coates, D. (1975) *The Labour Party and the Struggle for Socialism*, Cambridge University Press.

Crosland, C. A. R. (1956) *The Future of Socialism*, London, Jonathan Cape.

Drucker, H. M. (1979) *Doctrine and Ethos in the Labour Party*, London, Allen & Unwin.

Hodgson, G. (1981) *Labour at the Crossroads*, Oxford, Martin Robertson).

Holland, S. (1975) *The Socialist Challenge*, London, Quartet.

Howell, D. (1981) *British Social Democracy*, 2nd ed, London, Croom Helm.

Miliband, R. (1972) *Parliamentary Socialism*, 2nd edn, London, Merlin Press.

Biography/Autobiography
Bullock, A. (1967) *The Life and Times of Ernest Bevin*, vol. 2, London, Heinemann.
Burridge, T. (1985) *Clement Attlee*, London, Cape.
Donoughue, B. and Jones, G. W. (1973) *Herbert Morrison*, London, Weidenfeld & Nicolson.
Foot, M. (1973) *Aneurin Bevan, 1945—60*, vol. 2, London, David Poynton.
Harris, K. (1982) *Attlee*, London, Weidenfeld & Nicolson.
Marquand, D. (1977) *Ramsay MacDonald*, London, Jonathan Cape.
Morgan, K. O. (1975) *Keir Hardie*, London, Weidenfeld & Nicolson.
Pimlott, B. (1985) *Hugh Dalton*, London, Jonathan Cape.
Thomas, H. (1973) *John Strachey*, London, Eyre & Methuen.
Tsuzki, C. (1961) *H. M. Hyndman and British Socialism*, Oxford University Press.
Williams, P. (1979) *Hugh Gaitskell*, London, Jonathan Cape.

The Liberal Party

Bogdanor, V. (ed.) (1983) *Liberal Party Politics*, Oxford University Press.
Bradley, I. (1985) *The Strange Rebirth of Liberal Britain*, London, Chatto & Windus.
Clarke, P. F. (1971) *Lancashire and the New Liberalism*, Cambridge University Press.
Cook, C. (1976) *A Short History of the Liberal Party 1900—1976*, London, Macmillan.
Douglas, R. (1971) *A History of the Liberal Party 1895—1970*, London, Sidgwick & Jackson.
Emy, H. V. (1973) *Liberals, Radicals and Social Politics 1892—1914*, Cambridge University Press.
Freeden, M. (1978) *The New Liberalism*, Oxford University Press.
Hamer, D. A. (1972) *Liberal Politics in the Age of Gladstone and Rosebery*, Oxford, Clarendon Press.

Koss, S. E. (1976) *Asquith*, New York, St Martin's Press.
Matthew, H. C. G. (1973) *The Liberal Imperialists*, Oxford University Press.
Rowland, R. (1975) *Lloyd George*, London, Barrie & Jackson.
Wilson, T. (1966) *The Downfall of the Liberal Party 1914–35*, London, Collins.
Vincent, J. (1966) *The Formation of the British Liberal Party, 1857–68*, Harmondsworth, Penguin.

The Social Democratic Party

Bradley, I. (1981) *Breaking the Mould. The Birth and Prospects of the Social Democratic Party* Oxford, Martin Robertson.
Coates, K. (1983) *The Social Democrats. Those Who Went and Those Who Stayed*, Nottingham, Spokesman.
Owen, D. (1981) *Facing the Future*, Harmondsworth, Penguin.
Owen, D. (1986) *A United Kingdom*, Harmondsworth, Penguin.
Rodgers, W. (1982) *The Politics of Change*, London, Secker & Warburg.
Stephenson, H. (1982) *Claret and Chips. The Rise of the SDP*, London, Michael Joseph.
Tracey, N. (1983) *The Origins of the Social Democratic Party*, London, Croom Helm.
Williams, S. (1981) *Politics is for the People*, Harmondsworth, Penguin.

Minor Political Parties

Benewick, R. (1972) *The Fascist Movement in Britain*, 2nd edn, London, Allen Lane.
Billig, M. (1978) *The Fascists*, London, Academic Press.
Challinor, R. (1977) *The Origins of British Bolshevism*, London, Croom Helm.
Fielding, N. (1981) *The National Front*, London, Routledge & Kegan Paul.
Griffiths, R. (1983) *Fellow Travellers of the Right: British Enthusiasts for Nazi Germany 1933–9*, Oxford University Press.

Jupp, J. (1982) *The Radical Left in Britain, 1931–41*, London, Cass.

Kendall, W. (1969) *The Revolutionary Movement in Britain, 1900–21*, London, Weidenfeld & Nicolson.

Lunn, K. and Thurlow, R. C. (eds) (1980) *British Fascism: Essays on the Radical Right in Inter-War Britain*, London, Croom Helm.

Macfarlane, L. J. (1966) *The British Communist Party: Its Origin and Development until 1929*, London, MacGibbon & Kee.

MacIntyre, S. (1980) *A Proletarian Science: Marxism in Britain 1917–33*, Cambridge University Press.

Newton, K. (1969) *The Sociology of British Communism*, London, Allen Lane.

Nugent, N. and King, R. (eds) (1977) *The British Right*, Farnborough, Saxon House.

O'Brien, C. C. (1964) *Parnell and his Party*, Oxford, Clarendon Press.

Pelling, H. (1958) *The British Communist Party*, London, Adam & Charles Black.

Shipley, P. (1976) *Revolutionaries in Modern Britain*, London, Bodley Head.

Skidelsky, R. (1975) *Oswald Mosley*, London, Macmillan.

Taylor, S. (1982) *The National Front in English Politics*, London, Macmillan.

Walker, M. (1977) *The National Front*, London, Collins.

Wilkinson, P. (1981) *The New Fascists*, London, Grant MacIntyre.

Index